Aspects of mode

Social processes

GENERAL EDITORS

John Barron Mays
Emeritus Professor of Sociology, University of Liverpool

Maurice Craft
Professor of Education, University of Nottingham

ASPECTS OF MODERN SOCIOLOGY

General Editors

John Barron Mays Emeritus Professor of Sociology, University of Liverpool
Maurice Craft Professor of Education, University of Nottingham

This Longman library of texts in modern sociology consists of three Series, and includes the following titles:

THE SOCIAL STRUCTURE OF MODERN BRITAIN

The family
Mary Farmer
formerly University of Liverpool

The political structure
Grace Jones
Chester College of Higher Education

Population
Prof. R. K. Kelsall
formerly University of Sheffield

Education
Ronald King
University of Exeter

The welfare state
Prof. David Marsh
formerly University of Nottingham

Crime and its treatment
Prof. John Barron Mays
University of Liverpool

Structures and processes of Urban life
Prof. R. E. Pahl
University of Kent
R. Flynn
University of Salford
N. H. Buck
University of Kent

The working class
Kenneth Roberts
University of Liverpool

The middle class
Prof. John Raynor
The Open University
and
Roger King
Huddersfield Polytechnic

Leisure
Kenneth Roberts
University of Liverpool

The mass media
Peter Golding
University of Leicester

Mental illness
Bernard Ineichen
University of Bristol

The economic structure
Prof. Cedric Sandford
University of Bath

SOCIAL PROCESSES

Communication
Prof. Denis McQuail
University of Amsterdam

Stratification
Prof. R. K. Kelsall
formerly University of Sheffield
H. Kelsall
formerly Doncaster College of Education
L. Chisholm
University of Maryland, Heidelberg

Socialisation
Graham White
University of Liverpool

Social conflict
Prof. John Rex
University of Aston

Forthcoming titles will include:

Migration
Prof. J. A. Jackson
University of Dublin

SOCIAL RESEARCH

The limitations of social research
Prof. M. D. Shipman
University of Warwick

The philosophy of social research
John Hughes
University of Lancaster

Data collection in context
Stephen Ackroyd
and
John Hughes
University of Lancaster

BY THE SAME AUTHOR

Towards a Sociology of Mass Communications (1969)
Sociology of Mass Communication (editor) (1972)
Television and the Political Image (with Joseph Trenaman) (1961)
Television in Politics: its uses and influence (with J. G. Blumler) (1968)
Communication Models (with S. Windahl) (1982)

Communication

Second edition

Denis McQuail, MA, PhD, DipPSA

Professor of Mass Communication
University of Amsterdam

Longman
London and New York

Longman Group Limited
Longman House, Burnt Mill, Harlow
Essex CM20 2JE, England

Associated companies throughout the world

Published in the United States of America
by Longman Inc., New York

First published 1975
Second edition 1984

British Library Cataloguing in Publication Data

McQuail, Denis
Communication. — 2nd ed. — (Aspects of modern sociology. Social processes).
1. Communication — Social aspects
I. Title II. Series
302.2 HM 258

0-582-29578-5

Library of Congress Cataloging in Publication Data

McQuail, Denis.
Communication.

(Aspects of modern sociology. Social processes)
Bibliography: p.
Includes index.
1. Communication – Social aspects. I. Title.
II. Series.
HM258.M223 1984 302.2 84–890
ISBN 0–582–29578–5

Set in IBM Century 10 on 12 pt
Printed in Singapore by
Huntsmen Offset Printing (Pte) Ltd

Contents

Editors' Preface

The first series in Longman's *Aspects of Modern Sociology* library was concerned with the social structure of modern Britain, and was intended for students following professional and other courses in universities, polytechnics, colleges of education, and elsewhere in further and higher education, as well as for those members of a wider public wishing to pursue an interest in the nature and structure of British society.

A further series set out to examine the history, aims, techniques and limitations of social research; and this third series is concerned with a number of fundamental social processes. The presentation in each case is basically analytical, but each title will also seek to embody a particular viewpoint. It is hoped that these very relevant introductory texts will also prove to be of interest to a wider, lay readership as well as to students in higher education.

JOHN BARRON MAYS
MAURICE CRAFT

Foreword to the First Edition

I am grateful to the series editors, Maurice Craft and John Mays, for suggesting that I write this book, at a time when I happened to be concerned about the nature of communication as a field of study and its relationship to sociology. The period of writing has also coincided with a time when new courses in communication studies have been initiated or proposed in British polytechnics, and I have benefited from interesting discussion with some of those involved either as teachers or as fellow members of the Council of National Academic Awards (CNAA) Communications Studies panel. The book which has resulted may perhaps be read as a contribution to this process of development, although it may also suffer from the provisional nature of the subject. I have a particular debt to record to Joseph Trenaman, who was a pioneer in this field in Britain and who first introduced me to ideas about communication. Not least, he was to me, as to many others, a very kind friend, who is still missed. Finally, I am grateful to colleagues at the University of Tampere, Finland, especially Tapio Varis and Kaarle Nordenstreng, who have provided me with an opportunity to review what I have written in an agreeable and stimulating environment. If little has been changed, it is only because the changes might have been too great.

D. McQ.
University of Tampere

October 1974

Foreword to the Second Edition

I was very glad to be given the opportunity of revising this book but also daunted by the task, since so much has happened in the field of study during the last ten years. It would have been impossible to incorporate all new lines of thought or even the main findings of research, without writing an entirely new text. I have concentrated, therefore, on trying to make the original approach more accessible and more integrated, by rewriting the introductory chapter completely, adding a new summarising chapter (7) and confining a survey of more recent literature in a new final chapter. While for some purposes there is no substitute for an entirely new overview of the field, I am confident that neither the contours of the field of study nor the basic philosophical and scientific principles which should be applied to the study of communication have altered in ten years. The treatment chosen here follows the same humanistic-sociological approach as before, I hope more clearly and more explicitly. At a time when much attention is directed to the immense technical power and capacity of new means of communication it is worth reaffirming that the consequences for relationships of social power deserve rather more attention. That is certainly the main underlying 'message' in a book which does not otherwise argue a particular case. I dedicated the original edition to a pioneer in the subject, Joseph Trenaman, who was also a friend and my first teacher about communication. I would like, in recollection of him, simply to repeat that dedication.

D. McQ.
Schoorl, N.H.
January, 1984

Acknowledgements

We are grateful to *Journalism Quarterly* and the authors for permission to reproduce a figure based on material from 'A conceptual model for communications research' by B. H. Westley and M. S. MacLean (*Journalism Quarterly*, 34, 1957).

Communication process and society 1

Introduction

Within sociology, communication as a process has been neglected; at the same time, under other names, it has also been ubiquitous in the guise of interaction, relationship, change, influence, control, exchange, power, community and many more. This ubiquity stems from the fact that all social processes imply communication, so that of itself the term may seem empty of meaning. The continuing failure within sociology to specify communication as a recognised sub-field is partly attributable to this, partly to the division of labour which tends to allocate the study of individual behaviour to psychology and to refer structural and collective matters to sociology or political science. There is a tendency for important aspects of communication to fall between the two. While it is true that all communication may be ultimately reducible to individual acts of sending or receiving, to take this view exclusively is to lose sight of many causes, consequences and meanings of communication in its social context. There is no justification therefore for this neglect and this book is written on the assumption that a focus on communication as a process is necessary for the analysis of social life and that a sociological view of communication is just as vital as a psychological one.

A further assumption is that there are common features of communication at various levels of social life — ranging from the simplest case of the individual attending to and taking meaning from his or her environment or interacting with another person; through exchanges which take place in groups, associations and organisations; to the level of whole societies and relationships between states. The common terms and 'bridging' concepts are not yet fully articulated in any systematic or scientific way, yet they already exist in normal speech and it does not take too much imagination to see parallels and consistencies amongst relevant phenomena at different levels of social organisation. At each level, we can easily apply a rather similar framework with the shared features of the following: a set of 'actors' — individuals, organisations or states; a bounded area of place or subject matter within which the actors communicate; a set of relationships (of attraction or repulsion, co-operation or conflict, subordination or superordination, equality or inequality) which are to a greater or lesser degree structured and which shape the flow of communication; a common language or code; and finally a set of rules, formal or informal, for the conduct of communication. One aim of this book is thus to contribute to a development of concepts and ways of thinking. This leads to a more generally applicable, clearer and more formal theory for connecting the many fragments of evidence, observation, concept and speculation which at present make up the 'sociology of communication' or, more generally, comprise the field of a 'communication science'.

On definitions

It is easy to use the term 'communication', as I have already done, without seeming to raise serious problems of understanding, yet much time has been spent on the matter of defining communication. In normal use, the verb 'to communicate' usually refers to an action of 'sending' a 'message' about 'something' to someone who is a 'receiver'. In the case of this book I, the author, send a (rather elaborate) message, the contents, to a reader who is the receiver of the message. The whole event is one example of the general case of communication. That such an event can and does take place entails, however, some other elements and preconditions, which include the intention (on my part) to convey some information and ideas, a motive on the part of the reader and the existence of other persons, objects, events and ideas which are the subject matter (or referent) of the message. It also includes an activity on my part and that of the reader, a language which is sufficiently held in common between myself and the reader to allow me to expect some communicative effect and a certain relationship between us both, presupposing an appropriate mutual co-orientation and a measure of understanding. It also necessitates some sharing of time and experience, for we live in the same social and physical world, a technology which allows my message to be reproduced and distributed and a market for a certain kind of commodity (in this case a book). Finally, an effect or change of state is effected if the book is read and some meaning derived from it or some reaction produced. Most of these elements are present in all communication events and thus a commonsense understanding of what is meant by communication seems not too difficult to comprehend.

Even so, it is striking how many components have had to be named and it would not take much imagination to expand each of these into other sets of elements and points requiring further definition. The effort expended on defining communication is not simply a case of word-spinning for its own sake. There is a real complexity which defies covering by any single formula; a complexity stemming from several sources besides the mere quantity of elements and stages involved. In an overview of numerous definitions, Dance[1] identified fifteen types of definition, each of which places the emphasis on a different aspect or component. These can be summarily listed as follows:

1. Symbols, speech, language.

2. Understanding — thus the *reception*, rather than sending of messages.
3. Interaction, relationship — the active exchange and co-orientation.
4. Reduction of uncertainty — the hypothesised basic desire which leads to a search for information in the interests of adjustment.
5. Process — the entire sequence of transmission.
6. Transfer, transmission — connotating movement in space or time.
7. Linking, binding — communication as connector, articulator.
8. Commonality — increase in what is shared or held in common.
9. Channel, carrier, route — an extension of 'transfer', but with a primary reference to the path or the 'vehicle' (sign system or technology).
10. Memory, storage — communication leads to accumulation of information and we can 'communicate with' such stores of information.
11. Discriminative response — an emphasis on the process of selective attention-giving and interpretation.
12. Stimuli — an emphasis on the message as a cause of response or reaction.
13. Intention — stresses the purposeful nature of communication acts.
14. Time and situation — attention to context of the communication act.
15. Power — communication viewed as a means of influence.

A number of the questions raised by this list are taken up in later pages, especially in Chapter 2, but the list itself is a reminder of the diversity of communication events, acts or situations and of the many possible points of entry into an analysis. The basic choices are less than fifteen, but are still striking in their fundamental nature and their diversity. There are several oppositions or dimensions which must affect the form of any definition, and although no single definition will be offered these merit a short discussion.

First, there is the choice between communication as *sending or receiving*, since messages can be sent without being received and received without their having been consciously sent — as when we scan our environment and derive meaning from scenes, situations and unordered sense experiences. Second, and relatedly, there is the question of *intention*, which some definers like to include as characterising communication acts. There are degrees of intentionality in both sending and receiving, such that to set the presence of intention as a necessary condition excludes many seemingly relevant activities and situations. These include the use of gestures and expressions, time-filling conversation and much receiving, and even some sending, of mass communication. Third, we can emphasise communication either as *effect* or *cause* of a given set of social relationships and pattern of interaction. The contact pattern in family or neighbourhood could be an example of an effect, while communication might be seen as a cause of the formation of a public from among dispersed and divergently-thinking individuals. Fourth, communication can be treated as *linear* (one-way transmission) or as *circular* and interactive. Fifth, we can think of it as a source of *order, unity and cohesion* or as a cause of *change, fragmentation* or *conflict*. Finally, there is a choice between an *active* or *reactive* view, the former when we try to influence others or our situation, the latter when we accept influence and adapt to circumstances.

The simple definition of communication derived from the case of this book is misleading on one further point, since it suggests that the 'message' in human communication is usually recognisable as a separate thing or unit which is open to analysis according to known rules — which is largely true of written texts, acts of speech and some pictures. The messages we may have to consider are often not so easy to identify and include such things as customs, rituals, ways of dressing, gestures, touch, buildings, planned environments, gardens, ceremonies, flags, coins, performances, cultural genres and forms, and many others. Any cultural object or event has, by definition, a meaning (or meanings) embedded in it, such that it can 'store' meaning and recommunicate it, often over long periods of time. While this is partly to say that there are many types of language, it has a wider implication, since it points to the many choices for delimiting what we choose to study. The choice adopted in this book is to take a rather wide view and the following quotation from Edward Sapir[2] serves to introduce the chosen approach:

> While we often speak of society as though it were a static structure defined by tradition it is, in the more intimate sense, nothing of the kind, but a highly intricate network of partial or complete understandings between the members of organizational units of every degree of size and complexity, ranging from a pair of lovers or a family to a league of nations or that ever-increasing portion of humanity which can be reached by the press through all its transnational ramifications. It is only apparently a static sum of social institutions; actually it is being reanimated or creatively reaffirmed from day to day by particular acts of a communicative nature which obtain among individuals participating in it . . . every cultural pattern and every single act of social behaviour involves communication in either an explicit or implicit sense.

Society as shared meanings

Society can be treated conceptually in more than one way: as a set of people, concrete institutions and activities; as roles and relationships; as rules, norms, forms of control; or as a set of definitions and meanings. The last named has for long held a place in the study of society, but it has become especially salient during the last fifteen years along with the development of more 'subjective' versions of the practice of sociology, exemplified by symbolic interactionism, phenomenology and ethnomethodology. It has become a commonplace to view society as itself a social 'construction' rather than simply a social given, to which we react or adapt — an external force over which we have little control. Thus society can be seen as 'man-made' and much of what 'makes' it is symbolic activity — the giving of meanings and definitions to experience which may not have any unambiguous or objective reality apart from the definitions supplied in culture and society.

Much of the record of human culture is, in fact, the interpretation of experience and giving of significance, hence order and predictability, to birth and death and what happens in between. Much of art, religion, politics, philosophy and even science is essentially an interpretative activity which provides a framework within which sense can be made of diversity and discontinuity, choices made and objectives chosen. Insofar as social life can be thought about or described in any systematic way, it is such a framework of definitions which are inherited, shared and formed by members of a society, often reaffirmed consciously and unconsciously and transmitted or retransmitted to those who follow. Aside from partial definitions such as 'nation' or 'state', society is an abstraction, and, in this view, there is no society except in the meaningful behaviour of its members, in the ideas and objects which they can name.

This version of society clearly puts a central emphasis on communication and has a number of implications which allow one to make a communicative analysis of society. Most important, it means that society exists as a body of knowledge shared in varying degrees by members of the society. Thus, knowledge has a certain distribution in the statistical sense and there will be variations and discontinuities which are likely to reflect positions in society and social experience. The population considered to belong to the society will vary in experience and situation according to their age and social circumstances, their place of residence, their work, their beliefs, their class status and so on. Such differences are likely to produce systematic differences of perception, attachment conformity and consciousness. Thus, social 'knowledge' varies with social position and it may include a variation in what is acceptable or thought just, in norms and values, in feelings of identity or apartness. Behaviour which seems deviant or disorderly can be re-interpreted according to this perspective as reflecting an alternative definition of what is valued or relevant for a given sub-group or sub-culture. Instead of treating deviant minorities as 'problematic' from a dominant or majority view, we may be more inclined to view them as occupying a different social world, in which what passes for knowledge elsewhere has lower status or currency.

The social structure of communication

A more traditional sociological approach is to view social life as 'structured', thus shaped and held together in a stable form by a more or less generally available set of rules, roles and relationships. Applied to communication, it raises the question: who is likely to communicate with whom, for what purpose? Thus, from a knowledge of social structure — the regularities of social relationships — we should be able to predict something of the direction, frequency, context, purpose and, sometimes, effects of communication. The difference from the perspective just mentioned is that a certain determinancy is assumed; 'position' in a social structure is only, to a limited degree, open to redefinition or negotiation. Some of the conditions which are predictive of patterns of communication can be named. One is propinquity. People who are physically close, by virtue of residence, travel or work are more likely to communicate with each other than those who are physically apart. Another condition is similarity, for those who share social circumstances, interests, beliefs or activities are likely to communicate with each other more than are those who are different. Group membership is another condition of intercommunication, since, by definition, there is more communication within than across group boundaries and the direction of flow will be shaped by the relative status of group members and the different roles held. In practice, all kinds of co-operative activity have similar consequences for communication, often with more specification of purpose and elements of control.

In large-scale and society-wide activities, as within political and religious institutions, there are complex regularities of interaction and often particular communication roles — for instance, as information 'expert', 'relayer of information', 'opinion leader' or as grass-roots 'follower'. Wherever there is a complementarity of roles in groups, organisations or institutions, there are some prescribed patterns of communicative interaction. For instance, parents are expected to 'socialise' their children, supervisors at work are supposed to guide their assistants, political leaders are expected to help shape the opinions of their followers, and so on. In these and other cases there are, usually unwritten, rules understood by both parties, about the giving and receiving of messages with a predictable content and purpose. The awareness of these 'rules' for communication is part of the set of understandings which are socially distributed and they often include an allocation of 'legitimate' power to some role occupants.

On channels and networks

Where communication between individuals, or between roles, tends to recur, we can speak of the existence of a channel of communication — a pathway which is used over and over again. Of course it is an abstraction, although it may be represented by a physical link of some kind: a cable, a road, a frequency band, a speaking tube and so on. Even where there is a physical link we cannot assume the socially defined channel to be co-extensive with the physical link since the same physical link can serve more than one social communication channel. Thus a road system, a mass communication system, or a telephone link, will serve many different chains of social contact. The more open the access to a physical channel or network the more diverse will be the set of social contacts it represents. It is easy enough to appreciate that the structure of a society — the form of its social organisation — will often be represented and expressed through an observable pattern of communication channels and networks. For instance the centralised character of many modern states is revealed by the road map or the map of telecommunication facilities.

In order to understand and explain the form taken by the physical communication network and the actual use of that network we need to examine the social organisation of communication which it serves. Forms of social organisation and formal and informal patterns of human contact tend to shape the communication network in a distinctive way, and the latter has some effect in the reverse direction by constraining or making possible communication, as the case may be. The flow of communication as it is empirically observed and recorded has been regarded as a major datum for reconstructing and interpreting patterns of social life (as in sociometry). While one can question the value of such data in the absence of evidence about what actually flows in communication channels, there is no doubt that the latter vary with patterns of social activity.

As noted above, there are networks which do not conform to any physically observable patterns. These may be based on unwritten social rules about who may have access to whom — often matters of social status or other markers. Lines of informal, interpersonal communication are often confined within boundaries of social class, family, neighbourhood, religion or race. Other kinds of network or social circle are based on interest, knowledge, life-style, opinion or ideology. Thus, social channels, networks and circles are the result of the existence of some physical infrastructure or potential, a similarity of participants in social terms or a similarity of subject matter about which people communicate. In short, they can be based on channels and circumstances or people and topics.

On the means of communication

Considered in the widest sense, the 'means of communication' include all kinds of language and other symbolising systems which can be used for communication. A necessary condition for participation in social communication is the possession of certain skills or means and these, in turn, are usually subject to a particular pattern of allocation. In most 'modern' national societies there is a common public written language which satisfies this condition and enables basic institutional communication to take place for political, economic and cultural purposes. However, this is not always true of developing societies, and even in modern states there may be variations of access and competence. Some language variants are restricted to localities or sub-cultures, some are only acquired through long training or membership of elites. The result is much discontinuity, resulting in many barriers to communication relating to the general distribution of economic and political power. This has always been true, although the tendency of the democratic-bureaucratic form of state has been towards equalising access and reducing gaps and inequalities by way of education, mass communication and some 'levelling up' of standards. Even so, there remain many inequalities which threaten to increase as the volume and complexity of information flows also increase. The means of modern communication, whether sending or receiving, now involve expensive technologies, equipment and scarce skills — for instance in the use of computers. While past discontinuities were often the result of cultural and social class differences, they are now increasingly related to economic and power differences. Over and above what is available to individual members of a society in the way of basic communication skills and facilities there are specialist kinds of knowledge and means of communication. These, in practice, are only at the disposal of large commercial or governmental organisations, or a small minority of those well-trained or rich enough to have some access to these possibilities.

Communication and social change

It has already been observed that communication implies change and that it can be both the cause and effect of changes in social structure (ordered relationships between actors). It is also axiomatic that, if the social world as experienced is also a symbolic world, then there is an intimate connection between material changes and the meaning structure by which the material world is apprehended. In sociology, the term social change is generally understood as a long-term historical process involving fundamental rearrangements of culture and social institutions. A good deal of attention has been paid to identifying general stages of change in the basic forms of society as they have evolved from what are thought to be more primitive forms. We are dealing with processes which are collective and long-term rather than individual and short-term. Although the connections between communication and society are so intimate that one can hardly assess the relation of one to the other, it is worth naming several alternative lines of analysis and hypotheses about this relationship in the process of social change.

First of all, communication processes can be seen as causes, or necessary conditions of change, especially where the latter is thought of in terms of technological or social-cultural inventions. One might take printing as an example of the former and the newspaper as an example of the latter. Printing was an invention at a particular time and place (leaving aside the debate about which time and place) which was rapidly disseminated throughout Europe and, further, by travellers and movements of craftsmen and by the example of the product itself. The process was one of *diffusion* of a given innovation and later advances in print technology were similarly disseminated. The newspaper as a particular application of printing was a much later invention which depended on the political and social environment offered by early seventeenth-century western Europe and which was also, although much more slowly, disseminated in much the same way throughout the world. Both diffusion processes depended on the physical movement of persons and goods, sometimes individually and sometimes collectively and on a large scale as, for instance, through migration, invasion or colonisation. Essentially what is being diffused is an idea — of what is possible, of purposes to which it can be applied and of how it can be done. This process can refer to separate 'inventions' or to larger patterns of life and culture. It has been suggested (e.g. by Lerner[3]) that a primary mover in economic change in the present century is the transmission of a picture of a 'modern' way of life to societies which are both economically backward and culturally traditional.

Theory of the latter kind rests on a view of change as a more or less continuous social evolution leading to universally valued goals of higher production and of material consumption. An alternative view, while sharing a goal of material abundance, is rooted in Marxist interpretation of history as a succession of conflicts between economic classes. While communication is not the prime mover in such a version of social change, it plays an important part aside from its general contribution to industry and commerce. The development of an awareness of a common class interest and of identity as a class against other classes itself requires a complex process of inter-communication. Further, the mobilisation of support and the effort to secure political advantage is a matter of applied communication. Finally, the activity of a dominant class goes beyond either of these two and involves the control and direction of the means and content of communication to maintain its own legitimacy, to define the world in its own interest and, as far as possible, to undermine the efforts of a challenging class to achieve self-consciousness and formulate an alternative world view. While these processes in the modern period have mainly involved mass communication and public opinion, they also apply to the very nature of language and of symbolisation in general.

Third, there is a school of thought which attributes key developments in historical change, not to the substance of messages carried through communication channels, networks and processes, but to the basic technology of communication itself, thus to the *media* rather than the message. The most influential version of such 'media determinism' has its origin in the work of the Canadian economic historian Harold Innis[4]. He attributed the characteristic features of successive ancient civilisations to the prevailing mode of communication, each of which had its own 'bias' in terms of societal form. Thus, he regarded the change from stone to papyrus as causing a shift from royal to priestly power. In ancient Greece, an oral tradition and a flexible alphabet favoured inventiveness and diversity and prevented the emergence of a priesthood with a monopoly over education. The foundation of the Roman empire was favoured by a written culture on which legal-bureaucratic institutions, capable of administering distant areas, could be based. Printing, in turn, challenged bureaucratic control and encouraged both nationalism and individualism.

There are two main organising principles in Innis's work. First, as in the economic sphere, communication leads over time to monopolisation by a group or class of the means of production of communication and knowledge. In turn this produces a disequilibrium which either impedes change or expansion or leads to competitive emergence of other forms of communication which tend to correct the disequilibrium. Second, the most important dimensions of empire are space and time with some means of communication being more suited to one than to the other. Thus empires can persist for any length in time or extensively in space, depending on the available form of communication. Innis really had little to say about modern developments in communication and the theory, which is in fact very sketchy, takes little account of the institutionalisation of new *forms* of communication which may be more important than the underlying technology. Thus the poem, legal document, popular song, feature film, television news are examples of more complex *social* inventions than the technologies involved. Later writers have invoked a similar mode of explanation to explain or predict the consequences of a shift from print to audio-visual media during the last half century (for instance, McLuhan[5], Gerbner[6], Gouldner[7]). The consequences are variously thought of in terms of an emerging 'global culture', a decline in ideology, a greater vulnerability to manipulation and a decline in rationality.

Fourth, communication patterns and relationships are intimately connected with some fundamental patterns of change which sociologists and historians have exposed and documented. According to many social theorists, an archetypal beginning stage of human association, where members of more or less closed social groups shared sentiments and beliefs, lived in a self-sufficient way and engaged together in a limited range of basic activities, has given way to a large-scale complex society whose members are differentiated from each other in many ways and yet remain interdependent in new ways because of the division of labour. The greater freedom and individuality of modern society are sustained by an elaborate communication system which provides a mechanism of functional integration in an extensive society, superseding the normative integration of earlier, more communal forms of society. As Durkheim pointed out, in modern societies people are linked together more by their differences than their similarities, since these differences require complementarity and interdependence[8]. The need to collaborate and interact and the structures invented to organise new kinds of interaction are the bases of social solidarity.

While there is a measure of agreement on these points, there remains some conflict of interpretation. The growing individuation can be seen not as an increasing freedom, but as a growth of social fragmentation, leading to problems of isolation at the individual level and openness to manipulation by powerful organised groups at the collective level. The new 'higher level' unity of a society can thus be an illusory benefit. In these conflicts of theory, the mass media are often referred to either as the means for retaining a sense of national and cultural identity and a vision of the whole, or, alternatively, as a potent cause of the dissolution or weakening of social bonds. One should perhaps conclude that modern communications operate, at the same time, to promote the 'centrifugal' and the 'centripetal' tendencies in society.[9]

Conclusion

These several points which have arisen out of the quotation from Sapir serve to introduce the main concerns of this book. While it is about communication, it has also to be about society. We need to have a conceptual framework for analysing and comparing the many different kinds of communication activity and process which are involved in the business of entering and inhabiting a world of meanings which we share with other men. We want to make as many connections as possible between communication and the rest of social life. In particular we want to see how the structure of social relationships, the distribution of power in society and our experience of power differentials affects, and is affected by, communication. The aim is clearly over-ambitious, and the range of content too wide to allow enough discussion of detail, but the most important questions about communication and the scope of sociological analysis are such as to require an attempt to link the micro-analysis of communication with general questions about society.

Theories of communication 2

Elements of the communication process

We began with a simple view of human communication as the ordered transfer of meaning and looked briefly at the main elements implied by this view: the presence of a communicator or sender, a message, a language or code, a means of transmission or sending, a receiver who is able to 'read' or 'decode' the message. Any communication act involves a sequence of events which takes the basic form of a decision to transmit meaning, the formulation of the intended message into a language or code, and an act of transmission and of reception by someone else. This is the process of communication which can serve as a framework for a more detailed discussion of the constituent elements. At the same time, we should bear in mind that this view of communication may be highly misleading, however useful for exposition. Misleading not only because most communication events are much more complex than this model suggests, but also because of a bias written into this particular formulation. For one thing, it implies an underlying rationality and purposefulness about communication, an intention of achieving certain ends and hence the relevance of a criterion of communication efficiency. Second, it proposes a linear view of communication which is inconsistent with what frequently happens. Third, and correlatively, it suggests that communication always begins with a sender, and that it is the intention of the communicator which defines the meaning of a communication event. In secular rational cultures we are predisposed to think of human action and of communication in these terms, and it is a predisposition which needs to be corrected. The point is taken up again later (see pp. 33—4), but it needs particular emphasis.

Little need be said in general about the *communicator*, the source or point of origin of an act of communication. As we have noted, the communicator need not be a single individual, but could be a group or collective entity — a newspaper, a legislative body, a formal organisation, etc. We need also to bear in mind that communicators are also receivers although, in formally organised communication systems, the roles of communicator and receiver may be separately defined. And even in informal communication systems the distribution of roles of sender and receiver of messages tends to be socially regulated and related to the general distribution of values and power in the particular social context.

The next element for brief discussion is the *message*, first as regards content. The content of a message is the reference it contains to some object in the environment of giver and receiver of messages which is 'named' in the message. We call this the 'referent'. Communication is thus 'about' something — a minimal definition but one which saves us from the discussion of 'noise'. Our use of the word 'message' instead of 'information' bypasses certain questions which will be taken up later (pp. 42—4), though one can note that there are more precise definitions of what we are here calling the content of messages. For instance, Miller[1] defines information as referring to 'the occurrence of one out of a set of discriminative stimuli', a stimulus being an influence that is 'arbitrarily symbolically associated with some thing (or state or event or property) and that enables the stimulated organism to discriminate this thing from others'. This may be a definition of a 'name' when one is thinking of a communicator referring to (i.e. naming) objects for the benefit of a recipient ('stimulated organism'). It is a narrower version than our 'message' since it implies a particular criterion of meaningfulness — the degree to which the receiver finds it useful for discriminating. In information theory proper, communication is about the 'reduction of uncertainty' and the information is a quantifiable amount of uncertainty reduction (cf. Lin[2], pp. 23—34). The concept of a message is thus ambiguous, the ambiguity deriving from the arbitrary separation of content from form and from the possible discrepancy between what is intended by the originator and what is perceived by the recipient. Do we call something a 'message', whenever the originator regards it as indicating a referent, or do we restrict the term to cases where 'uncertainty is reduced' for the receiver? The message of one person may be noise for another. Our approach does not require us to make an exclusive choice between these alternatives (but see below, p. 33).

The business of 'encoding', of putting ideas into the appropriate message form, has already been raised. A language or code is, following Morris[3] (pp. 35—6), a plurality of signs which have a common signification to a number of interpreters, and which are producible by these interpreters. The signification of language signs must be relatively constant in different situations and the signs 'must constitute a system of interconnected signs combinable in some ways and not in others in order to form a variety of sign-processes'. We can widen Morris's definition so as to include sign systems other than the language of normal speech or writing — for instance systems which make use of sounds like the morse code, or visual representation like traffic lights, or pictures like road signs and so on. A code or language system in this sense consists both of units (the signs, etc.) and of patterns (the rules of combination), and its essence lies in matching patterns of sense data with patterns of meaning. As an activity, 'encoding' inevitably varies in the extent to which it is deliberate and conscious and in the degree to which it constitutes a separate stage in the communication event or process. Thus in everyday speech we put thoughts into words with little care or attention, but when speech is used very purposefully we frame expressions with more attention to the likely interpretation and effect. Where messages originate with collective sources which are formally organised for communication, the encoding process may be a specialised activity, requiring particular knowledge of the appropriate code and of the means of transmission. The rules or conventions which govern the encoding process are not only 'linguistic' rules — they are also the rules and conventions of the area of social life within which the communication occurs. For instance, prayers, scientific theorems, poems, legal documents and strip cartoons are produced according to conventional requirements which are peculiar to different institutional settings.

Transmission calls for little comment at this point. It covers any of the possible ways of gaining the attention of, and making messages available to, others — by speaking, writing, using electronic devices, films, sculpture, painting. All these are *media* of communication but, more particularly, means of transmission. Physical materials and/or energy are always involved and these vary in their accessibility. They are often scarce goods, subject to many kinds of institutional control as to their supply and use. While the regulation of sign systems may be thought of as primarily a matter of culture, the regulation of transmission is predominantly societal and institutional.

The term '*receiver*' in our basic communication model is in many ways misleading. It has a very limiting connotation, implying as it does a passive role, one defined primarily in terms of reaction or response. It also appears as a role defined largely in terms of the expectations of the communicator and hence lacking in autonomy, as if it could not exist apart from a sender. When we ourselves receive messages, we have quite a different view of what the word implies. The receiver is, more often than not, also an initiator, both in the sense of originating messages in return and in the sense of initiating processes of interpretation with some degree of autonomy. The receiver 'uses' and 'acts on' the information available to him. In another important sense he is an initiator, in that he has chosen to attend to some sources and messages rather than others. We are both responding to and acting on our environment when we receive messages and this more or less continuous 'scanning' of the physical and social world takes precedence as a human activity over the originating of messages for others. In a real sense, communicators are themselves 'responding' to an environment, which includes their 'receivers', when they put messages together. The sequence or process of communication with which we started could be represented in the reverse direction, with the activity of receiving as the point of initiation, without violating the reality of communication.

Conditions and effects

This description of the constituent elements of a communication event does not exhaust the full meaning of communication as a social process. There are prerequisites for, and consequences of, communication which have yet to be mentioned. Communication has been defined as a process which increases commonality, or what is shared between participants, and it is certainly this. But it also requires elements of commonality for it to occur at all. There must, first of all, be a shared 'environment' — a social, physical and temporal space within the boundaries of which the participants are located. The essence of a shared environment in all three senses is the shared experience of the world of referents which messages are about. Messages can only have meaning if they concern matters within, or close to, the experience of both senders and receivers. There is some latitude in this requirement since communication frequently extends the boundaries of shared experience by using known referents to convey meaning about others unknown to the receiver. The sharing of physical space is also a matter of degree. Some communication processes occur within a very restricted space, others occupy the territory of a whole society or beyond. Nevertheless, where communication occurs, there are usually some acknowledged physical boundaries which can be drawn around participants, and these boundaries depend both on the means of transmission (the range of access to the communication network), and on the area of relevance in the physical world.

The sharing of time–space is also a matter of degree since, by definition, communication must occur through time and cannot strictly be instantaneous. The period of time is variable, but there is always some measurable limit to it. The military command and response, or the friendly greeting, occupy a short space of time and the participants have to 'be there' together for communication to be accomplished. The publishing and reading of a newspaper takes somewhat longer and requires less sharing by sender and receiver of the same time–space while events like artistic communication or the spread of a religious belief have long time spans and little contemporaneity among those involved. Nevertheless, we retain the rather elastic concept of a shared time in the form of different units — a passing moment, a day or two, a generation, an historical era, and so on. Such a concept is universally embedded in our understanding of what communication is. It is always time-bound, subject to decay, inertia, completion or cessation. Space, time and social relevance all interact with each other as variables of the common environment which sustains the communication process. The common language which, as we have noted, is essential for the transmission of meaning is the outcome of a shared environment, and the sharing of language extends beyond the fact of knowing the rules of combination of signs to include common awareness of conventions and covert indications. We can find examples of communication which violate some of these general assertions, for instance the deciphering and response to some symbolic artefact of a remote culture or the case of a foreign invasion, but it is more correct to regard such examples as marking the boundary points between distinct communication processes.

A feature of all communication process which has been noted in passing, and is implicit in much of what has been said, is that all communication involves change. Wherever there is communication there is a change of state — something happens in the course of communication which alters the situations of participants in relation to each other, or to the external environment. This is another way of saying that communication has effects, but it avoids the implication that the effects of communication need to be conceived in terms of the intentions of the communicator. Effects of communication should also be thought of as changes of probability about the future. Thus a communication event which has the immediate effect of confirming an existing situation or relationship (for instance a conversation between friends) has consequences for the probable duration of the friendship by keeping latent feelings of attachment in being. The proposition of 'no communication without effect' is a sound one, although it depends on a broad view of what to consider as effects. The dynamic nature of the communication process also creates difficulties for those who want to study it since, as it occurs, it is constantly changing and immensely hard to put on record or to reconstruct after the event.

Communication always presupposes or establishes a social relationship between those who participate. Weber[4] (p. 88) defined social action in the following terms: 'Action is social in so far as, by virtue of the subjective meaning attached to it by the acting individual, it takes account of the behaviour of others and is thereby oriented in its course.' The communicator, in sending a message, has a receiver in mind and shapes his actions with conscious reference to this person; similarly, the receiver, in attaching meaning to messages, is orienting himself to a human source. While we would have to regard all communication relationships as social relationships, the reverse is not true, the former being a subcategory of the latter. There are many ambiguous cases. When parents punish their children, is this a communication relationship? Or when we visit the cinema do we establish one with actors and film-makers? It is not important to classify individual cases, but it is useful to have a view of what distinguishes the communication relationship from the social relationship in general. We would tend to find the distinction in the definitions of the situation supplied either by the participants or by others. Is the relationship defined or interpreted as directly concerned with the transfer of meaning, or only incidentally so? Communication relationships often give rise to, and arise out of, other sorts of social relationship, but remain distinctive for purposes of analysis. The fact of a relationship, a co-orientation between sender and receiver, is important for our view of communication, and essential to understanding the differences between theories and models of social communication.

Communication models

It is one thing to be able to list the main elements involved in communication, but another to show how they are related to each other. The study of communication over two or three decades has produced a number of attempts to express the relationship between the elements just described, sometimes in the form of a model or physical representation. In looking at some of these attempts, we do not propose to give an exhaustive account nor to evaluate them and choose the best solution. Instead, the aim is to indicate the dilemmas posed in the conceptualisation of communication. It is a complex process, open to alternative philosophical interpretations and almost as variable as are the examples of communication phenomena in social life.

Perhaps the most influential model of communication is that of Claude Shannon[5] (Shannon and Weaver), a model developed to assist in the construction of a mathematical theory of communication which would apply to any situation of information transfer, whether by men, machines or other systems. This model depicts a basic sequence of the kind already discussed, which begins with a *source*, from which a *message* is passed to a *transmitter* where it is *encoded* into a *signal*, which is subject to *noise* on its way to a *receiver*, where it is *decoded* and then passed to a *destination*. More or less contemporaneously with this work, another information theorist, Norbert Wiener[6], was proposing a general science of communication which would apply equally to men or machines, to be called cybernetics, a word derived from the Greek for 'steering'. In cybernetics, the emphasis is on the 'feedback' in a communication system, the procedures for control which enable a system to adapt to changes in the environment. A communication source, similarly, can respond and adapt to information about the results of the messages it transmits. Feedback typically has a modifying and guiding effect on the encoding and transmitting activities of a 'communicator' and takes different forms, depending on the type of communication event. It might, for instance, be the 'other half' of a conversation, the results of examinations in an educational system, the audience research statistics of a broadcasting organisation, the reviews of a book, the facial expression of an interlocutor and so on. In discussing the nature of human communication, Schramm[7] stresses the fact that feedback makes the process of communication circular rather than linear and one-directional, and no representation of the human communication process can omit this key element. All representation of communication in social system terms (e.g. DeFleur[8]) or social systems in communication terms (e.g. Deutsch[9]) depends on the concept of feedback. When we include it in the basic model of information theory we have the essential components of a social organisation which can survive, change, adapt to an environment and be much more 'efficient' in its internal operation.

The social system model of communication can be applied to any situation where there is some persistent relationship between the constituent elements — senders, receivers and environments. A simple model of a communication process which illustrates the system approach is suggested by Newcomb[10]. This is based on the 'initial assumption that communication among human beings performs the essential function of enabling two or more individuals to maintain simultaneous orientations to each other *and* towards objects of an external environment'. The model is a triangular one, the points of the triangle being taken up by two individuals, A and B, and an object in their common environment, X. Both individuals are oriented to each other and to X, and communication is conceived of as the process which supports this orientational structure, in the sense of maintaining the symmetry of the relationship between the three elements by transmitting information about any change and allowing adjustment to take place. The model assumes that at any given moment the *ABX* system is 'at rest' or balanced.

A further modification of the Shannon and Weaver model has been required to take account of the fact that communication, especially in large systems, has to be looked at as a flow of 'information' or messages along a network, a chain or set of channels. From this perspective, what is of primary interest is not the efficiency of the encoding and transmitting facilities in overcoming 'noise', or the integration and articulation of the whole system, but the discontinuities in the flow of information and the process of selection which occur at various points. Selection occurs at the source, at the point of transmission, at the different stages in the 'journey' of the message, where intermediaries are involved, and at the point of reception. There is no single dominant model of communication which is addressed to handling this problem, although Lewin's[11] work, which gave rise to the concept of 'gatekeeper', has been influential, and studies of the diffusion of information like that of DeFleur and Larsen[12] or of news flow like that of Galtung and Ruge[13] have developed or relied on such a model.

In the analysis of mass communication, where the process is essentially one of relaying messages in a very open system, a model suggested by Westley and MacLean[14] has been widely adopted (see below, p. 171). They take Newcomb's '*ABX*' model as their starting point and interpose a fourth element to stand for the activities of the mass communicator who is an intermediary in the channel between *A* and *B*. The latter are, respectively, those who have something purposive to say (the sources of communication) and the audience or public. The new element, *C*, is a 'channel role' which acts at the same time as an agent of the would-be communicator and of the audience. The effect of *C*'s presence in the system of communication is to extend the environment of *X*'s to which the audience member can be oriented, to bring *A*'s into touch with *B*'s which would be otherwise out of reach. The *C* role also accomplishes the task of selecting among the *A*'s, or would-be communicators, those whose messages are believed most relevant to the needs of *B* or which meet some other criteria of selection. The authors propose this as a model which could be appropriate to any communication system which transcends the face to face situation. For present purposes, it is useful in calling attention to the various stages at which selection takes place — in the choices made by *A* about what to communicate, in the choices by *C* among potential communicators, in the selections which *B* has to make in attending to mass communication content.

Perhaps the most comprehensive attempt yet to specify all the component stages and activities of communication is Gerbner's[15] general model of communication; in the way of description, little or nothing has since been added. In its verbal form, the model is expressed as follows: 'Someone perceives an event and reacts in a situation through some means to make available materials in some form and context conveying content of some consequence.' The aim is to specify and relate areas for study in the field of communication, but a number of important points are stressed and have been taken up by the same author in subsequent work. Our attention is drawn in particular to the following points.

1. The great variability in the perception of an event by a communicating agent and also in the perception of a message about an event by a receiver. In general terms, this variability can range from an extreme 'transactionist' position which 'stresses the structuring effects of (the communicator's) assumptions, point of view, experiential background, and other related factors upon the perception' to such an extent that the event is 'almost "created" in the act of perceiving' to a nearly opposite or 'psychophysical' view which sees the 'world of material events, sounds, shapes, forms as "in control"'. Gerbner's model does not assume either extreme view, but does attempt to take account of 'the creative, interactional nature of the perceptual process, avoiding any implications of either solipsism or mechanism'.

2. The importance of the *situation* and context in which the stimulus to communication and the actual process occurs, in the sense both of physical as well as social circumstances.

3. In discussion, Gerbner contrasts the *open* nature of human communication with the closed sequence of mechanical or automatic communication systems. Human communication is open in that events and objects in the environment do not automatically generate signals or communicative reactions and the whole process of communication is open at many points to variable and unpredictable effects of perception and human choice. The analogy with a programmed device like a thermostat in a heat control system is misleading: human communication systems are not homeostatic and 'feedback' has a different connotation.

4. Content is always 'meaningful' and the meaning of content cannot be derived solely from either the intentions of the transmitter or the perceptions of the receiver alone but is a 'relational pattern' to be interpreted in the light of the whole sequence of events in a particular case of communication. While the model is essentially descriptive and taxonomic it does something more than provide a framework for com-

parative study and it opens the way to more focused theoretical approaches and to a discussion of communication in normative terms.

Another model which has been especially influential during one phase in the study of mass communication is that offered by Riley and Riley[16], based on a sociological interpretation of accumulated research. Their overall concern is to locate the working of mass communication within the wider social structure, and the empirical research findings reviewed do indeed yield striking support for a view of the mass communication process as very much subordinate to the structure and process of the social system. Thus the audience member is located in a nexus of primary and reference group memberships which are interrelated and which strongly affect his selection and response to the messages made available from the mass media. The 'mass communicator' is, likewise, not an individual acting at random but 'part of a larger pattern, sending his messages in accordance with the expectations and actions of other persons and groups within the same system'. Both communicator and audience member are also interdependent and have an interactive relationship within a common normative and institutional framework provided by membership of the same society. The model, which is essentially conceived in system terms, can serve as a corrective to misleading ways of thinking about the mass communication process — in particular, formulations which represent the messages of mass media as coming from 'outside' the social world of the audience.

Of models which develop distinctive theoretical perspectives on communication subsequent to the main work of the 1940s and 1950s, we might mention two in particular. Barnlund's[17] 'transactional model of communication' stands at one pole of the dimension noted by Gerbner. Barnlund says of communication that 'it is not a reaction to something, nor an interaction with something, but a transaction in which man invents and attributes meanings to realise his purposes

. . . meaning is something "invented", "assigned", "given", rather than something "received"'. The model he develops seeks to incorporate this essential characteristic and to take account of other related features of communication: its dynamism, complexity, continuity, circularity, uniqueness, irreversibility. The model sets out the basic processes which occur both within the person and between persons, as environmental cues and the situation itself are perceived, interpreted on and acted upon in ways which influence subsequent stages of the process. There is little that is novel in the terms or elements employed, but the strong emphasis on perception and attention-giving gives the model as a whole a distinctive character. Second, we can note a suggestion (Dance[18]) for modifying our model of communication to take account of the fact that the communication process 'is constantly moving forward and yet is always to some degree dependent on its past, which informs the present and the future'. Dance proposes that the appropriate geometric image of the communication process is neither the straight line (emphasising forward direction of flow) nor the circle (emphasising feedback) but the helix or spiral. A helical model of communication flow has the advantages of stressing the change of state which is involved in communication and the 'reflexive' character of communication. That is to say, communication acts upon itself. The image is certainly a useful one, and to have it in mind acts as a corrective to static or equilibrium models of communication which suggest a return, perhaps after 'feedback', to the starting position.

However brief and selective this discussion of alternative models, it will have drawn attention to some of the main issues in communication theory and to the variable elements in any conceptual framework for studying communication. A model which tried to reconcile all the conceptual possibilities would be something of a monstrosity and would certainly lack utility or interest. But the foregoing discussion suggests a limited set of basic choices about the representation of the communication process which can be formulated as a series of questions, the answers to which indicate the range of perspectives which need to be considered.

Basic questions about the communication process

Is the process one-directional or interactional?

The answer depends both on the salience of 'feedback' in the process and on the degree of circularity (or spiralling) implied. A casual interpersonal conversation or a process of verbal bargaining is essentially circular and interactional. Each act of communication is a response to a prior one and open to modification. The participants are equal and interchangeable as communicators and receivers. In the unidirectional case, the communicator has the initiative and is either unable to respond to the results of his communication or unprepared to do so. The former tends to hold in mass communication, while the latter arises in institutionally defined situations where the communicator is not constrained by his interlocutor or is even obliged to ignore response. Thus in military or some educational or correctional contexts communication might take this latter form.

Is it open or closed?

The difference lies in the degree to which the outcome of the communication is predictable and planned or subject to uncertainty from various sources. The extreme contrast is between most cybernetic machine systems, which are programmed in specific ways to take account of certain kinds of 'information', and most human communication processes, which are subject to unplanned modification and interference from outside the system. But human communication systems also vary according to the degree of closure. Military command systems and formal networks and channels of communication in organisations are relatively closed in the sense of working according to established definitions of who the participants should be, how they are related in terms of precedence, what effects to expect and what kinds of information are relevant to the system. On the other hand, artistic communication, mass communication and informal interpersonal contact are open.

Are meanings fixed or 'transacted'?
The variable of transactionality relates to the tolerance of different meanings as intended by the communicator or perceived by the recipient. Some messages are unambiguous and open to only one interpretation, while others are not, and communication situations vary according to the acceptability of ambiguity. In artistic communication and informal conversation, ambiguity is high and the experience is highly negotiable for the recipient. There is a relatively high tolerance for variable and subjective perception in these situations and the receiver of communication is understood to be structuring his own social world through his reception of communication. In scientific communication, or in communication concerned with guidance and control, the process is not normally transactional in this sense.

Is it to be seen from the perspective of the sender or the receiver?
The question arises from the existence of alternative definitions of communication, some of which describe it as a matter of sending messages and influencing other people, while others describe it in terms of response (Nilsen[19]). Thus, whether we find meaning in our environment or acquire meaning, as intended, from the deliberate messages of others, some 'transfer of meaning' has been accomplished. But the fact that a communicator has transmitted a message with the intention of conveying meaning is not sufficient to constitute an accomplished act of communication. The former view of communication as *response* is more inclusive and less restrictive. But to adopt one view rather than the other is to give a

biased account of the communication process. From the point of view of the receiver, communication is a matter of observing, scanning, perceiving, interpreting. From that of the sender it is a quite different sort of activity.

Is it purposive or non-purposive?

A communication process, whether we think of it as the sending of messages or the acquiring of information, may vary according to its intention and instrumentality. Where there is a specific objective, criteria of effectiveness will be relevant, conscious motivation and more planning and structuring of the activities will be involved. Thus mass communication is often conceived (as by Westley and MacLean[20]) as essentially non-purposive communication — a matter of 'making available' what might be usable by unknown members of the public. It has this character from the perspective of the media organisation, although a particular message may be highly purposive from the point of view of an advertiser or propagandist using mass media channels. The same communication process may be purposive for some of its receivers and non-purposive for others. This does, however, create a difficulty for the model builder, since a model representing both aspects simultaneously must be flexible and very general.

Is the process system-linked or system-free?

The question posed here concerns the function of particular communicative events for other processes of social life. Communication is systematic where successive acts of sending and receiving messages are related to each other in a deterministic way and similarly related to the context in which they occur, in that contextual circumstances may cause communication to occur and the results of communication then feed back to modify the context. The underlying model is one of need-generation and solution and of system-adjustment through communication. At the personal level, we might find an example in the need of an individual to talk to someone, after moving to a new district — a need arising out of loss of previous social ties and of having to adjust to a new environment and obtain information about it. The satisfaction of this need restores the social system, as experienced by the person, to its former normal working and 'well adjusted' state. We can contrast this with communication which is random or arises out of spontaneous acts and therefore cannot be accounted for in terms of prior needs or causes. Some processes of communication, as in formal organisations, are designed to incorporate systematic features and promote integration and adjustment. In some cases, however, we are free to choose whether or not to treat a communication process in functional terms. For instance some writers view mass communication as a 'mechanism' for integrating and faciliting the individual, cultural and social system (e.g. Wright[21]; DeFleur[22]), while others contest this view (see McQuail and Gurevitch[23]). Whatever the merits in particular cases, the choice is a vital one for the communication theorist since the two formulations are irreconcilable.

It will have become clear that the various choices posed in these questions are related to each other, despite the separate focus of each question. In particular, it can be seen that the first mentioned of each pair of alternatives all tend to go together. Thus there is an implied contrast between a polar type of communication process as unidirectional, closed, unambiguous, sender-oriented, purposive and systematic and one which represents the reverse characteristics. This provides a single conceptual dimension along which acts and events of communication can vary. The dimension has more heuristic than practical value but its existence helps to explain why no single working model of communication has ever been produced and why it would inevitably be misleading if one were attempted. It would be equally mistaken to formulate two alternative models based on the dimension just described. The range of situations in social life in which communications occur is so wide that we can rely neither on a single reductionist view of the communicative act nor on a single model of communication.

The communicative act and the communication relationship — alternative theories

The passive-active dimension

The difficulty of choosing any single most appropriate and economic model to represent the social process of communication does not stem from disagreement over facts or over the range of elements which have to be taken into account. It derives, first of all, from the great diversity of social events which would have to be accounted for and, second, from the fact that communication events are open to quite different conceptualisations. Social scientific views of phenomena are selective, and different perspectives produce different versions of what is going on. It is useful, however, to try and develop some conceptual bridge between the two kinds of variability which have been mentioned, the one empirical, the other theoretical. One dimension or continuum which can be used in order to map different events and different conceptions of events can be described as that of 'activity-passivity'. It is close to, and sums up, other distinctions of a similar kind, such as that between what is manifest and latent, intentional or casual, 'acting on' or 'being acted on'. The value of this kind of distinction derives from the fact that it underlies and points to both the *empirical* differences between communication events and the *theoretical* differences in ways of looking at such events. It is especially helpful in placing, relative to each other, alternative conceptions of the communication act and the communication relationship. If we apply the dimension to the perspective of both the sender and receiver of communication and cross-classify the resulting dichotomies we arrive at a simple typology of the four basic kinds of communication situation, as follows:

	Perspective of	
	(*a*) *Sender*	(*b*) *Receiver*
Communication situations:	1. Active	—Passive
	2. Active	—Active

3. Passive — Active
4. Passive — Passive

What this does is to treat the communicative act as falling empirically into the class of either 'active' or 'passive' and to regard the resulting classification as identifying different kinds of relationship between participants, which we would expect to have basically different meanings for them, and to involve situations which are quite differently defined.

The first situation (active-passive) is familiar as the model of the intentional transfer of information as defined by the sender, but without the positive commitment of receiver to this definition of the situation. The case of the advertiser and his 'target' audience or the propagandist and his public are examples, as are some institutionally defined learning situations where the pupil is uninterested and lacking in motivation. Such situations are, in principle, one-directional and imbalanced, with greater weight on the side of the sender who is using superior social power or resources to define the terms of the relationship and to act according to this definition.

The second situation (active-active) is most clearly represented by the case of exchange or interaction where both partners act in turn as sender and receiver. The conversation, the encounter, the bargain, the debate are familiar examples at the interpersonal level. But we would include teaching situations where the receiver is motivated and responsive. The criterion of success, the measure of effectiveness, the 'purpose' have to be established in terms of the mutual satisfaction of the participants. Such relationships are generally symmetrical and the participants are equal.

The third situation (passive-active) occurs where there is an active and purposive *search* for information — the model is that of the 'scanning' of the environment. We engage in such an activity more or less continually, sometimes prompted by the need to solve particular problems, sometimes in a less directed and specific way. We find solutions and construct meaning out of the messages we 'read' in the environment. Such a situation implies, or allows for, a good deal of freedom for the individual to choose among available messages and meanings and to adopt a personal view.

The fourth type of situation (passive-passive) is a residual category for occasions where latent and casual communication occurs on an undirected basis, purposeless from the point of view of both sender and receiver. Communication relationships which arise on such a basis will tend to be temporary, unstructured, lacking in clearly defined meaning, unlikely to produce much change and having low salience to participants. Such cases may, nevertheless, be important in their aggregate effect, since they occur frequently and their outcome will be to reinforce a framework of meaning and of relationships.

This typology indicates something of the continuum of actual communication events which lie along the active-passive dimension. It helps also to pose the questions with which the remainder of this chapter is concerned. We begin with questions of why people enter into communication, either as givers or receivers; second, with the meaning which participants attribute to the communication situation; and third, with the way in which senders and receivers orient themselves to each other and define their relationship. The circumstances of the particular case will obviously determine the specific answer to such questions, but there are certain alternative perspectives and theories which shape the general character of the answers. It is these alternative frameworks which we are now aiming to explain and, in doing so, we are ordering them in terms of a dimension which can also be labelled as 'passive-active'. This similarity between the principle which distinguishes theory relevant to communication and the principle which helps to order the actual communication events is the 'conceptual bridge' noted above. The value of this device is not merely heuristic, since it shows clearly enough that different versions of the communication process do not simply arise out of confusion or arbitrary disagreement.

The range of available paradigms or models is inevitably wide, and choice will be related to an overall philosophic or scientific position. The distinction underlying the continuum is, for example, related to that which in sociology separates views of society and social action emphasising consensus from those emphasising conflict, or separates the primary concern with order and 'reproduction' of society from the concern with change. In psychology, too, there is an underlying intellectual tension between those who favour the strictest form of empirical behaviourism and those who acknowledge cognitive and mentalist elements. The debate in psychology takes a different form, uses different terms and rests on a different set of assumptions but it has similar elements. It is inevitable that if we look at an aspect of social life as central as communication we enter the same areas of dispute that divide sociologists and psychologists on other matters.

The following discussion of some alternative perspectives and theoretical models in psychology and sociology moves from the more 'passive' to the more 'active' formulation. As a result, psychological approaches have been mentioned first because psychology tends to focus more on behavioural, organic and 'mechanistic' aspects of human action while sociology is concerned more with questions of meaning and interpretation. Nevertheless, it may be misleading to suggest that psychological approaches are inevitably more 'passive' in their implications. There is a range of positions within each discipline, an area of overlap between them and the possibility of a sociologist providing a more determinist and thus, in our sense, more 'passive' set of answers than a psychologist.

Learning theory

The psychology of learning offers a number of different

versions of the mechanisms and processes of human learning and in doing so provides one basic form of a theory of communication. Despite the differences of approach, and especially the varying emphasis as between cognitive and behavioural elements, virtually all theory in the psychology of learning gives an important place to association as the underlying principle of effective communication. Briefly, the relationship between stimulus and response is seen to provide the key to both learning and communication (in the sense of teaching). A stimulus is some physical object or event in an environment which is able to affect the sense organ of an organism and the response will be some overt and measurable act. Stimulus-response learning or 'connectionism' is familiar to most people as classical conditioning of the kind demonstrated by Pavlov when he succeeded in 'teaching' a dog to salivate in response to a sound which had become associated with food. There are several variants of stimulus response theory, such as instrumental conditioning where an animal is 'taught' by conditioning to do something in order to obtain some reward, or discrimination learning where conditioning can produce the ability to respond differentially to specific stimulus conditions. It is evident from the work of experimental psychologists that knowledge of classical conditioning and of the manipulation of rewards and punishment can produce learning results of a complex kind.

Different theorists have emphasised different elements in the learning process; for instance Hull[24] stresses drives, Thorndike[25] reward, Tolman[26] the cognitive element, Skinner[27] reinforcement, but all seem to share a general framework of concepts which is also a framework for understanding how communication works. This general view or framework includes the assumption that the organism is in a systematic relationship with its environment such that a change of state in either organism or environment (which may be other organisms) will have mutual consequences and produce mutual responses. Every action may be conceived of as a response, which presumes a preceding stimulus. The response behaviour 'triggered off', or otherwise caused, by any stimulus has consequences which are ultimately accountable in terms of a reduction of tension, a return to equilibrium or stasis which is the 'normal' state of the organism and of the larger system of which it forms part. Human communication, in this view, is that process which links individuals to each other and to their environment. In summarising his account of communicative acts, Newcomb[28] defines these as 'outcomes of changes in the organism — environment relationships actual and/or anticipated. Communicative acts are distinctive in that they may be aroused by, and result in, changes anywhere within the system of relationships between two or more communicators and the objects of their communication'. Hence, communication, whether as transmission or reception, originates in an experience of tension and should be explained in terms of its function, actual or anticipated, in reducing the state of tension. It has causes and it has effects. In the terms of Skinner's extreme behaviourist version of S-R theory, apparently 'random' or 'spontaneous' acts of communication are simply examples of 'emitted' responses or 'operants', where the stimulus is simply unobserved or unobservable. Communication, in this perspective, is either response to a prior stimulus (feedback) or a given datum which forms the starting point of a new sequence of S-R associations. Communication process is essentially a *reaction* process and even seemingly 'expressive' acts of communication are to be viewed as reactions. It should be stressed that this is not the only formulation of the meaning of communication among psychologists who accept basic stimulus response and conditioning theory. For instance, the social psychologist Maslow[29] makes a distinction between 'coping' behaviour and 'expressive' behaviour — the former an 'interaction of the character with the world, adjusting each to the other, the latter an epiphenomenon of the character structure'. Where communication is a matter of 'coping', the stimulus response model applies, where it is expressive, the model is only partially relevant.

Implicit in this whole approach to communication are some answers to the general questions raised earlier, and only the aim of exposing these answers can justify this inadequate sketch of such a large part of psychology. First, on this view, we suppose that people enter into communication relationships as a result of an experience of tension within a shared environment: some prior stimulus exerts pressure on them to transmit information or to respond to information which comes to their attention. Second, the communication situation will be interpreted as one where the needs of participants are satisfied in a calculable way – its 'meaning' derives from the needs of the participants and of the wider system of which they form part. Third, the relationship between participants is a functional and mechanistic one, either useful or unavoidable. The sender relates to the receiver either instrumentally, to achieve some planned and predictable response and effect, or out of necessity. Similarly the receiver attends because it is useful or because he is conditioned to do so. While random and spontaneous elements may be present, our first presumption will be that such elements, when we come across them, are the result of faulty observation or inadequate evidence. This whole behaviourist perspective is clearly a very powerful explanatory paradigm which can generate propositions not only about these particular questions but also about the processes by which meaning is given to phenomena, the development of language and other sign systems, and about attention, perception and effects. Our concern however is at this point only with the conception of a communication act and a communication relationship as it is formed by the participant or the observer.

Information theory

Consistent with the approach which has just been described is a view of communication as basically a processing of 'information' by organisms, and information theory provides the components of such a view. It is primarily concerned with the problem of defining and measuring the quantity of information in any message. The definition of information comes from its opposite: randomness or 'entropy'. According to the founder of cybernetics, Norbert Wiener, 'we are always fighting nature's tendency to degrade the organised and destroy the meaningful'[30]. While nature promotes uncertainty, information helps to reduce it. According to Frick[31], the insight which led to the development of information theory was the realisation that 'all the processes which might be said to convey information are basically selection processes'. Thus, the mathematical theory of information provides an objective approach to the analysis of communicative activity, whether in machines, man or other systems. The basis for objective quantification is the binary coding system, the yes/no decision. All problems of uncertainty can ultimately be reduced to a series of either/or questions and the number of questions required to solve a problem (the number of items of information) provides the necessary measure of quantity for the application of the theory to communication analysis. Message content can be quantified in this way, as can the capacity of communication channels and the 'efficiency' of coding, receiving and decoding processes.

Information theory is a formal mathematical theory, based on probability and without any value for empirical prediction, or need for empirical validation (Frick[32]). It is not itself a model or theory of communicative behaviour, but it has been extremely influential in formulating problems, and shaping models for the study of communication processes. As Frick notes, 'the information-theoretic approach reflects an attitude, or opinion'. In relation to the electronic communication systems to which the theory was first applied, this attitude led to an assumption (*a*) that the process was statistical, and (*b*) that the significant feature of the process was the *difficulty* of communicating. Frick concludes that:

> the formalism of the theory is directed at the determination of the efficiency of the communication and the application of information theory to psychological data implies an interest in the efficiency rather than the structure of the process under study. The theory is, in this sense, normative.

We can see that, although it is only a tool or technique, information theory also has a tendency or bias in respect of the questions which we asked above. One tendency is to imply that communication is normally purposive and intentional, concerned with 'reducing uncertainty'. This particular formulation leads the observer to one particular definition of the communication situation and he may tend to attribute this interpretation to participants. The difficulty arises in that some communication situations, such as casual, interpersonal contact or artistic experiences, may be aimless, or creative, or productive of new meanings and ambiguities. While any message can be translated into information theory terms for analysis, to do so is liable to violate the understanding participants have of what is happening and of the orientation they have to each other. Information theory implies that the relationship between sender and receiver is essentially an instrumental one, and hence it offers an answer to our question in this respect consistent with, although distinct from, that which is implicit in the perspective of behavioural learning theory.

Congruence theory

The basic premises of congruence or balance theory are simple enough. Among the several variants, all stemming originally from Gestalt psychology, the earliest form of the theory relevant to communication is that of Heider[33]. This holds that in the case of two people who have an attitude of like or dislike to each other and to an external object, some patterns of relationship will be balanced (as when the two persons like each other and both like the object or when one person dislikes both the other person and the object) and some will be unbalanced (as when a person dislikes the object which is liked by a liked person, etc.). The theory proposes that where there is balance, the participants will resist change, and where there is not attempts will be made to restore 'cognitive' balance. Newcomb[34] has suggested a 'strain to symmetry' model resting on the same principle which posits communication as the main procedure for the extension of the area of agreement and of consistency. The dynamic for communicative acts is the tension produced by inconsistency. Elsewhere, Newcomb[35] also observes that communication is a 'learned response to strain'. In this view, communication follows 'system disequilibrium' and tends to restore the state of equilibrium until it is disturbed by the receipt of new information, and so on. The principle of consistency which has been mentioned is described by Zajonc[36] as holding 'that behaviour and attitudes are not only consistent to the objective observer but that individuals also try to be consistent to themselves'. The striving for internal consistency is a major factor which shapes the pattern of receiving and interpreting communication content.

Festinger's theory of Cognitive Dissonance[37] is the most developed version of balance theory and its main elements are summarised in the following way by Zajonc[38]:

1. two elements of knowledge are 'in dissonant relation if, considering these two alone, the obverse of one element would follow from the other';
2. dissonance, 'being psychologically uncomfortable, will motivate the person to try to reduce dissonance and achieve consonance';
3. ' . . . in addition to trying to reduce it, the person will actively avoid situations and information which would be likely to increase the dissonance'.

The theory has a number of implications for the communication process. Since communication is the main way in which balance in this context is maintained, sought or restored, the theory states a number of conditions relating to motives for the sending or receiving of messages and the pattern which shapes communicative behaviour. It predicts that people will seek out information which confirms their existing attitudes and view of the world or reinforces other aspects of their behaviour. Similarly, it predicts that people will avoid information which is likely to increase dissonance. They will selectively perceive and interpret the information they receive in accordance with the existing structure of their view, organising new information accordingly. They will be more open to receive communication from those sources to which they are favourably disposed. The primary application of this theory of communicative behaviour has been in the study of communication effects on attitudes, but in the present context it offers a general view of what the communicative relationship is about. It is a process which helps to maintain and develop a pattern of interdependence and co-orientation which is the product of pre-existing or external constraints. It tends to see the communicative relationship as secondary to, dependent on, and shaped by other circumstances, while at the same time the shape of relationships, the content of cognitive fields, the direction of ties between people are in some degree the outcome of communication behaviours. Nevertheless there is some flexibility about the approach, some attention to the transactional nature of human communication.

This discussion of some essentially psychological approaches to the study of communication illustrates the relevance of the active-passive dimension posited at the outset. It is not a term which would have much meaning to the proponents of the theories discussed, but, in our view, the more mechanistic and system-dependent the representation of communication, the more passive the conception of communication: passive only in the sense that the individuals involved are responding rather than initiating; accepting given definitions of the situation in which they relate to each other rather than giving new meanings to it in the sense of 'creating' an event and a relationship which was not latent in the preceding circumstances and the context. Sociological perspectives on communication can also be represented in terms of this dimension, although in sociology the terms tend to be recognised and used explicitly in the sense just outlined.

Social system theory
This offers a sociological perspective on communicative acts which is closest to the psychologistic and rather mechanistic accounts presented above. Talcott Parsons has been the main exponent of social system theory and, while he does not deal with communication at length, we can extract from the body of his work, especially *The Social System*[39], a consistent view of the communication process. He views social action in general as being distinguished by a motivation to achieve some goal. It is 'related to the attainment of gratification or the avoidance of deprivation' (p. 4). In addition, action occurs in a situation to which the actor orients himself and in which he is guided by norms, values and other constraints of the particular social environment. Parsons refers specifically to an 'activity-passivity coordinate' (p. 8) which differentiates the actor's concern with the development of a situation over time: 'The actor may at one extreme simply "await developments" and not actively attempt to "do anything about it" or he may actively attempt to control the situation in conformity with his wishes and interests.' A future state which is passively regarded is termed an 'anticipation' by Parsons, while one which is actively sought is termed a 'goal'. Parsons is also at pains to distinguish both extremes of this continuum 'from "stimulus-response" in that the latter does not make the orientation to the future development of the state explicit'. Earlier in his discussion he notes that 'it is a fundamental property of action . . . that it does not consist only of *ad hoc* "responses" to particular situational "stimuli" but that the actor develops a system of "expectations" rela-

tive to the various objects of the situation' (p. 5).

These points would all apply to communicative acts, although Parsons does not write specifically about communication in the same context. Where he does write about communication, he is mainly concerned with the emergence of a symbolic culture on the basis of interaction between human actors. Thus:

> Where there is social interaction, signs and symbols acquire common meanings and serve as media of communication between actors. When symbolic systems which can mediate communication have emerged we may speak of the beginnings of a 'culture' which becomes part of the action systems of the relevant actors (p. 5).

Systems of communication arise out of 'interaction with social objects', but in turn, developed forms of social behaviour depend on communication:

> it is quite clear that the high elaboration of human action systems is not possible without relatively stable symbolic systems whose meaning is not predominantly contingent on highly particularised situations (p. 11).

We should also note the connection which Parsons makes between the communication media and social control:

> A symbolic system of meanings is an element of order 'imposed' as it were on the realistic situation. Even the most elementary communication is not possible without some degree of conformity to the 'conventions' of the symbolic system (p. 11).

While it is evident that this general approach to social behaviour and to communication in particular in some sense 'takes off' where behaviourism ends, this way of thinking is not entirely different; it is more the focus of attention which is different, and the level of analysis. Thus while Parsons emphasises the distinction between social action and 'reactive' behaviour, as well as the free orientation to the attainment of chosen goals in the future, he tends to concentrate on the constraints — the limited range of goals which are culturally available and of modes of orientation to these goals, the regulation by the norms appropriate to the particular institutional context, the need to conform to culturally approved means of expression and so on. The communicative behaviour of an individual is thus frequently adaptive and functionally related to the social environment and to other actors. Social theory, as written by Parsons, aims with at least some success to achieve a reconciliation of those elements of Durkheim's work which emphasise the constraint exercised by social facts with Weber's view of human action as the making of meaningful choices in a universe of infinite variety. The element of subjective interpretation and the development and exchange of meaning is clearly present, hence differentiating human action systems from mechanical or organic processes, but the end result of a total social system theory is to bias attention towards system-maintenance and equilibrium. The answers to our starting questions about communication consequently suggest a view of the communication relationship as the outcome of ongoing systematic social processes, in a situation which has a largely predetermined social meaning, with relatively little freedom for the participants in relating to each other.

Symbolic interactionism

Another body of theory which takes us further along the continuum from the system perspective derives from the work of G. H. Mead[40] and has come to be known as symbolic interactionism. As its name implies, it is primarily concerned with the process of social interaction through symbols and it focuses quite directly on communication. While Mead's work is historically precedent to that of Parsons, and although he was a social psychologist rather than sociologist, and a 'behaviourist' as well, it has become influential as a successor or alternative to both the structural functionalism of the social system approach and to the methodology of early empirical sociology. Its rise to favour is connected with the interest in phenomenology which is discussed later. Mead's pupil, Herbert Blumer, has been influential in introducing the work of Mead into sociology. He describes some distinctive features of the approach as follows:

> under the perspective of symbolic interaction, social action is lodged in acting individuals who fit their respective lines of action to one another through a process of interpretation . . . as opposed to this view sociological conceptions generally lodge social action in the action of society or some unit of society[41].

Blumer further opposes this approach to those based on the social system which sees action as 'an expression of a system either in a state of balance or seeking to achieve balance'. He then criticises these approaches on the grounds that they ignore a 'view of group life or of group action as consisting of the collective or concerted actions of individuals seeking to meet their life situations'. Blumer also stresses the freedom of choice of action within a framework of social order: 'From the standpoint of symbolic interactionism the organisation of a human society is the framework inside which social action takes place and is not the determinant of that action' (p. 87). He emphasises that such elements as culture, social system or social stratification set the conditions for action without determining it: 'People . . . do not act towards culture, social structure or the like, they act towards situations.' Thus, in Blumer's view, there are two basic points about social action: it occurs within situations shaped by social organisations but is itself oriented to the situation and not directly to the determining features themselves. It is a conception which allows for more freedom and diversity than the social system approach.

Within this general framework, Mead's social psychology also offers a view of communication behaviour which informs Blumer's outlook when he underlines two basic points: the primacy of communication and the 'reflexivity' of the communicative act — the capacity of the individual person to converse 'with himself' from the standpoint of others. In this 'internal conversation' and its outcome, the person gives shape to society instead of merely being shaped by it. Communication is thus, essentially, creative in the sense that its outcome is the unique and unpredictable product of the act itself. On the primacy of communication, we can quote from Mead as follows:

> Wundt presupposes selves as antecendent to the communication process in order to explain communication within that process, whereas, on the contrary, selves must be accounted for in terms of the social process and in terms of communication (in Strauss[42], p. 161).

And again:

> The importance of what we term 'communication' lies in the fact that it provides a form of behaviour in which the organism or the individual may become an object to himself.

The essence of Mead's position lies in his conception of the individual as communicating with himself from the point of view of society:

> The human self arises through its ability to take the attitude of the groups to which he belongs — because he can talk to himself in terms of the community to which he belongs (ibid., p. 33).

It is this ability to 'enter into the attitude of others' which makes complex human society possible.

This process of self-formation and of acting on society depends on the development of language or systems of significant symbols. The connection between gesture and language is made as follows by Mead:

> The gesture is that phase of the individual act to which adjustment takes place on the part of other individuals in the social process of behaviour. The vocal gesture becomes a significant symbol when it has the same effect on the individual making it that it has on the individual to whom it is addressed (ibid., pp. 157—8).

This is a critical point in Mead's argument and important for its view of the nature of human communication. Communication is the essence of participation in social life because when we speak, use vocal gestures, we are producing the same effect on ourselves as on others. It is virtually a definition of the 'significant symbol' that it should have the property of having the 'same effect on the individual making it as on the individual to whom it is addressed' (ibid., p. 158). The elements of Mead's approach to communication and its outcome in the structuring of self and of society are as follows: from childhood onwards a person participates in group activities on the basis of a set of meanings and significant symbols which denote the objects and others of the world and are shared with other participants in social life. In giving and receiving communication, the person is not only acting on others, he is acting on himself, standing outside himself, as it were, and treating himself as an object. Through communication he becomes able to take on the attitude of others to himself. The 'other' in this context is sometimes referred to as the 'generalised other' or the 'representative of self in society'. Sometimes it is the 'significant other', a valued and respected person. Through inter- and intrapersonal communication and through contact with 'significant' (meaningful) objects of the social world a person develops a coherent view of himself and of his relations with others which is largely consistent with the perception which others have of himself.

Mead's remarks add up to an important statement about the communication process which does more than simply underline the importance of communication for social life. In particular, it helps to resolve the paradox of continuity and change in society. Continuity is achieved by the intrusion of the generalised other in the formation of new 'selves', while change comes from the relatively free dialogue within these new selves. Communication between persons or between society and persons is in part unpredictable in its outcome because it is only in part a process of adjustment and response and has elements of creativity and freedom. Change and variability would be more rare if communication were merely reaction and anticipation. Mead's work both helps to answer the question of why people communicate and also offers a way to avoid the distinction between giving and receiving in communication. Thus in 'sending' messages a person is also receiving them (his own) and responding to them; in receiving he is also managing a communication between the external social world and himself. For example, Mead comments on the 'astonishing' degree of interest which people take in stories, movies and novels, and in news of people who are unknown to them. In Mead's view this interest is accounted for by the individual's capacity and wish to 'take the attitude of the group to which he belongs'. Attending to such phenomena is thus a matter for the person of 'talking to himself in terms of the community to which he belongs' (ibid., p. 33).

The perspective of phenomenology

In phenomenology, and particularly in the work of Alfred Schutz, we can find an approach to communication which is consistent with symbolic interactionism and takes us nearer to a view of the communicative act as spontaneous activity. Schutz's phenomenological sociology has been described as 'an attempt to synthesise the phenomenology of Husserl with the sociology of Weber' (Wagner[43]). The former aimed to establish a philosophy without presuppositions — one which would derive from the immediate sense experience of human beings living and acting in a 'world' which is shared with others and has a common meaning to all who experience it as a set of external objects. The aspect of Weber's sociology most relevant to the concerns of Schutz was his view of meaningful social action, conduct which is invested with meaning by its author and oriented forward in time to the conduct of other human beings.

Schutz's basic perspective has the following main elements. The individual experiences a 'life-world' which he takes for granted and seeks to make sense of in terms of an acquired 'stock of knowledge' derived from experience. In interpreting and making sense of this world of experience he acts upon it and to some extent constructs his own unique world. He selectively attends to the world of experience according to what is of relevance to him at the time and the world consists of receding 'zones of relevance'. The vast amount of possible sense experience is selectively attended to according to principles of relevance, and handled by means of 'typifications' — accepted meanings which render less problematic most of the objects of experience he encounters and which make possible interaction with those who share the world. The sharing of the world with others — the 'intersubjectivity' of the world — is facilitated by the belief which people have that others experience the world as they themselves do, and by the capacity to take another's point of view, to understand each others' motives and perspectives. A person is able to act in relation to others in a subject—object way (the Thou relationship) and also to act with them as object or subject (the We relationship). He can also relate to others as typifications, occupants of other roles not directly experienced (They relationships). The action of such an individual in the social world is essentially free and oriented to the future, planned in its course; the meaning or explanation of human action is essentially a matter of this reference to the future.

Contained within this theoretical framework, we can find the answers to a number of our key questions about communication. First, we have a view of the nature of the communicative act as essentially purposive. 'Every action', writes Schutz[44] (p. 57), is a spontaneous activity oriented towards the future.' And 'It is essential to every act that it have an extrinsic goal — the in-order-to-motive, the aim that the person addressed take cognisance of it one way or another.' At this point Schutz distinguishes the 'expressive act' where communication is intended (not necessarily by using verbal forms) from the 'expressive gesture', where it is not so intended, even though an observer may attribute communicative intent. On the reasons for communication, for engaging in 'expressive' acts, Schutz has also something to say. One reason is simply the free choice of the person: 'He who lives in the social world is a free being: his acts proceed from spontaneous activity' (ibid., p. 146). But purpose is also presupposed, some orientation to the future: the 'project'. Most expressive acts occur as part of the individual's exploration and making sense of his world. He attends to matters of relevance, those close to his life interests, and it is about these that he communicates to others. The fact that it is apparently a shared world and that to live in the world we have to engage continually in relationships with other men is sufficient to account for most communicative acts. We communicate, broadly, to achieve future ends and to participate in social life, to handle the world of experience.

The preconditions for communication are discussed in some detail by Schutz (in Wagner[45], pp. 203–4). He begins by saying that

> communication . . . is based on purposive signs, as the communicator has at least the intention of making himself understandable to the addressee if not to induce him to react appropriately. But certain requirements have to be fulfilled to make communication possible.

The most important preconditions are as follows:

1. the signs must be held in common and have a common meaning:

> Communication requires under all circumstances both events in the outer world, produced by the communicator and events in the outer world apprehensible by the interpreter. In other words, communication can occur only within the reality of the outer world.

2.

> The sign used in communication is always pre-interpreted by the communicator in terms of its expected interpretation by the addressee . . . communication presupposes that the interpretational scheme which the communicator relates and that which the interpreter will relate to the communicative sign will *substantially* coincide.

3. Full coincidence is impossible because of differences in biographical experience and the different structures of relevance of participants, but the greater the differences between

systems of relevance the fewer chances there are for successful communication.

4. A set of abstractions or typifications must be held in common by communicator and interpreter.

Finally, Schutz's work contains an answer to questions about the results or effects of communication. These must be judged, in the first instance, according to the intentions of the communicator. In general, however, communication results in a wider currency of typifications, a change in the social distribution of knowledge, a greater sharing of the social world, reciprocity of understanding, a greater concordance between the stock of knowledge of different individuals. The construction of society is the outcome of diverse acts and processes of communication.

In conclusion, we shall call attention to the emphasis on the communication relationship in the phenomenological scheme of things. Communicative acts cannot be autistic, whether they are acts of sending or receiving. They are essentially *intersubjective*. Schutz's comments on musical communication occurring between a long dead composer and a living listener illustrate this conclusion. He uses the expression 'tuning in' to express the concordance between communicator and receiver:

> All possible communication presupposes a mutual tuning-in relationship between the communicator and the addressee of the communication. This relationship is established by the reciprocal sharing of the other's flux of experience in inner time . . . by experiencing this togetherness as 'We' . . . communicating with one another presupposes, therefore, the simultaneous partaking of the partners in various dimensions of outer and inner time — in short in growing older together. This seems to be valid for all kinds of communication (in Wagner[46], p. 216).

This is a sketchy and very selective view of sociological perspectives on communicative behaviour, designed only to present one dimension of analysis and to record the main concerns of sociology with communication phenomena. Perhaps the most serious omission is a discussion of the work of Erving Goffman[47] which has developed into a major presentation of the motives and forms of interpersonal communication. Goffman explores the complex rules and occasions of symbolic exchange between persons, showing both the elaborate structuring of contacts and many strategies for handling them and making the best of them. In terms of the continuum that has been discussed here, it is difficult to place his work, since Goffman deals in situational constraints as well as cases of negotiation of relationships through optional action. But the emphasis is on intersubjectivity, spontaneity and creativity, despite the fact that many of his terms and categories imply a use of communication for managing tense situations, restoring equilibrium, or engaging in rituals of exchange (e.g. 'supportive' and 'remedial' 'interchange', 'facework', 'social control', 'tie-signs', 'normal appearances'). What Goffman also reminds us is that communication and communicative acts cannot just be conceived of as 'information transfer', although they can all be *reduced* to that. A communication event is a complex social occasion, often highly particular to the circumstances and individuals participating, although patterned according to culture or subculture.

Conclusion

What can be said by way of a summary about the three questions posed earlier in this chapter (p. 38)? What implications do alternative theoretical perspectives have for an answer in general terms to each? On the first question, the *why* of communication, one might note a continuum of answers. At an extreme point to the 'left' of the continuum one would treat communication as a response, a conditioned reaction to external stimuli. Moving along, the explanation would suppose an element of conscious choice, but the 'need' to adjust or release tension is still the guiding explanatory principle. At a further point, choice of goals is assumed, but these are conceived in much wider terms than simply as forms of tension-management. The individual chooses ends among those made available by the social system, and patterns of communication are governed by norms and conventions. Finally, we have at the other extreme a view of the act of communication as a spontaneous and creative act directed to some freely chosen future state which may involve a modification of norms and conventions. These points are illustrated in Fig. 1.

	(*psychological*) ----------			(*sociological*)
	1 **Extreme behaviourist position**	*2* **Social-psychological position**	*3* **Social system position**	*4* **Interactionist/ phenomenological position**
1. **Why communicate?**	**Conditioning; instinct**	**Reduce tension; orient to environment**	**Achieve approved goals by approved means**	**Express free choice; act *on* the environment**
2. **What is the meaning of a communication situation?**	**Reaction as determined by the system**	**An experience of tension or discomfort**	**A situation of choice among goals and means**	**An occasion for innovation and creation**
3. **What is the relationship between participants?**	**Partial; mechanistic**	**Functional; instrumental; holistic**	**Institutionally defined complementarity**	**Intersubjective; negotiable**

Fig. 1 Summary of alternative answers to the main questions posed about the communicative act, in terms of the Passive–Active continuum

Our question about the *meaning* of a communication situation also produces alternative answers, as Fig. 1 shows. At the left, or more 'passive' end, the meaning of communication lies outside the control of the individual participant. The situation is defined for him, is not open to variable perceptions, and he responds according to past experience and as the logic of the situation requires. A second position to the right has some of these elements, but communication depends on the perception of tension and ways of resolving it. Thus, the predominant 'meaning' is in terms of an experience of discomfort, calling for some action. Further along our continuum, we can think of communication situations as having a complex meaning to participants, especially in respect of the alternative goals of action and the value judgments involved in choosing between these alternatives. Thus the predominant 'meaning' suggests a situation of free choice, structured according to cultural and institutional values. At the furthest extreme, on our right, the meaning of a communication situation is still characterised by choice of goals and means, but without the element of constraint, predictability and calculation. A communication situation is one which offers the possibility of changing and restructuring the environment — that is, it is not a response *to* the environment or an act *in* an environment, but an act *on* it.

Finally, an answer to our third question, about *relationships*, can also be found at different points along the continuum. The relationship between givers and receivers at the left-hand extreme is a mechanistic and temporary one, with only small elements of co-orientation. A participant in communication, according to this view, is essentially reacting to an external stimulus and the relationship is consequently partial and limited. Further along, according to versions of balance theory, one would posit a much more holistic relationship, but still one based on an assumption of functionality and of unavoidable interdependence emerging out of contiguity. The degree of intersubjectivity is limited and we would still be thinking in terms of discrete organisms finding some mode of joint operation. Sociological versions of the communicative relationship vary according to the amount of external constraint and role determination involved. At one pole, a relationship is defined in terms of role-complementarity, at another it is highly active and negotiable, and communication is a sensitive vehicle for the process of interaction.

Ways of communicating 3

Acts of communication as well as the social process of communication as a whole can occur only through the application of techniques or technology, ranging from the very simple to the very complex. Communication necessitates the conscious manipulation of physical forces and objects according to agreed rules and conventions. While one must give prior attention to the purposes of the giving and receiving of messages, to the meaning and structure of situations in which communication occurs and to the consequences of communication, the question of how communication is accomplished is not simply a residual or unimportant one. The means of communication which are available are varied, they differ according to the level of development of the society and, in their use, they are always subject to social and cultural regulation. It is also true that in the widest sense, they affect who communicates with whom, how often, how well, and the substance or content of communication.

Several quite different things have to be taken into account under the general heading of 'means of communication'. First, there are language systems and codes: the formal systems of signs and rules for their use which constitute the physical content of messages. Under this broad heading there is also much diversity. Second, there are activities, techniques and devices for encoding messages: the formation of sounds, the visual representation of images and signs. Third, there are techniques and activities concerned with the 'transmission' of messages: the turning of symbolic material into forms which can be consulted over time and distributed over distance. The technologies of telegraphy or printing and the social inventions for distributing multiple copies of messages by way of the press, the cinema or television fall under this heading; so too, do the simple skills of speech, letter writing, etc. Finally, there are the skills, activities and techniques associated with the reception, 'reading', or 'decoding' of messages: interpreting film and photograph, reading words, receiving radio and television, etc.

Our interest is, for the most part, limited to a discussion of the ways in which technique and technology (in the broadest sense) interact with social and cultural factors. There are a number of general ways in which this interaction occurs. First, through the coincidence of societal and group boundaries with the boundaries of a language system or a code. Thus we use the term 'speech community' collectively to designate the users of a particular language, implying that the sharing of a language normally goes with having other things in common — values, an environment, patterns of association, etc. This coincidence of boundaries occurs within societies as well, since groups within a single speech community, which have their own distinct linguistic usage or argot, are also normally groups which have a separate identity in the social organisation and share other things. Another aspect of social regulation is the institutionalisation of meanings and usages. Thus there are sanctions of varying degrees of formality and strength which control the relationship between language or code and the reality, or external phenomena, to which the language refers. Third, the skills and knowledge relating to communication and the degrees of access to giving and receiving messages are also socially distributed. Fourth, in the other direction, we can expect that language systems and technologies of transmission will affect the content and the social relationships of communication and hence the nature of social life, by influencing the selection of cultural objects for attention and the definition of contact situations.

Language

The primary means of human communication is the spoken language, in the sense of its being historically precedent and also the form of communication still most used as well as providing the model for other communication forms. Language is a universal fact of human society and in basic essentials it has the same characteristics in all its main examples. The origin of language is obscure since it existed before there were any self-conscious attempts to study it and we have little evidence of development of language itself, although there is a known history of methods of representing it. While we cannot say much for certain about the origin of language, the process by which it emerges can be understood from observation of contemporary social life, since we can see how variations in, and modifications of, linguistic use originate, and see the functions of language in social interaction. We can presume that its origin lies in the interaction of people in a common environment which is encountered and manipulated. For people to cooperate, or simply to cope with environmental facts, agreed ways of denoting experience must be arrived at. Sounds become associated with certain experiences and can be said to have meanings; as a result of this association their utterance gives rise to the image of the experienced object. The basic similarity of languages across time and space and their relative immutability supports this view of language as arising out of a response to a common environment. The facts of human life in the relatively short period of human existence are fairly universal and give rise to the same processes of perception and response in different places and times.

What are the basic characteristics of language in this universal form? The answer which follows is based mainly on Dinneen[1]. First, it is 'linear', or sequential, in that the sounds which compose it are produced by successive movements of the speech organs and can be represented by a linear succession of symbols paralleling the sequence of emitted sound. A more important feature of language is that it is systematic and governed by rules. Thus there are a limited number of sounds in the language which can be combined in a limited number of ways. The form to be taken by the sounds and the ways in which they can be combined are determined for a given language, just as the association between the sound sign and the object to which it refers is determined and subject to rules of grammar, syntax and vocabulary. 'Systematic' thus refers to the lack of randomness in the usage of sounds and the exclusion of casual or idiosyncratic alterations; it also refers to an element of logical consistency to be found within most languages. Third, language is a system of differences or contrasts: it is basically concerned with distinguishing one object, experience, concept from another, sometimes by subtle variations of sound or order. Languages vary according to the range of differentiation of which they are capable or which they actually exhibit, depending on the culture and environment of their location. This basic characteristic makes it possible to translate language into a form suitable for handling in digital computers since all differences of meaning can be accommodated by binary coding. Fourth, a language is said to be arbitrary in that there is no necessary or objective connection between the nature of the thing or idea and the linguistic unit which refers to it. Hence the incomprehensibility of languages to those outside the speech community. It is possible that some words, by their sounds, convey an impression of the object to which they refer, but it is also clear that very little of experience is open to this sort of representation. Written languages in the form of ideographs or pictographs may be representational but, even here, the connection is more often than not conventional. The conventionality of language is a further main characteristic — that is, the language rests entirely on the implicit and informal agreement of its users to abide by rules of meaning and usage. The arbitrariness of language is made possible by this underlying and complete agreement, so complete that the speech of any one member of a speech community is representative of all others.

Certain other points should be made clear about language and about the terminology of linguistic use which has become embedded in communication study. The study of language itself is, of course, peripheral to our present purpose and we need in particular to distinguish between language as a system of sounds and language as a means of communication actually in use. The threefold distinction of Saussure[2] between *langage*, *parole* and *langue* is relevant at this point. In his view, *langue* is language in its formal properties as we have described, open to examination as a fixed object. *Parole* is the language as it is spoken, while *langage* is the sum of these two elements. When we look at some of the social correlates of language we need to focus primarily on *parole*, since in actual usage there is the greatest amount of variation, especially between subcultures, within the same speech community. The main concern of sociolinguistics, for instance, is with variations in use of the same language by different groups and with the consequences of this variation.

Language (*langue*) was regarded by Saussure as a 'deposit of signs' and this description calls for some further comment, if only because language is the necessary starting point for any review of the means by which communication is carried out and the standard against which we can judge other modes of communication. In using the word 'sign', Saussure was thinking of a complex phenomenon composed of an 'acoustic image' and a concept (the thing signified). Thus a word or a combination of words in a language refers to, or indicates, some externally existing thing or idea. This is now the customary meaning of sign in discussing language communication. The sign is arbitrarily (in the sense described above) and conventionally associated with some concept and when it is used it conjures up a mental image of the concept. This simple account is complicated by the fact that there are not only different kinds of signification (for instance denotational or connotational) but also other kinds of sign in use in communication. Raymond Firth[3] (pp. 74—5) distinguishes four such different concepts which deserve to be noted. These are: index, signal, icon, and symbol. An index is a sign which has a direct relationship in fact to what is signified — for instance, the footprint which shows that someone has passed or the smoke which shows the existence of a fire. A signal is a sign with an emphasis on 'consequential action', a stimulus requiring some response. An icon is a sign which has a sensory likeness to what is represented. An example would be a sculpted or painted 'likeness' or possibly music which reproduced some essential characteristic of an experience — birdsong or wind or a storm, etc. A symbol is a sign with a complex series of associations which are conventionally understood to convey some thought or emotion or event. This version is taken by Firth largely from Charles Peirce[4], who saw the meaning of a symbol as being allocated 'depending on habit, convention or agreement, or natural disposition of the interpreter'. More will be said of communication by means of symbols, but it should be stressed that processes of communication based on indices, icons or symbols have a different reach and a different power from communication based on conventional sign-based language. For one thing, they are not confined within the same group of users, but can convey meaning across the normal boundaries of the speech or language community. They are suitable also for media of expression and transmission other than speech and writing which are the only media for communication through language, as normally understood.

There is at least one other major form of expression which can support communication and has a different distribution in use than language, and that is the language of gesture, movement, and physical posture (see also below, p. 73). Observers of social interaction have noted regularities in the use of bodily movements and positioning, facial expressions, gestures which indicate the unconscious use of what is sometimes called a 'paralanguage' which at least expresses states of mind, emotion, intention and often acts to convey meanings in as efficient a way as formal spoken language. The study of such 'paralanguages' has reached a point where one can be sure of the fact that members of the same culture or group unconsciously, or 'instinctively', make use of a non-verbal means of communications which is well understood, consistent in use, apparently resting on much the same conventional agreement as language proper and open to reliable observation and notation.

Our earlier discussion of basic features of language helps to put in perspective the significance for the communication process of these alternative modes of communication. The factors which are of most interest for the sociological study of communication are related in different ways to these other communicative devices. We are interested, in particular, in three things: the degree of coincidence between social group and mode of communication; the skills and competence involved and their social distribution; the availability to senders and receivers of the means of communication. On the first of these, it is generally the case that language is the property of a (generally large) clearly defined population with little probability of movement across boundaries because of the long-term nature of language endowment. On the second, we know that within the same speech community there are differences of skill in the use of language and these differences coincide with differences of power and esteem in society; on the third aspect, language is associated with high availability and accessibility. In developed societies, there is great institutional pressure towards the universalisation of language skills and competence in their application to reading and writing as well as speaking.

Of the other modes of communication which have been discussed, three are of particular importance: the symbolic, the non-verbal and the iconic. Each differs in respect of the points mentioned. Thus, symbolic communication has a largely unknown range and potency. Its power will be variable and dependent on subjective factors. The relationship with societal and group boundaries is present but very complex. Non-verbal communication has a range determined more by culture than society, and it may often be very localised. It involves skills which must be unevenly distributed, but the lines of division may coincide more with personality than with social structural factors. These skills are not generally open to formal teaching or diffusion and are largely intuitive. Iconic modes of communication, because of their representational nature, are the most universal, least subject to boundary-drawing, involving fewest skills which can or need to be taught. All they require is some common experience of what is represented.

Language and social structure

There has recently been a revival of interest among sociologists and students of language in the social patterning of language use, with the coining of a term 'sociolinguistics' to describe the new field of study (see below, p. 69). While the main-stream linguistic tradition has been to treat language for working purposes as an object which is *sui generis* and context free, it has become increasingly difficult to ignore the connection between variations in speech behaviour and the underlying structure of social relations. Linguists, partly under the influence of ethnographers and anthropologists, have come to recognise that the link between social groups and language use is a problem for investigation, not a fact that can be taken for granted and ignored. For their part, sociologists have been moved to study language, both out of a growing concern with the detailed management and control, by people, of their social relationships and of the social reality they inhabit, and also out of a more long-standing concern with problems of social differentiation and inequality which cannot be solved without reference to the variable of language use.

The connection between sociological concerns and communication through language is implicit in the concept of the 'speech community'. This has been defined as 'any human aggregate characterised by regular and frequent interaction by means of a shared body of verbal signs and set off from similar aggregates by significant differences in language usage' (Gumperz[5]). This definition does not merely refer to national societies but to many subcollectivities within societies whose similarities of language use are related to different kinds of social experience and separate patterns of interaction. Thus, for the sociologist, speech communities are not mere 'aggregates'. Gumperz notes that 'most groups of any permanence, be they small bands bounded by face to face contact, modern nations divisible into smaller subregions, or even occupational associations or neighbourhood gangs may be treated as speech communities, provided they show linguistic peculiarities that warrant special study'. The evidence for the development of special languages associated with intensive and relatively exclusive types of social interaction is very impressive. Sometimes these language differentiations are the familiar outcome of regional differences and spatial isolation; sometimes they derive from alien ethnic origins, as in the case of the gypsies or Jews; sometimes they relate to specialised occupations which have their own argots — for instance railwaymen (Cottrell[6]), thieves (Sutherland[7]) or jazz musicians (Becker[8]); sometimes voluntary associations, such as street gangs, give rise to speech differences. Frequently differences of language use are simply of historical or circumstantial origin. The more interesting cases of consciously developed and maintained speech habits seem to relate to the need to mark group boundaries, to 'symbolise' membership, or promote solidarity and integration. They are an essential part of the culture of a group, and the more permanent, isolated and salient the group, the more likely are speech differences to be pronounced. Of occupation-based languages, Miller and Form[9] (p. 263) say that 'part of the occupational culture is the development of jargon and a technical language and argot'. They also say that 'jargon is developed more extensively among highly skilled workers' because everyday language is inadequate to refer to objects and occurrences at work. But a technical vocabulary is only one element in the situation. One should also note that these kinds of special language are always additional to the standard language of the society to which the users also belong.

A further aspect of the relationship between language and social structure is the fact of an intimate connection between status in a social hierarchy and language use. This manifests itself in so many ways as to defy any brief summary, but there are two main aspects to the connection. One relates to the points just made and suggests an explanation in terms of culture. A status group in a society, normally differentiated by the degree of its access to power, is also a community and in part a speech community. Hence, for example, the continued difference between a small upper class in this country and others in the way they speak and use language. An illustration would be the 'U' and 'non-U' forms of speech described by Alan Ross and popularised by Nancy Mitford. Second, there is an explanation relating to language use as a scarce and valuable skill. Thus in ancient civilisations, a literate élite of administrators and religious experts was able to maintain itself as a centralised bureaucracy. Both in ancient and medieval times it was likely that literacy (i.e. the ability to read and write) was a caste-like possession which did not belong either to kings and rulers or to peasants and ordinary people. The former, as members of a warrior class, might look down on their literary experts, while depending on them; at the same time, the latter had no means of access to skills in speech and writing except by recruitment from above. Goody and Watt[10] quote from Childe the remark of an Egyptian of the New Kingdom: 'Put writing in your heart that you may protect yourself from hard labour of any kind.' They also make the interesting point that the élite literate group, whose interest was in maintaining the social order and their place in it, had a strong tendency to maintain a writing system of a particular kind: 'pictographic and logographic systems are alike in their tendency to reify objects of the natural and social order; by so doing they register, record, make permanent the existing social order and ideological picture'. By contrast 'phonetic writing, by imitating human discourse, is in fact symbolising not the objects of the social and natural order but the very process of human interaction in speech'. For this reason, the invention and diffusion of this form of writing is much more likely to be responsive to social change, more accessible to outsiders, and also more reflective of group and cultural differences.

The tradition of association of special literary skills with power and status has remained. It continued in the use of Latin as the language of administration and law into very recent times in Europe; in the retention of the European language of colonial powers among the educated of ex-colonial societies, or in the continued valuation of a classical education for ruling positions in Britain well into the present century. Another illustration of the link between language and social status is provided by the process of 'sanskritisation' which is still important in India as a means of upward social mobility. Members of a caste or group move up the social hierarchy by adopting the sanskritic culture and values. The educated urban Indian seeks to acquire English as a social accomplishment in much the same way (Beteille[11], p. 116). It has become very hard to disentangle the elements of utility from those of status in any of the modern examples of connection between spoken and written language competence and differences of power. The general direction of change has presumably tended to emphasise the useful and rational basis of such associations, especially in relation to written language. The differences of spoken language use which remain have more to do with differential patterns of association, with the social isolation of some groups and with varying needs to use spoken language at all. For example, Hymes[12] has observed that:

> Peoples do not all everywhere use language to the same degree, in the same situations, or for the same things; some peoples focus upon language more than others. Such differences in the place of a language in the communicative system of a people cannot be assumed to be without influence on the depth of a language's influence on such things as world view.

The context of this remark is the Sapir—Whorf[13] thesis that language itself shapes culture and perceptions of the world. Gumperz[14] comments on a similar phenomenon:

> Control of communicative resources varies sharply with the individual's position within the social system. The more narrowly confined his sphere of activities, the more homogeneous the social environment within which he interacts, the less his need for verbal facility. Thus, housewives, farmers and labourers, who rarely meet outsiders, often make do with only a narrow range of speech styles, while actors, public speakers and businessmen command the greatest range of styles.

This has always been, and continues to be, so. It becomes a 'problem' largely because of the bureaucratic organisation of modern industrial society in economic and political matters which requires a universal minimum level of spoken and written verbal performance.

In looking at the social distribution of communicative skills and facilities, it is important to take note of a long-term historical change in the form and location of social control. In the past, control focused on access to communication at the receiving end by limiting the ability to read and understand or the chance to make wider social contact than was institutionally provided for. At the present time, societal arrangements foster and promote the reception of communication by encouraging literacy and education, by making radio and television accessible, by encouraging travel within and between societies. The consensus view in most societies, whether overtly stated or not, is that the more 'access' in this sense the better. At the same time, there is more care to ensure control over the 'transmitting' end of communication chains and networks, by licensing, by regulation, by finance and other less formal ways. The social distribution of the power and ability to transmit, or participate in forming, the content which circulates in society's communication channels has become the key issue.

One case study which provides an interesting example of the close connection between language and changes in social life is that of the history and use of the pronouns 'you' and 'thou' in English and in several other European languages. Brown and Gilman[15] tell us that 'the interesting thing about such pronouns is their close association with two dimensions fundamental to the analysis of all social life — the dimensions of power and solidarity'. According to them, the two forms of singular pronouns of address originate in the Latin *tu* and *vos* and the use of the plural form to address a single person is found first in an address to the emperor at a time (fourth century) when there were two emperors. Use of the *vos* form then developed, generally in relation to anyone of superior power, and indicated respect and deference. The singular, or *tu* form, conversely, was gradually confined to use to address either inferiors, or equals in intimate circumstances: 'the power semantic is simply non-reciprocal; the superior says *T* and receives *V*'. This usage for many centuries characterised the relationships between parents and children, nobility and commoners, masters and servants, priests and penitents, men and animals, God and his angels. The 'T' form is described as the pronoun of solidarity because of its use between those whose relationships are symmetrical in terms of power: friends, workmates, siblings, etc. However, in recent history, there has been a considerable change in societies where the two forms remain in use (as they do not in English). First, where power is asymmetrical, the *vos* form is used on both sides of the relationship: it has become reciprocal. Second, there is evidence of a widening of the sphere where the *T* or solidary form is mutually in use. Both trends are consistent with greater democratisation of society and of personal relationships.

Sociolinguistics: some issues

So far as sociology in Britain is concerned, sociolinguistics has tended to focus on the question of social class and language use, with particular reference to problems of equalising educational experience. Even the brief foregoing discussion will have shown this to be an unduly narrow focus, and some of the disagreement and sterility associated with this approach in sociology seems to reflect a lack of perspective. A recognisable precursor to recent British work concerned with social class and language use may be found in Schatzman and Strauss's[16] study of speech examples of respondents in Arkansas. They reported patterned differences between the speech of working-class and middle-class respondents. Working-class speakers were distinctive for tending to relate events only from their own perspective, making no allowance for the fact that the interlocutor had not been present; using names and pronouns without explanation; not offering qualification or elaboration; giving concrete information; digressing in their narrative. By contrast, middle-class respondents employed other perspectives than their own; supplied a context; took account of the interlocutor's absence; provided qualifications; provided coherently ordered accounts. These differences are explained in terms of life-styles and habits of thinking: thus a working-class person normally deals with 'listeners with whom he shares a great deal of experience and symbolism'. Middle-class speakers, on the other hand, are more used to communicating in formal, impersonal situations and with strangers whose different location they are able to take into account. The importance of this work is that it proposes the existence of fundamental differences of kind between 'working'- and 'middle'-class language which are not a matter of degrees of inferiority, but related to social situation and life-style.

This field of study is associated in Britain with the later, though independent, work of Bernstein which reached similar, though more fully worked out and supported conclusions. Bernstein[17] (p. 78) proposes that 'associated with the organisation of particular social groups are distinct forms of spoken language'. He is primarily concerned with a difference between what he terms a middle class and a lower working class, and a difference between two forms of speech use, two languages or codes. His class differentiation is highly ideal-typical in that he abstracts the main elements of a 'traditional', 'family centred', 'communal', 'non-instrumental', 'affective', working-class life-style and culture and contrasts it with another abstraction of elements of 'middle-class culture': discipline, rationality, orientation to the future, stability, formality, self-control and so on. His analysis of language use, based on empirical observation and research, contrasts two ways of using language, one called either a 'restricted speech code' or a 'public language', another an 'elaborated code' or a 'formal language', the former associated with working-class occupation and life-style, the latter with middle-class culture. The restricted code, or public language, is simpler, more repetitive, involves short commands and questions, and infrequent use of impersonal pronouns as subjects, has few adjectives and adverbs, is unstructured and is a language of 'implicit meaning'. An elaborated code, or a formal language, is more complex in structure, more organised, richer in qualification, controlled, complete as a form of reference. It is a language or speech form which is highly effective and self-contained as an instrument for rational action. As one would expect, it is the language of education, business and administration.

For Bernstein, the important point to understand is the

intimate connection between form of language, socialisation process and the rest of life experience. From the point of view of practical policy, especially in education, the implication is clear enough. The formal language, which is available to the middle-class child, is the one required for success at school and work. The middle-class child can have this as well as have access to the other code and hence has an advantage. It is the causes and consequences of this fundamental linguistic fact about social classes which lies at the core of Bernstein's work. He argues (op. cit., p. 200) that speech differences are closely related to socialisation on the one hand and, on the other, to a person's subsequent potential in society. Class structure limits access to elaborated codes and hence tends to limit access to forms of social action which are relatively context-free, universalistic rather than particularistic, less tied to local structure and generally more autonomous. The whole body of work is a complex web of proposition, theory and evidence which ties language and social experience together in an interactive relationship. Typical class and family experience produces a certain form of use of speech, which in turn reinforces certain elements of the culture. In a society which selects certain cultural elements for valuation above others (as do all) those who have only the restricted code are at a permanent disadvantage.

Variations in speech and the use of language within the same society have been looked at in the context of Negro—white differences in the United States. The work of Labov[18] contains a warning against an uncritical application of Bernstein's analysis (especially in its early forms) to the situation of the American urban Negro. In particular, Labov is concerned to refute the concept of verbal deprivation and to reject the value implication that lower working-class language is an inferior version of standard English. Essentially, what Labov is concerned to demonstrate is that the typical language of American Negroes is a non-standard form of language with its own rules, its own subtleties and range, a perfectly adequate capacity for the economic expression of abstract thought. Of the Negro speech community, as it appeared from his work in the ghetto areas, he writes:

> We see a child bathed in verbal stimulation from morning to night. We see many speech events which depend upon the competitive exhibition of verbal skills . . . a whole range of activities in which the individual gains status through his use of language. . . . We see no connection between verbal skill at the speech events characteristic of the street culture and success in the schoolroom.

Labov's case against the concept of verbal deprivation as applied to Negro speech is a convincing one. There is little doubt, equally, that there are some important social class-related differences in the use of language in Britain and that these have a connection with patterns of socialisation and with early interaction between mothers and children. The evidence is still somewhat sparse and restricted in range, but as summarised by Robinson[19] (p. 181) it leads to the general conclusion 'that the learning opportunities offered by the mother are determinants of the verbal behaviours of children'. The empirical evidence tends to confirm the basic thesis of Bernstein, especially in finding an absence, among working-class mothers, of the use of language in 'discipline situations' except in the form of direct commands:

> Language is used as a medium for the direct control of behaviour by commands or to define roles. Middle-class children also receive such prescriptions, but in addition are given verbally expressed reasons for certain behaviours and information about the material and social environment in general (ibid., p. 178).

The kind of work which has been described tells us a good deal about the mechanisms and the social factors which produce language, and especially speech, variations between subcultural groups in the same society. The fact that these groups tend also to be social-class groups and that many of the causal influences stem directly from the characteristics of a class-divided society turns the issue into a social problem.

While linguistic deviance of this kind can be tolerated as welcome diversity in some contexts, there is strong social pressure to eliminate rather than adapt to this particular expression of deviance. In his efforts to preserve and respect non-standard forms of language, Labov may be fighting a losing battle, but his position deserves a good deal more notice from would-be reformers than it has so far received.

Paralanguage

While language is the basic means of communicating and the key invention or development in the 'evolution' of man's communicative capacity, it is not, as we have seen, the only mode of communication between people. In some circumstances it can even be subsidiary. Its uniqueness comes from its great power compared to other means, its capacity for development and the causative influence it has had on human history and culture. The modes of communication we must now attend to are those which are prelinguistic, 'paralinguistic' or 'extralinguistic' — those forms of behaviour which are used for transmitting meaning and are open to meaningful interpretation but do not use words or linguistic sign systems. The terms 'non-verbal' communication or 'paralanguage' are the most frequently used terms for these phenomena. The first is simply a way of describing all behaviour which communicates without the use of a verbal language, the second has a somewhat different implication and it is more difficult to decide which phenomena should be included or excluded from its reference. Laver and Hutcheson[20] (p. 13) define paralanguage as:

> All those non-linguistic, non-verbal features (both vocal and non-vocal) which participants manipulate in conversation.

They add that the interpretation of these features, as in the case of linguistic features, is subject to conventions which are shared with other members of one's culture. The idea of government by convention implies some degree of codification and hence justifies the comparison with language. Similarly, this definition draws attention to cultural patterning and hence to the idea that there are 'paralinguistic communities' as well as speech communities, with somewhat different boundaries. Another definition, by Abercrombie[21], limits paralinguistic features to activities which '(*a*) communicate and (*b*) are part of a conversational interaction'. Abercrombie notes that all animals communicate with each other by noises, movements and postures but that human beings, who also have language, have mixed these 'more primitive communication activities' with spoken language. Hence the term 'paralinguistic' since these activities are aids to, or adjuncts of, language proper.

Our present interest in paralanguage must be confined to a brief discussion of its nature, the functions it serves in processes of communication, the ways in which usage is socially patterned and the relationship between these means of communication and more developed forms. Evidently non-verbal communication is very extensive and important to people, but it is also confined mainly to direct interpersonal contact and especially to interactive situations where exchange and management is actively occurring. We can note, but leave out of our discussion, the important problem of intent, meaning and interpretation since, without evidence to the contrary, we may have to assume that much 'non-verbal communication' is simply unconscious reactive behaviour which is not used as means to a goal or is not in any real sense manipulable. We must certainly distinguish non-verbal behaviour from non-verbal communication. Harrison and Knapp[22] suggest a set of defining characteristics of the latter: '(*a*) a socially shared signal system or code; (*b*) an encoder who makes something public via that code and (*c*) a decoder who responds systematically to that code'. This is useful, but possibly over-restrictive.

What features are generally included under the heading of

'non-verbal communication'? They divide into those which are vocal and those which are not. The former may either be behaviours such as laughing, crying, groaning, yawning, etc., or matters of intonation, voice quality, emphasis, intonation, etc., and there is little doubt that variations on these lines are commonly understood as reinforcing verbal meanings or are associated with particular meanings. Non-vocal means of communication take a number of different forms, but principally the following: facial expressions; gestures, especially hand movements; bodily movements; postures taken up; visual orientation, especially eye-contact; physical contacts such as handshakes, kissing, pats on the back; proximity and distance positions. All these have been subject to some investigation and summaries of research evidence (e.g. Argyle and Kendon[23]) show that in each case there is some justification for regarding these features as to some degree meaningful in themselves or significantly associated with verbal meaning and open to interpretation.

In terms of the threefold distinction which has been drawn (by Laver and Hutcheson[24]) between information which is 'cognitive' or concerned with interaction-management or 'indexical', non-verbal communication falls mainly into one or other of the two latter categories. Thus, indexical information is provided to convey some essential point about the self which the originator wishes to present to another. This may be done by means which are not paralinguistic (e.g. language itself, dress, badges, ignoring or noticing, etc.) but often the means is paralinguistic, for instance the chosen degree of proximity, the directness or obliqueness of positioning which is adopted. Such things express a view of one's own relative status or friendliness. All the devices mentioned may be used in the management of an interaction, for instance the direct gaze to attract attention, the bodily shift to keep it, the gesture to reinforce or supplement words or convey reaction, the variation in distance associated with stages of interaction, and so on. These one may think of as the functions (intended consequences) of various forms of non-verbal communication. They have mainly to do with the initiation, steering, continuing and closing of the encounters, or the presentation of the self in an encounter, or the establishment of an image in relation to another. The ability to use such forms of communication and the need to use them depend on personality and social position, and also on the particular features of the actual situation in which the encounter occurs.

Most of the features we are here concerned with have the character of *signals*, behaviours which have a single unit of meaning and call for some response. They are also very much tied to their *context* in that their meaning derives from an association with a particular type of situation. Sophisticated ways of recording and notating paralanguages have been developed with some success (e.g. Birdwhistell[25]) but it is also clear that these paralanguages differ from language proper in a number of respects: the skills involved are much more localised and variable, there is much more improvisation and invention, much more scope for individuality in use; and much less standardisation and systemisation, much more association with personality difference. For the student of communication, one of the most interesting features of paralanguage (by contrast with ordinary language) is its interactiveness and non-*linearity*, hence the appropriateness of circular, helical or intersubjective models and concepts of communication process. A communication process between individuals, if it is observed correctly, cannot be accounted for in terms of a sender and receiver model in which signals are received and reacted to in sequence, according to agreed rules, and open to accounting in terms of efficiency (Birdwhistell[26]). The anthropologists, ethnographers and psychologists who have reported on interpersonal interaction reveal an extraordinarily complex and indeterminate *joint* activity in which behaviour is not sequential but continuous for both or all participants. There is exchange and calculation, but it is carried out at a number of levels concurrently.

The social distribution of paralanguage has been mainly accounted for in terms of cultural variations in the typical meanings of non-verbal signals and in terms of variations which accord with differences of power and status. LaBarre[27] provides a large amount of evidence to show the cultural relativity of even the most common and unsubtle forms of non-verbal communication, such as nods, shakes, laughs, silences, gestures of greeting and farewell. E. T. Hall[28] and Robert Sommer[29] have done much to demonstrate the variable meanings of different kinds of physical distances and the differences between cultures in their interpretation. Hall, for instance, documents the typical discomfort of Americans at the violation of cultural norms of positioning by foreigners who come much closer to strangers in conversation than is understood as appropriate by Americans. There are cultural understandings of the difference between intimate and public distances. Hall's evidence is mainly of interest in confirming the extent of a tacit understanding of the rules of what he calls 'proxemics', but of other paralanguage too. He writes:[30]

> Communication of this sort, operating outside awareness as it does, appears to be an extraordinarily persistent form of culturally specific behaviour which is responded to with considerable effect whenever people encounter patterns which are at variance with their own. It is also a rather basic form of communication, many features of which are shared with other vertebrates (p. 287).

Symbols and social communication

The discussion so far has reviewed those means of communication which are available to individuals, as members of the same society or community, for exchanging meaning with each other and for facilitating interpersonal contact. Languages and paralanguages are the primary means of such communication. In extending the discussion to certain non-verbal modes or 'body languages' we have widened the scope of this study to include communicative events where the transfer and exchange of meaning is not the primary purpose of the interaction, nor is the process of communication as such always salient. But in a discussion of *ways* of communicating this extension is necessary since the means of communication mentioned are available and are sometimes used for deliberate communication, especially in those situations which are not merely concerned with cognitive information or its efficient transfer.

One could have gone further, to talk of other ways in which individuals express something about themselves — 'convey indexical information' and use a culturally agreed and 'coded' set of signifiers (the distinction made above between sign, symbol, index, signal is hard to maintain here). For instance, if one confines oneself to possibilities for signifying which are chosen and manipulated for conscious purpose, one could instance the following and only begin to tap the range of possibilities: badges and uniforms to indicate membership of a group; styles of dress and personal appearance in the matter of hair, cosmetics, etc., which may either act to signify membership of a group (e.g. the cropped hair, boots, etc., of skinheads, or the distinctive dress of various ethnic groups in Chicago, described by Suttle[31]) or to express some mood or convey an intention; furnishings, cars, decorations of one's home and possessions which express meaning; the numerous kinds of behaviour which can be used to express or reinforce social distance. All these, and others too, are modes of conveying indexical and expressive meaning to individuals directly and to other people collectively. Their use depends just as much on common cultural understandings as does language, although the difference from language as a sign system is also clear enough.

Such means of communication are normally more local, temporal and ambiguous than language. They are prelinguistic or extralinguistic, non-systematic, normally unrecorded and learnt and unlearnt in informal ways. They are modes of communication open to creativity and free choice, directly related to personal experience and social interaction, to the concrete material world of objects which men inhabit. There is still an element of arbitrariness about the signifiers, but it is much less so than is the case with language signs. The connection between signifier and meaning is often quite direct but ambiguous. Thus sun-tan in northern societies directly conveys the idea of leisure and access to a valued and scarce good, but at the same time the connection between sun-tan and the idea of beauty is arbitrary, since pallor in some settings has the same connotation and dark skin has an association with inferiority.

We are evidently at a fringe area between, on the one hand, the use of devices for interpersonal communication according to conventionally assigned meanings and, on the other, the sphere of symbolism, which takes us to the communicative relationship between people and their society. Relatively little space can be given to a central question of the study of social life — the relationship between society as a whole and its members. While we might agree, in general terms, that society has an existence and a reality independent of any of its individual members (though not without them all) there are a number of alternative ways of conceptualising the link between the two. For our immediate purpose it is sufficient to assume that there is a relationship of a complex kind between them which is open to observation and mediated by a variety of institutional devices, patterns of activities and forms which carry meaning. A brief comment on the latter is all that can be attempted. Three kinds of communicative device can be mentioned: symbols, myth, rituals. One could distinguish others, but since even these three can be treated under the general heading of symbolism, to go further is unnecessary for our exposition.

What can be said of symbolisation in general? We are thinking of it as a process whereby, first, meaning becomes associated with specific objects, concepts, practices, narratives, or with representations of all of these. Second, by these means ideas and images which are variously complex, potent, emotionally charged, abstract, unapproachable, sacred, deeply significant and extending beyond immediate experience in time and space are conveyed in an economical and fairly reliable way, to those who have been socialised within a culture or society. Symbolism works as a mode of communication in those spheres where language and paralanguage are too restricted to sensory experience, too exact, too formalised or too emotionally inadequate, too little known, to serve as a vehicle for meaning. It brings into experienced reality certain meanings which are not easily observed and grasped in physical terms. Hence its crucial place in the connection between man and the collective entity of a society or the unexperienced world of a deity. Symbolisation is an essentially collective process. While an individual can choose from available symbols and manipulate their use to try to express sentiments or evoke them in an audience, he cannot invent new symbols. In using symbols to communicate an individual is calling on the collective store of meaning which he shares with his interlocutors.

Symbols are, of course, expressed in a language of signs or of icons, or signals, but it is the physical objects or events to which the language refers which properly constitute the language of symbols. To give specific examples, the flag with its colours and emblems signifies the identity of a nation or community and in itself embodies the idea of the nation itself; the sword as a symbol of justice, law or the military; the Cross as symbol of salvation of Christ, of christianity in general; the monumental building as symbol of wealth, power or civic spirit; the ritual as a symbol of certain religious ideas — for instance the breaking and eating of bread in the Catholic Mass as signification of the relationship between God and his followers; the phoenix and the associated myth as symbol of rebirth; the lion as a symbol of strength and courage; the pelican as a symbol of self-sacrifice. Even from this brief and arbitrary list two things are plain: symbols, whether in the form of objects, practices or myths, have a concrete material form while relating to an abstract idea; second, they are the property of a collectivity (not of an individual) and act to connect the individual to that collectivity whether it be the community of a religion, or a society or some more particular form of association. The important point here is the limitation of the range of symbolic expression to certain space-time boundaries and the fact of its *mediating* properties for the collectivity.

In his review of theory, Raymond Firth[32] tells us something of the range of alternative perspectives on symbols. His discussion of Durkheim is of particular interest. According to Firth (p. 131), Durkheim looked primarily at symbols as modes of expression and wished to examine their effect upon other members of a society: 'He drove home the idea of society as a system of active forces involved in, and conditioned, by the symbolising process.' For Durkheim the social sentiments are largely dependent for their existence on the symbolising process: 'social life, in all its aspects and at all moments of its history, is possible only thanks to a vast symbolism' (Durkheim[33], p. 331). The symbol, for Durkheim, is an object which concentrates upon itself all the fervour that properly belongs only to the ultimate reality it represents (Firth, p. 133). The key to understanding what a symbol is probably lies in this concept of shared beliefs or 'social sentiments'. The symbol is a directly experienced object or activity which is associated with general concepts and ideas which cannot themselves be experienced directly, but which are important to the functioning of a group or a collectivity.

Two further and connected points which Firth makes deserve to be emphasised. One has to do with the symbol as a 'store' of meaning. This helps 'to cope with problems of communication over time, aiding recall and obviating to some extent a need for reformulation of ideas' (p. 81). The symbol is consequently a considerable cultural asset, especially for preliterate or culturally and linguistically diverse societies. Its value will depend, however, on the range of interpretation which obtains in a given case. As Firth says, if a 'symbol is to be an effective instrument of communication it is essential that it should convey much the same thing to people involved' (p. 81). Paradoxically, this requirement conflicts with a feature of the symbol which may otherwise be advantageous — its essential ambiguity and allusiveness. The advantages have to do with flexibility of handling by the individual. The symbol enables the user to refer to, act in relation to and in some degree understand, what is usually a complex entity. Because of its iconic or indexical quality, it helps to bridge the gap between experienced physical reality and abstract notions, without exposing the essential weakness of such links.

Technological advances in communication and their social consequences

The discussion of means of communication has so far been confined to those skills and techniques which have been available throughout the entire history of organised social life. While the origin of the spoken language is distant and obscure, one can locate approximately within known human history the beginning of the first major communicative advance beyond systematic speech: the development of writing. During several millennia before the Christian era, more and more effective ways of representing speech in a material form were devised, beginning with certain aids to memorising simple codes (such as notched sticks) and progressing through pictographic forms (picture-writing) and ideographic writing (abstract and connotative) to phonetic scripts which are a graphic counterpart to speech, and finally to alphabet writing which can be traced to the Near East at about 1000 B.C. (Diringer[34]). The essential property of writing was the ability to preserve over time and distribute over space a physical record of a communication much more efficiently than speech allowed. Obviously speech can be organised to ensure communication over time and space, but much less certainly than writing. It would be hard to distinguish the consequences of the development of writing from the causes which led to its invention and diffusion, but one can note certain correlates. For one thing it involved some cost and skill and hence an association with better-off individuals or special castes or élites. For another, the keeping of written records over time implies some relatively complex and stable form of social organisation. The distribution of written records equally requires and implies some institutionalised and organised activity associated with the exercise of political, religious, economic or military power. For another, there is an associated conservatism, a resistance to change made more likely by the continuity of the document. Things are more likely to become fixed, because they are not dependent on individual memory and agreement. Documents rather than people are consulted for legal or administrative purposes. While one believes that in the pre-writing era many spoken languages came and went leaving no trace, the coming of writing 'fixed' languages in such a way that only those languages which could be written could survive. Writing as an invention was also associated with great empires and religious movements, and the boundaries of political, cultural and religious movements are marked by the diffusion of written forms of language.

During the age of writing which preceded the invention of printing, the most significant technical innovations had to do with the materials and the devices for inscription, adding to the quantity and the range of diffusion of written records and to their aesthetic value. Inventions such as that of paper in China, about A.D. 105, are clearly important and the transition from engraving on stone, wood or clay to the written books which could be circulated and stored economically in medieval times is also of immense significance. One must also note the growing diversity of *forms* of written record which became established, especially during the Greek and Roman eras and which seem to represent an enormous cultural advance from the civilisations which produced writing. These changes are connected both with the greater accessibility of writing and the enlargement of the community of readers and with the differentiation of societies and the growth of individual consciousness. Writing changes from being a magical thing associated with the most sacred core of the society and its power centres and becomes a means of interpersonal communication and private intellectual and moral development, though still confined to small minorities of members of a society. While no proof of a causal kind can be established, it is hard to doubt the intimate connection between the availability of writing and the cultural and institutional forms of communication which proliferated during the classical period, which were not extinguished during the 'dark ages' (dark at least in northern and western Europe), and continued into modern times to shape western European culture.

No summary can adequately convey the crucial social and cultural developments which are entwined with the history of communicative devices, but several elements have to be distinguished: the coding systems (e.g. language, symbols, iconic conventions); the material and technical aspects of recording and distribution and their social organisation; the cultural *forms* for the expression of messages (e.g. letters, poems, narratives, accounts, laws, songs, plays, edicts, maps, histories, prayers, inventories, portraits, memorials, charters, etc.). The modern era of communication begins with the development of the second set of elements, and especially in the sphere of reproduction and transmission. But the change has been more quantitative than qualitative and the other elements seem to have resisted any proportionate alteration. There is nothing to compare with the invention of writing or the development of iconic representation in painting, sculpture or music and new forms of cultural expression have not yet been widely adopted.

Perhaps this does less than justice to the importance for society and human experience of the new means of communication, and they deserve some closer attention. The mid-fifteenth-century invention of movable type and its application in printing was the first major advance in communication since the invention of alphabetic writing. The basic ideas and technology had been used before in the stamping of money and the reproduction of woodcuts on paper, and one might well speculate about the failure to apply these ideas to relieve the labour of hand-reproduction of manuscripts. No doubt there is some connection between this fact and the élitist, static and highly stratified characteristics of medieval societies which operated well enough with limited access to a written culture. The diffusion of ideas of the European Renaissance and the ferment in religion were a powerful stimulus to invention. Much has been said about the incalculable social and cultural effects of printing, and McLuhan's[35] views on this subject are fairly convincing, although cause and effect cannot be properly separated. The use of printing certainly had a number of major consequences for human communication. It enabled the individual writer or thinker to reach an audience or public without the blessing of an institution of Church or state, in itself diversifying the available culture. It invited, however, supervision and control by those same authorities and by the law. It enabled the individual to become a private 'consumer' of thoughts, ideas, literature, encouraging an individualism of spirit and thought. It encouraged the formation of groups of likeminded private individuals around the printed output of essayists, scholars, playwrights, poets, political and religious propagandists. It was a force both for the preservation of thoughts and ideas (given the greater ease of recording) and also an impetus for change and replacement (for the same reason). It established a new mystery, interposing between thought and speech on the one hand and attention on the other a technology and an organisation, the activity of other men. It established the social invention of institutionalised *publication*. It was and remained unusual for people to publish their own thoughts. The process of going through another agency (ostensibly for economic and technical reasons) was a legitimating process. The habit of mind which looked for the ratification by authority was not, and has not been, fundamentally changed.

Much of what could be said about the social significance of printing at the present time would be no less true with reference to the sixteenth or seventeenth centuries. In one respect, however, there has been a significant change, arising from a combination of material and sociocultural change: the rise of a 'mass press', a printing and publishing industry devoted to disseminating enormous quantities of printed matter to very large numbers of readers. The seventeenth-century forerunner of the newspaper, a sheet containing advertisements, news and curiosities (see Frank[36]) established the printed periodical as an accepted form, but it was not until the nineteenth century that a significantly large reading public, a more relaxed attitude by the state, combined with railway transport, brought the mass press into being (Williams[37]). The new form of press retained existing functions but was essentially different in purpose, in the time scale of its activities, and in social meaning. As a means of communication, the press in its modern form can be said to be oriented more to reception than to communication, as far as the majority of people are concerned: the larger the scale of distribution, the less accessible as a platform for the ideas of an individual. The mass press accustoms people to being communicated to and to being an audience of spectators. But it is the institutional form — centralised, highly market oriented and heavily capitalised — which accounts for this result rather than anything in the nature of print as such. The experience of 'being in communication' as well as major features of the communication process are distorted (or shaped) by these features of the mass press which have been mentioned. It must be added that such tendencies are not only the result of the mass press. The agencies of mass education have shaped expectations in a consonant way, accustoming and training people to be receivers and at best critics of what they receive, not originators.

Technology has, even so, facilitated interpersonal communication between individuals in their private capacity, particularly through the cheap postal system and the telephone. Both, though especially the former, have made available to ordinary people, as an amenity of everyday life, a facility which had been a luxury and privilege of rulers and élites. While the social effects of mail and telephone have never been studied in a formal way, there is little doubt of their intimate connection with other features of modern society — mobility, individuation, privacy, division of labour. They must encourage, facilitate and yet also act as antidotes to these tendencies. They make possible intercommunication and self-expression. They oblige their users to initiate as well as to receive. Intercommunication by way of the mail depends on a degree of competence in reading and writing which is not evenly distributed. Intercommunication by telephone depends on the economic development of a whole society as well as on individual income standards. It is likely that the development of the telephone reduced the use of mail for contact between private individuals or halted its extension. While mail and telephone services do facilitate interpersonal communication, they also make private individuals more accessible to organisations, and the mails especially can become a form of 'quasi-mass communication' (Menzel[38]), where advertising matter, propaganda, appeals, etc., can be directed simultaneously to large numbers of people.

The most striking developments in communication of the present century have been in the sphere of reproduction and distribution. Thus the capacity to multiply copies of the same aural or visual message has increased enormously together with the capacity to deliver these messages to very large numbers of people. The technology which was developed out of basic scientific discoveries was open to application in more than one institutional form. The one actually adopted, and which has shaped our expectations and definitions of what public social communication should be like, has followed the model of the centralised nation state, of hierarchical political control and of market economics. The model of the manufacturing firm, of the production and marketing process has shaped the application of new communication technology. The most immediate cause of this has been the constraint of capital expense involved in film-making and radio and television dissemination. The money has had to be found either in the private market or from public funds and either market determination or political control or both have been inescapable. Whatever the cause, the near universal form of production and distribution of film, radio, television, press and records has, embodied in it, the image of the centralised and authoritative source connected with a large number of separate receiver units. This cannot be sufficiently explained in terms of any technical necessity. Rather, it is a choice of pattern which is favourable to the dominant form of organisation not only of whole societies, but of other institutions within society: businesses, bureaucracies, schools, hospitals and so on. What is important, in the present context, is the fact that these chosen distribution structures favour certain kinds of communication relationship. Developed ways of communicating have come to determine the content of communication and the structure of communicative relationships to a greater extent than in the historical time preceding the invention and application of printing and other mass dissemination techniques. The earlier division between the literate and the illiterate, correlated as it was with the distribution of social power, certainly had some determining effect on forms of social organisation. But the new ways of communicating which have followed on the elimination of this division in economically developed societies embody unequal social relationships in a much more extensive and monolithic way and are less open to challenge.

It remains to be seen whether these predominant forms of mass communication can themselves be changed. One potential source of change would seem to come from the increasing availability to private individuals of the technology which underlies the mass media industries, in the form of film cameras, computers, video recorders, television cameras, tape recorders and so on. People can increasingly make their own content and establish new technologically mediated relationships. They are also able to be more selective by acquiring and using their own recordings from several sources. The model of book publishing and the library could gradually replace the one we have described and thus reduce the element of central control.

How far such a movement will go is hard to say, given the limitations imposed by cost, inertia and the possible moves to organise this new type of dissemination and use which we can come to expect. We may also derive some lessons from the fate of private technologies which have been available for some time: photography, typewriting, tape-recording, mail, telephone. While these have grown in use and had their own significant social consequences they have not produced any challenge to the basic form of social organisation. Rather, each technology has acquired a rather limited definition of its appropriate use and the majority of users conform to this definition. Photography, for instance, came into wide use as a form of cheap portraiture and has remained largely within the sphere of the family. As a form of self-expression beyond this, it has had a limited flowering, but it has been little used by private individuals in connection with any other aspect of their social life, despite its potential. In the case of each technology, we find informally established controls and conventions about their appropriate use and it is reasonable to expect much the same in respect of television facilities in private hands.

Conclusion

This chapter has been concerned in part with the relationship between the form and the content of communication. How does verbal language itself, or writing, or paralanguage reflect and shape the message and the relationship between intercommunicants? How do these things relate to our experience of the world? In this connection a few more words should be added with reference to these new means of reproducing and transmitting messages. First, it is obvious that the sheer quantity of available and received messages has increased in societies where the new media are in use. Second, film and television have altered the balance from verbal/abstract to pictorial/iconic representations and reports of experience.

The effects of the much extended use of visual imagery in modern communication are very hard to assess. Although some may discern a tendency towards the separating out of two cultures, the one based on pictorial and graphic media, the other on print, it is doubtful if this is a new development and not simply the old phenomenon of unequal distribution of verbal skills, under a new guise. The different media are still very interdependent: films and television rely very much on 'literary' conventions, while print communication has learnt to benefit from new illustrative possibilities and the diffusion of iconic images. There is probably some development in the direction of new visual 'languages', as film and television mature, but as yet these do not seem to have made much impact on what is disseminated for general consumption by the public, where old narrative forms still predominate. So far, it has mainly been a question of the establishment of new symbolic conventions for representing or illustrating concepts which cannot be directly shown. The visual display governed by computer opens up some new possibilities for change, but its tendency seems to be towards a new integration of the various language forms rather than either to threaten print culture or stimulate visual culture.

The structure of communication process 4

This chapter is concerned with the basic factors which shape the pattern of communicative interaction between individuals, in other words with the social forces which influence the direction and frequency of a communication flow and account for certain typical forms of communication network, to use a visual image. By using the word 'structure' we infer the existence of a thing which can be visually represented, has some stable existence and consists of separate elements or units which are related to each other in spatial terms. In dealing with this subject matter we are faced in an acute form with the problem, already touched on, of distinguishing social interaction in general from communicative interaction as a special aspect of the former. The problem cannot be adequately resolved, except by trying to focus on communicative aspects of forms of social organisation which themselves cannot solely be treated in communication terms. The relationship between social structure and communication structure is, however, interdependent. In some circumstances, communication as an autonomous process may lead to the development of stable forms of social organisation; in others, prior forms of social organisation determine the structure of communication patterns. The difference is largely coincidental with the difference between informal and formal patterns of interaction, in that all structures of interaction arising primarily on the basis of communication are informal, although they may subsequently become in varying degrees formalised. Examples of informal communication structures include the friendship or neighbourhood group arising out of casual contact in a common environment, or the cliques that form within a group, or the interactive structures which develop on the basis of rumour or the passing of information between strangers. We are concerned here both with cases of this kind and with those where formal organisation is served by channels and networks of communication which largely reflect a prior structure of social relationships.

Communication in social life occurs as the outcome of certain needs or causal conditions and it also takes place within certain boundaries. We can approach the question of communication structure either in terms of its causes or in terms of its variable extent and location. It will be least confusing to organise the material according to the latter. Thus communication takes a characteristically different form in the context of the primary group; or of the formal work organisation; or the association based on locality, class, or interest; or an institutional activity such as politics or religion. Generally speaking, the contexts mentioned imply an ascending order of scale and dispersion. They also differ according to the degree of formality in respect of the definition of roles, the allocation of marks of membership and the location of the boundary around participants. It will be easier to take account of the 'causes' of communication while discussing these different kinds of context.

Among the factors which either facilitate or give rise to communication, we would include: *spatial nearness*; *social nearness* or similarity; *association*, meaning the pattern of contact which arises out of engaging with others in the same everyday activities such as travelling, shopping, working; *cooperation* and collaboration; and *conflict*, in that relations between conflicting parties necessitate a form of communication, as one sees in industrial conflict, in warfare, in policing, as well as in disputes between individuals. Each of these factors will have consequences for the structure of communication, but since the consequences will depend on the level and kind of social organisation of the specific context in which they operate, it is the context which must take precedence as a framework for illustrating and exemplifying the forms of communication structure.

Communication in informal groups

A group may be defined, as it is by Homans[1] (p. 1), in terms of human communication: it consists of a 'number of persons who communicate with each other often enough over a span of time and who are few enough so that each person is able to communicate with all the others, not at secondhand through other people but face to face'. The essence of group life, according to Homans, is a dynamic interrelationship between several elements: activities, sentiments, norms, interaction, and communication. Sentiments of attachment between members grow out of contact and cooperation; interaction and intercommunication lead to the acquisition of common norms and an attachment of a solidary kind to the group; emerging patterns of communication reflect and sustain a structure of differentiated status internal to the group and a particular distribution of sentiment of attachment on the part of members for each other.

We cannot easily separate out communication as a distinct element for analysis, since all interaction is in some sense communicative and since both interaction and communication have a two-way causal relationship with sentiments, norms and structure. That is, the processes of communication in themselves give rise to sentiments of attachment between individuals and to the group; to agreement on norms; to the internal status structure. Each of these elements in turn decides who communicates to whom and how often. The most we can do is to concentrate on certain aspects of the group communication process and state some general propositions which can be illustrated or demonstrated. Small informal groups have been intensively studied, both in natural and experimental settings for a good many years, and since communication behaviour is the most easily observed and recorded aspect of group life, there is no lack of data. This is a disadvantage as well as an advantage, since observed patterns of contact and communication are not self-explanatory and can be misinterpreted. Their meaning may be no clearer to the investigator than the sentiments and power relationships which they are taken to reveal. Certain relevant points can nevertheless be pieced together.

Group cohesion

The process of communication is most germane to two main aspects of small groups: their solidary or cohesive character and their internal differentiation. Communication serves cohesion in a number of ways. One is by providing a mark of membership, in the form of a common 'language' or of conventions of verbal or non-verbal address. Most small groups are too temporary or non-institutionalised to develop anything more than minor variations of the language of the subculture to which the members belong anyway, but there are often private modifications of language, tacitly understood, which grow out of close association. This can be found in families, or gangs, or in groups of children, the consequence being to enhance the sense of sharing a private world and to emphasise the boundary against outsiders. To be accepted, one must know how to use and interpret special forms of communication. Cohesion in groups also follows from communication because of what Homans (p. 112) calls the 'mutual dependence of interaction and sentiment'. His analysis of data about group behaviour led him to formulate the hypothesis that 'if the frequency of interaction between two or more persons increases, the degree of their liking for one another will increase and vice versa'. The corollary of this is that conflict or dissension within groups is also reflected in patterns of communication flow. However, it is not simply that the more deviant members of a group receive less communicative contacts. Conflict with other group members or potential deviation from group standards may *promote* communication. Berelson and Steiner[2] (p. 337) sum up the situation as follows:

> The response of a group to deviation from its norms for behaviour is, first, discussion and persuasion to bring the dissenting minority into line: second, disapproval of the dissenters; third, lowered ranking for the dissenters; and fourth, their expulsion or induced resignation from the group.

Thus dissension initially increases intercommunication, but the same authors also conclude (pp. 346ff) from studies of interaction in groups that the relationship between dissension and communication varies according to whether the group is characterised by high emotional attachment or not. Where emotional attachment is high (as in family groups) dissension inhibits communication; where it is low, communication is promoted. A partial explanation is that, in the former case, tension may be increased by communication and the group members will not risk breakdown, while in the latter case, communication on disputed topics can occur without personal involvement, and the risk of failure is acceptable.

Communicative interaction in a group setting is related not only to the development of sentiments of attachment but also to the emergence of group norms — in the sense of expectations and understandings about behaviour: the more people are in communication with each other in group situations, the more likely are shared norms to develop. Festinger *et al.*[3] show this principle at work in their study of the formation of tenants' associations in a small housing development. They say (pp. 130—1) that 'once a social group is formed, the connections within it also function as channels of communication along which information and opinions flow. This process will tend to make the social grouping more and more cohesive.' Within the group studied, there was more communication about matters relevant to its functioning than about other matters. Group standards also tended to develop around these more relevant matters and exerted some pressure to conformity. Correlatively, it was found that matters which were not the subject of group communication (such as politics) were not regulated by group norms. The authors observe later (p. 167) that:

> the development of a friendship also implies the development of an active channel of communication between two people. The more intimate the friendship the greater the range of content which flows through this communication channel and the lower the restraining forces against communication. The opening of such active channels of communication thus means that there will be a sharing of information, opinion, attitudes and values.

It is partly because of this process that the rate of intercommunication between members of a group is generally taken as an index of group cohesiveness and separate identity. Groups vary both according to rates of intercommunication and to the ratio of within-group communication contacts to those which cross group boundaries. Both are related to cohesiveness. As Deutsch[4] summarises it, 'cohesiveness is consistently associated with greater communication between group members'.

We may also apply this same proposition to the fact of variation in individual participation. It is unusual for members of a group to participate equally in communicative contact. According to Hare[5], in 'free communication situations a gradient of activity rates among members is the usual thing rather than equal participation. Members who talk most, generally also receive the most interaction.' Those who are least involved in the group communication network as senders or receivers are also likely to be less well integrated, less liked and potential deviates. The study by Festinger *et al.* already cited provides some support for this generalisation. While acknowledging the difficulty of separating cause from effect, they say (p. 113): 'there is abundant evidence that the attractiveness of the group and the amount of communication between the member and the group are major determinants' of whether or not a person deviates from group opinions. One final implication of this line of reasoning which should be noted relates to group size. The larger the size of the group, the more physical constraint there is on diversity and frequency of communication, but the greater the extent of 'psychological freedom' (Mills[6], p. 64). That is, there is a tension between increasing group size and increasing cohesion and identity stemming directly from the difficulty of communication between large numbers. There will be other reasons, but this particular one has some general application to our study of communication process.

Status differentiation and leadership

The question of individual variation in participation brings us directly to the second focus of our interest in informal groups, the question of structure and differentiation. The discussion so far has left out of account a universal feature of small groups as observed, that they develop internal differentiation according to status and mutual regard. Thus, group cohesion apart, there are variations in group structure related (i) to stratification and leadership and (ii) to the formation of pairs or cliques of members within groups. We are here concerned with communication and should remember that this is only one aspect of structure, analytically distinct, for instance, from the work, friendship, power and prestige structures. Nevertheless, communication is related to, and reflective of, each of these and a person who holds a central position in the communication structure is likely to hold a central position in others (Deutsch[7]). Groups tend to evolve not only norms but also relationships of leadership and systems of prestige. These are, indeed, logical consequences of the development of norms. The leader in a group, as Homans[8] (p. 141) shows in his discussion of the Bank Wiring Observation Room, is the person who most embodies and conforms to the norms of the group. Similarly, W. F. Whyte[9], in his study of the Norton Street Gang, found that the gang leader was 'the one, who, on the whole best lives up to the standard of behaviour that the group values'. Prestige is related both to conformity to norms and to popularity or likeability. Being a leader, or being liked, has consequences in turn for the frequency and direction of acts of communication. Thus one of Homans's[10] generalisations states that 'the higher a man's social rank, the larger will be the number of persons that originate interaction for him, either directly or through intermediaries. Men that are not highly valued must seek others rather than be sought by them' (p. 182). At the same time, in a given case of interpersonal interaction between two persons of unequal rank, the person of higher social rank, 'originates interaction for the latter more often than the latter originates interaction for him' (p. 145). Thus, higher authority and esteem in an informal group is accompanied by the following communication correlates: a greater tendency to initiate communication with a given other of lower rank; a tendency to receive more communications than those of lower rank; a wider range of contacts, vertically and horizontally, within the group. These general points are related to the findings of Bales *et al.*[11] derived from numerous experiments with informal social groups, which indicate that 'if participants in a small group are ranked by the total number of acts they initiate they will also tend to be ranked: (1) by the number of acts they receive; (2) by the number of acts they address to specific other individuals; (3) by the number of acts they address to the group as a whole'. These general tendencies also have implications for the rate of communication between equals in social rank. As Homans[12] puts it: 'the more equal in social rank a number of men are, the more frequently they will interact with one another. Or . . . interaction is most frequent where social distance is least' (p. 184).

Homans uses data from W. F. Whyte's[13] study of the Norton Street Gang to test these propositions, and presents a diagram taken from Whyte showing the status relationships and the channels of communication between the thirteen members of the gang. The diagram 'sums up hundreds of instances in which communication between the men in the group took place in these channels'. It shows the interconnection between the leader Doc, and his two lieutenants, Mike and Danny, and lines of communication from each of these three downward to two others, Nutsy and Angelo who each provided the entry to a communication chain linking two small subgroups of three and two respectively. There was another slightly detached pair linked through Nutsy to the leadership and also Long John, a relative isolate but high in status, who was connected directly by communication to Doc and his lieutenants. When Doc was not present, the gang tended to fall apart into the two smaller groups which had relatively little intercommunication. Homans[14] summarises the position of the gang leader in the communication process as follows:

> Communication flows towards the leader. It flows towards him in general conversations; it also flows towards him in private ones. The followers come to him with their problems and confidences. Thus he is better informed than anyone else about what is going on in the gang. . . . If communication flows towards the leader, it also flows away from him. He is the man who makes the decisions, who starts action going, and he is expected to do so (pp. 170–1).

Finally we can note one other point made by Homans in this connection. Where one has in a group acknowledged differences of rank or esteem between members and a corresponding pattern of communication channels reflecting this, one has a system of 'lines of influence' which act to control and direct activity even where these are not formally laid down.

Conclusion

This short discussion of small informal groups helps to emphasise the intimate connection between communication process and some key features of social structure and dynamics. At this 'micro' level of social life we find a reflection and expression of some of these basic features of social life, such as the marking of boundaries; the setting of social distance; the emergence of normative cohesion, of like-mindedness and mutual attraction; the differentiation of relative position; the exercise of power and influence. Without intending to imply that the small group is a microcosm of society, we can find much support for the view that changing patterns of communications will be very closely related to changes in society. The principles established for groups need to be modified for other social settings and new factors introduced, but what happens in small groups is paralleled in one way or another at macro-social levels.

Communication in formal settings

We can add to what we know about the communication process if we look at settings, especially formal organisations, where a good deal of communicative activity is structured and planned for independently of the spontaneous wishes and interests of participants. One of the basic facts about places like hospitals, business firms or universities, where people cooperate on some complex task on a continuous basis in an institutional setting, is that both formal and informal communication occur together, sometimes overlapping, sometimes in quite separate channels. This observation provides a central theme for our discussion of communication in formal organisations. It also enters into the consideration of other issues, such as the relationship between communication and cohesion; between work-related and personal content of communication; between horizontal and vertical channels of communication; and the interaction between status differentiation and communication processes.

All formal organisations have an officially instituted chain or network of communication channels, designed to expedite the attainment of goals and to coordinate and control essential activities. Typically, this chain is vertical, spreading 'down' from the centre of highest responsibility, where decisions are taken, to functional areas of the organisation;

here information is in turn received from 'lower down' and processed for transmission 'upward'. The organisation has, in effect, the equivalent of a neural system and Weber's[15] ideal type of bureaucracy presupposes such a vertical communication process linking functionally separate work tasks and levels of varying authority in the hierarchy. If the communication process worked exactly as the organisational blue-print sets out, there would be little to learn about human communication from studying what actually happens. However, all students of formal organisation are agreed that the blue-print rarely, if ever, corresponds exactly to the actual process of communication flow, partly because of communication flows which are additional to the official version and partly as a result of various barriers and impediments. There is a good deal of evidence on this matter, the greater part being concerned with the implications for organisational efficiency.

Communication, integration and efficiency

To begin with the question of cohesion, we should, of course, expect the social forces at work in informal groups to operate in a similar way in organisational settings. Indeed, some of the most extensive and significant evidence which we have about informal groups relates to the industrial work setting. Wherever people come into contact with each other on more than a temporary basis, we should expect interaction and intercommunication to promote agreed norms and relations of esteem and liking which, in their turn, reinforce a particular pattern of intercommunication. However, the evidence for this comes mainly from studies of self-contained task groups. When we look at more typical work situations, especially the shop-floor of large factories, we find conditions which are likely to be inimical to the formation of informal communication ties, and hence to cohesion. The spatial arrangement of work, the demands of machines and the predispositions of workers themselves have all been shown to militate against the formation of solidary group relations.

This is a matter of concern both to management, for whom cohesion means greater efficiency, and to trade unions for whom solidarity means stronger worker organisation. Argyle[16] describes a number of factors which inhibit communication and, in turn, cohesiveness. These include the lack of physical closeness; the dissimilarity of work tasks; the heterogeneity of the individuals working together; and the existence of incentive systems which may limit group activity.

Assembly line work, in particular, is associated with failure to form group allegiances in work contexts. In their study of assembly workers, Walker and Guest[17] found that virtually no social groups emerged among these physically separated workers. More recently, Goldthorpe *et al.*[18] (I, 48–50) confirmed this finding, showing the formation of friendships at work to be related to technological factors in the factory. They asked their sample of factory workers how much they talked to their workmates. They found that more than half of setters and assemblers talked to their workmates 'a good deal', while only 22 per cent of process workers did so, with craftsmen and machinists having an intermediate position. In explanation, they note that setters and assemblers are brought into contact more frequently with others on the line. Of process workers, the authors say that 'the development of group relations was largely precluded; that is to say, individuals were prevented from sharing in common networks of social relationships, set off from others by more or less distinct boundaries'. These investigators confirm the earlier comment of Kelley[19] that the more unpleasant the job the more essential it was to try and communicate with fellow workers, especially on matters not related to work. We should also note, with Goldthorpe *et al.*, that technological factors are not the only explanation of low group-involvement. They say (p. 52) that 'the workers in our sample *as a whole* have a notably *low* degree of affective involvement with their workmates'. This is as much a matter of the general orientation of such workers to their job as to the actual work situation.

There is also a suggestion in studies of work organisations that the tendency to form solidary groups is related to position and status in the work organisation. Cohesion and solidarity based on work generally increase with status in the hierarchy and this is reflected in patterns of communication. For example, Etzioni[20] (p. 47) reports findings which show higher amounts of informal communication at higher levels of the work hierarchy — a fact to be explained partly by the more favourable physical situation of white-collar or managerial workers and partly by the greater commitment to the organisation which managerial staff tend to have. Etzioni also links this observation to the attenuation of family and neighbourhood ties among people who are typically more socially and geographically mobile than shop-floor workers (see below, pp. 120—1). Friendships are formed on the basis of proximity and identity of interest and work on the factory floor is less likely to encourage this.

Two related aspects of communication process in work groups, which bear on the question of cohesion, should also be noted. One has to do with the physical shape or pattern of the network of communication, the other with the presence or absence of feedback. On the former, there is experimental evidence (e.g. Bavelas[21]) to show that arrangements for inter-communication which allow all members of a work group to communicate to all the others are more conducive to solidarity and satisfaction than are alternative patterns. The more equalitarian pattern seems to promote morale and creativity, although it is not necessarily more efficient than the centralised or linear arrangements. This will depend on the nature of the task. The importance of feedback to satisfactory communication is of wider significance. Studies of informal groups show that a high proportion (more than half) of communications which occur are actually some form of feedback or response. As we would expect, in formal situations where communication is directed to the performance of tasks and is hierarchical or vertical in character, feedback is much more restricted than in informal situations — only a limited amount is functional for the defined purposes of the organisation and it is costly in time. There is clear evidence, from field experience and experiment, that this is a significant loss. Thus Leavitt and Mueller[22] show that 'the completion of the circuit between sender and receiver (feedback)' increases accuracy and confidence and reduces doubt and hostility in the sender—receiver relationship. Of particular importance is their conclusion that 'free feedback seems to permit the participants to learn a mutual language, which languages once learned may obviate the necessity for further feedback'. As Bales *et al.*[23] (p. 404) comment on these findings 'one-way communication prevents not only expressive catharsis, but also the opportunity for building new understandings and norms by which the members manage their social relationships and their process of communication'. We are brought back to the central finding about communication in group situations that it is the key to the development of micro-social elements: common norms, languages, cultures and sentiments.

Lateral versus vertical communication

As we have seen, the flow of communication in an organisation is mainly vertical in direction rather than horizontal, but a number of writers (e.g. Simpson[24]; Burns[25]) have commented on the undue neglect of the lateral flow of communication in accounts of organisational communication systems. There are several reasons why horizontal flow should occur more often than is acknowledged. One has to do with the effect of mechanisation. According to Simpson, levels of mechanisation of a medium degree require little close supervision or vertical communication since the machines rather than foremen set the work pace and in these conditions horizontal communications may be extensive. Where mechanisation is very high, lateral communication is difficult and where it is low, vertical communication replaces it. A second reason for the importance of lateral communication is the greater tendency for status equals to talk with each other, rather than with superiors or inferiors in the organisation. This is true mainly, but not exclusively, of matters not directly related to work. For example, Berkovitz and Benniss[26], in a study of nurses, distinguished between communication content which was 'task-related', 'organisational' and 'interpersonal' and concluded that interpersonal content tended to go 'sideward rather than up or down'. The study also found a good deal of 'sideward' flow of task-related and organisational content.

Another explanation of lateral flow can be derived from Blau's[27] study of a law enforcement agency, where agents were understandably reluctant to take problems to superiors, but, instead, developed partnerships with their colleagues for this purpose. Burns[28] was concerned with the importance of lateral patterns of communication in a departmental executive group — there was as much time spent by members with other staff as with those with whom they had line relationships. He concluded that the mainly informal lateral system was 'yet essential to the proper functioning of the system'. These different findings show the direction of flow in informal settings to be affected by several variables, some related to technical factors, some to spatial and social nearness, some to do with the organisational structure. In some cases, lateral communication may simply be permitted by the work setting, in others it may be encouraged by it or even contribute to the efficient working of the whole system.

The grapevine

This brings us directly to the question of informal channels of communication, especially the phenomenon known as the 'grapevine' which is found in nearly all organisational settings. It is not simply a matter of the exchange of gossip between equals, but of a chain or network of communication which acts to transmit rumours or information in advance of, or additional to, the formal communication channels. The existence of the grapevine reflects the inadequacy of formal channels for meeting the communication needs of participants in an organisation and also the fact that any group of people in structured relationships will develop their own communication pathways. Davis[29] has described in some detail the grapevine as it operated in one particular industrial firm and has drawn some interesting conclusions. First, the grapevine is fast. Second, it can be highly selective and discriminating in who gets acquainted with what; its operation is not, consequently, inconsistent with the preservation of confidentiality. Third, it operates mostly at the workplace and can be used by management for the effective transmission of information. Fourth, the 'formal and informal communication systems tend to be jointly active or inactive'. Thus where the formal communication system is active, so also is the grapevine and vice versa. This suggests a general tendency for a given amount of communication to generate further communication. Davis also observed the existence of distinct patterns of communication flow in the grapevine. One he describes as a 'chain', in which there is a sequential flow between a succession of contacts. Another is a 'random diffusion', in which any or all of a set of contacts might or might not pass on an item. But the predominant type is what Davis calls a 'cluster chain', describing the situation in which an item of information is passed on to several, of whom only one passes it on also to several others and so on:

> The predominance of the cluster chain at Jason [the firm] means that only a few of the persons who knew a unit of information ever transmitted it — what Jacobson and Seashore[30] call the 'liaison individuals'. All others who received the information did not transmit it; they acted merely as passive receivers.

From the same study we can see that rumour tends to flow either downwards or sideways — subordinates would tend not to pass information to their superiors. It is also clear from this and from other studies directly concerned with rumour transmission (e.g. Festinger *et al.*[31]) that the grapevine tends to leave out certain individuals — the isolates. Physical separation, ethnic difference, lack of integration in a friendship chain, organisational detachment, can all account for exclusion from the informal network of communication.

Hierarchy and status differentiation

Formal organisations have, by definition, some form of hierarchy and status division affecting relationships between members and the effect of hierarchy on the flow of communication has received a good deal of attention, mainly because hierarchical communication may in some cases be beneficial and in others prevent the fulfilment of communication needs (Blau and Scott[32], pp. 124ff). While, in general, leadership and centralisation in groups cooperating on work tasks seem to further coordination and problem-solving, Blau's own study of a federal law enforcement agency offers a reverse example. In this case, status differences actually impeded consultation with supervisors, because of agents' anxiety about revealing their own difficulties in situations where they were free to act on their own initiative. The system of partnerships of mutual consultation among equals which was established led in turn to a differentiation of status among the formally equal group of employees: 'The processes of consultation among peers give rise to an informal differentiation of status, because some members of the colleague group earn more respect as consultants than others' (Blau and Scott, p. 134). As the same authors go on to note:

> such emerging distinctions of informal status also create obstacles to the free discussion of problems, just as formal status differences do. These obstacles may further redirect the flow of consultation, so that the highest frequency occurs between persons of equal informal as well as formal status.

The interaction between status and communication is a close one and may be functional as well as dysfunctional.

Thus Chester Barnard[33] (p. 66), writing about the functions of status differences, claims that these are important for giving authority to messages and for ensuring an appropriate language for communication. As Wilensky[34] comments, 'without stable, comfortable and certified ways of talking and writing, without the observance of rules of deference and demeanour, people of different rank or different function do not easily maintain harmony' (p. 44). However, the emphasis has generally been on the harmful consequences of barriers to communication imposed by status differences. For instance, Revans[35], in studies of hospitals, found relationships between measures of patient satisfaction and even average patient stay in hospital and variations in the tendency for different kinds of staff, especially doctors and nurses of different rank, to communicate with each other and with patients. Much of the evidence we have about status and communication comes from hospital settings, where good and rapid communication is both essential and at the same time impeded by traditional status differences between staff groups.

The main problem, as Wilensky[36] observes, relates to getting satisfactory upward communication: 'if an organisation has many ranks and if in its administrative style and symbolism it emphasises rank, the greatest distortion and blockage will attend the upward flow of information' (p. 44). In the department studied by Burns[37] there was a marked tendency for interaction to be initiated downward rather than upwards and, typically, formal organisations legislate more extensively for this kind of flow. Hierarchy is especially restrictive of the upward flow of complaints and criticisms, for reasons which are obvious enough (Kelley[38]). In the study by Berkovitz already cited it was found that the initiation of communication was negatively related with status — the nurse would initiate the majority of her contacts with subordinates rather than with superiors and confine non-work related content to equals: 'Communicating social and intimate content across hierarchical levels may attenuate the formal role structure of the organisation; therefore in order to maintain one's superior status one would not transmit interpersonal content to subordinates'. Rosengren[39] makes a similar point about the risks of such attenuation in a therapeutic setting:

> One of the salient consequences of the ethic of maximum communication is the increased difficulty among the staff to maintain the posture of the professional and, as a reciprocal of that, the increased difficulty among the inmates to assume the posture of the patient.

However, the empirical evidence suggests that in most organisations, and certainly in hospitals, the tendency to restrict communication within status levels is damaging to therapeutic aims. Mishler and Tropp[40] document the operation in a hospital context of a 'general sociological law that the extent of interaction is an inverse function of the distance between status levels'. Four groups of hospital employees, doctors, nurses, technicians and attendants who are shown to have a mutually acknowledged status gradation, were asked about the extent to which they talked to each other on a range of topics, some to do with work, others not. According to the authors, 'the findings completely accord with the status-interaction law'. Thus:

> for each occupation group, a higher rate of intra-group interaction is reported than of any inter-group interaction. Second, the rate of interaction between any two groups is an inverse function of the status difference between them, e.g. nurses report a higher rate of interaction with technicians than with attendants. . . . Finally, for each group in turn, there is less restriction imposed on the content of communication in discussions of members with each other than is imposed by the member of any other group in discussion with them . . .

The formal organisation is at the same time a social structure designed to achieve certain ends and a setting in which the normal processes of social life operate. Communication in organisations reflects this and has a dual character in conse quence, with two sets of channels and contents supplementing, complementing and interacting with each other. Communication relationships are thus of very varied kinds, sometimes predefined and system-determined, sometimes freely chosen and self-defined. While the organisational membership provides a boundary for both types of communication it is worth noting that communicative exchange of both kinds cross the boundaries, linking an organisation with other organisations and linking individual members with other individuals who are outside the boundaries of the organisation. Here, as with other communication processes, the boundary assigned to networks and contexts of communication is real enough, in being acknowledged, but fictitious in that it is so frequently crossed.

Communication and local community

For further evidence about the structure and flow of communication we can consult selectively a very large literature, based on empirical investigation, of actual communities in both rural and urban settings. That much communicative exchange should have as its setting, not the primary group or the organisation, but the locale of everyday activity is to be expected. The place where we live provides us with personal contacts in addition to our family and kin, provides the subject matter for communicative exchange in the common situations of life and generally sorts us out into relatively homogeneous or compatible sets of people in terms of culture, status and even life-cycle position. The combination of all three factors of physical nearness, common concerns and similarity is a potent force, as previous discussion has made clear, for the initiation of communication and the development out of this of a structure of social relationships and even a local social structure. We can learn from studies of community, neighbourhood or locality something of the variable factors which influence the formation of communication patterns or networks.

Social networks

The idea of a network, introduced into urban and community sociology by way of social anthropology, is of particular relevance. The work of Barnes[41], of Bott[42] and of Frankenburg[43] provides us with a consistent view of what network stands for in this area of social analysis. It is an analogy which expresses the fact that lines of contact between people in any social setting can be drawn to represent a network of varying degrees of connectedness and closeness of mesh. When used in this way, network has an egocentric implication (Boissevain)[44]. That is, it refers to 'chains of persons with whom a given person is in actual contact, and their interconnection'. Boissevain also says that the links between a given person and a number of others are *potential* communication channels. He adds that a 'social network is more than a communication network, for the messages are in fact transactions' (p. 25).

Bott[45] has shown that a close-knit or highly connected social network exists where a given family has a set of relatives, friends and neighbours, many of whom individually also know each other. This approaches the condition of a social group, which by definition consists of a set of people in interaction with all others within a single boundary. Social networks of this 'connected' kind can be found especially in small, long established, mainly rural settlements, although they also occur in urban areas, especially in traditional working-class parts of towns and cities. By contrast, according to Frankenburg[46], in 'a new housing estate in a conurbation we would expect a predominance of loose knit networks' since the residents would tend to have relatives and friends living elsewhere and rather casual and random social contacts in their immediate locality. This way of thinking and the basic proposition of a connection between type of residential settlement and communication pattern provides the starting point for our discussion. At the outset we should not expect a too strong or general determination of communication pattern or social network from the physical environment. Typically, urban social life takes place at several levels, with a communication pattern appropriate to each. The residential quarter is only one sphere of activity. There is a wider sphere which encompasses the use of shops, schools, leisure facilities, the place of work and political life. It is no longer common for the activities of social life and the range of contacts one has with others to be contained within the narrow spatial boundaries of a local community or even a single city or town.

Proximity and communication

It is, nevertheless, a common assumption of urban planning and architecture, with some basis in evidence, that primary social contacts, and thus the nucleus of social life, are located in the immediate area of residence and influenced, if not determined, by the characteristics of this local place. Since time budget data indicate that the average adult spends more than fifteen out of every twenty-four hours at home, the assumption is understandable. We can call this expectation an ecological hypothesis: that the membership of a given social network, the composition of a person's set of social contacts, those with whom he is in communication, will be a function of physical closeness and locality. The work of Festinger *et al.*[47], on the pattern of relationships in a new housing project for ex-servicemen at college, supports this view fairly unequivocally, at least as a statement of probability. They conclude that:

> data from two differently designed housing projects show a strong relationship between sociometric choice and physical distance. In both projects the greatest number of choices were made to people living closest to the person choosing and the choices decreased continuously as distance from the home of the chooser increased (p. 43).

The setting for this research was hardly typical, but the precision of measurement is impressive and there is plenty of evidence from elsewhere that physical proximity is a factor in the initial formation of patterns of intercommunication. Lenz-Romeiss[48] (p. 103) tells us that 'courtyards, houses lying opposite one another, shared lawns, drives and service installations can become crystallisation points for social relationships'. She also points out, however, that the physical arrangement of buildings is only one factor, among many, which influences the pattern of relationships, and she quotes the findings of a study in Munich which found 'no correspondence between architectural arrangement and the spatial distribution of circles of contact' (ibid., p. 104). We can explain very little of the main forms of communication network by looking at opportunities for contact. As the same author remarks, 'communication relationships require the existence of certain specific social preconditions if spatial proximity and architectural arrangement are to have their effect' (p. 104). It is from the exceptions to the ecological hypothesis and from the variant expressions of ecological effect that we can learn most about communication process.

The locality of the home provides a variable proportion of a person's friends and social contacts, and there are other things beside the fact of neighbourhood on its own which account for the pattern of contact — for instance, kinship. There is a good deal of evidence for supposing that kinship continues to play a very significant part in social contact patterns in modern British towns. Rosser and Harris[49], for example, in a study of Swansea report that about 70 per cent of their married respondents had seen a parent within the week previous to interview. That part of Bell's[50] sample of housing estate residents that he describes as 'local' had similarly close contacts with family members after marriage. The national sample interviewed for the Royal Commission on Local Government[51] in 1969 provides further evidence, since 51 per cent reported the presence of one or more adult relatives or in-laws within ten minutes' walk. The same survey gives some indication of the relative importance of the home area as the locale of social contact. Thus, of the sample as a whole, 44 per cent had no relatives living in the 'home area', but only 13 per cent had none of their friends living in the home area. Those with relatives and friends in the home area reported quite high rates of contact — 60 per cent saw their relatives in the home area to speak to two or three times a week or more often, while for friends the comparable figure is 70 per cent. The study also investigated the degree to which informants' friends in the home area also know each other — in effect the 'connectedness' of the network, in Bott's terminology. It showed that 'over three-quarters of those electors who had friends in the area claimed that most or all of those friends knew each other'. The study concludes that this 'may further be seen as confirming the factor of friendship and acquaintance as a very potent aspect of community structure'. The findings of this study, given the fact of its being based not on a homogeneous local sample but on a national sample, are striking confirmation of the continuing importance of the place of residence as a determinant of social contact.

Needs to communicate

The formation of communicative contacts is evidently related to the presence or absence of a wide range of needs. These may be of a collective kind, as when a residential group is in a situation of conflict with outsiders, for instance over threats to its amenities, or to claim an improvement; or it may simply relate to the small size and interdependence of a community where there is an obligation to participate in every organised activity. A second kind of need situation which influences communication patterns relates to the essential and involuntary intercommunication between very close neighbours. They cannot avoid some contact and there are matters which require some regular consultation as householders. Mogey and Morris[52] show this to be a different interaction system from the friendship circle which is confined to voluntarily chosen local contacts and extends over a wider area, and different again from the contact pattern based on the need to supervise the activities of children, who in turn make their own contacts. Other kinds of personal need situation should be mentioned, which involve voluntary and fairly stable patterns of social relationships. First, the situation of initial occupation of new housing developments. There is a good deal of evidence that new occupants of an area experience a need to establish local friendships, partly for the intrinsic satisfaction of having human contact or avoiding loneliness (Mogey[53]; Bell[54]; Gans[55], etc.). Second, it is clear that in new and in established residential areas there are need situations which give rise to exchange relationships and to networks of communication. These relate to such matters as baby-sitting and the borrowing of household commodities, tools or the exchange of advice on household matters.

The extent and the form of organisation of networks based on these needs depends on there being similarities of life-cycle position and homogeneity of income and status levels among residents of a locality. In addition, the pattern of exchange is evidently affected by the nearness of relatives. In his study of middle-class suburban housing estates, Bell found quite a difference between those respondents who belonged to the locality and had relatives near and those who had not. The former, the 'locals', did not make the same investment in the social relations of the estate. They had other friends and kin in the locality and so did not have to rely on the estate either to provide their day to day contacts or their personal needs and, as Bell comments, 'need is the key to a great deal of the social relations on the two estates' (p. 136). The non-local residents (or 'mobiles'), unlike the 'locals', drew their daily contacts from other estate residents. This difference is forcefully illustrated by the existence of two distinct gossip networks involving locals and non-locals respectively. Bell's data show that non-locals gossipped about each other and locals about other locals, with very few 'cross-cutting alliances', except as created by very close propinquity, as for instance where a common garden fence is shared. The flow of gossip was also found to be influenced by its content. Bell gives most information about one main topic, that relating to occupation, career and mobility, which was especially prominent in the non-local network. Very detailed information would be exchanged by husbands in pub conversations, then passed to wives and in this way enter the estate gossip channels and be widely diffused. The other main topic of gossip, that concerning family and kin, was more prominent in the gossip network of the 'locals'. The division that runs through Bell's study — that between locals and non-locals — had been noted in earlier investigations in one form or another. Thus Watson[56] made a distinction between 'spiralists' and 'burgesses', Seeley *et al.*[57] differentiated the socially mobile from the immobile in their study of Crestwood Heights, Gans[58] wrote of 'transients', 'mobiles' and 'settlers', and Merton[59] coined the terms 'cosmopolitans' and 'locals' to explain two types of influentials in a small American town, the former orientating themselves to the wider society and its concerns, the latter to the town and local affairs, with a resulting difference in patterns of contact.

Effects of social differentiation

The importance of social status as an influence on the formation of communication networks has been implicit in much of what has been said. In formal organisations, high and low status persons are connected by communication links, while in residential areas, especially the more dispersed ones and in the large-scale and individuated settlements typical of modern urban society, social status differences limit contacts or form the boundaries of networks which are essentially voluntary and informal in character. The reasons are obvious enough. Physical separation tends to follow the lines of class, status and income differences; as do connections based on family; as do interests and life-styles. There is less to talk about across status boundaries than within them, and less chance of contacts being made deliberately or by chance. That propinquity by itself should be a poor predictor of communication pattern was shown by Stacey[60] in her study of Banbury, a town small enough for several distinct groups to live quite close together. She describes the different 'areas of communication' which characterise the social class and status groups of Banbury. Thus, the traditional upper social status groups (county and gentry) had no, or very slight, connections inside the town of Banbury and no members of their social circles drawn from neighbours:

> It is remarkable of the upper class that they have practically no contact with Banbury itself; any contact they have is limited to acts of patronage, presidencies of Banbury associations for example. Nor are immediate neighbours of any account in the upper class: a neighbour is a member of the same class within a radius of about thirty miles (pp. 154–5).

This wide basis of the upper-class face-to-face group is attributed to the availability of means of communication, cars and telephones in particular, and also to the greater command of language associated with this social class. By contrast, the 'middle class' has Banbury as the basis for its friendship circle, a circle 'principally drawn from members of their own class with like interests to themselves living in the town or nearby villages' (p. 155). Stacey goes on to say that the 'geographic horizon of the working class is more restricted again. The majority form their most important friendship groups in the street where they live and often within a part only of their street.' These findings are summed up in the proposition that 'the size of the geographic area within which relationships at the face-to-face level are maintained also increases with social status'. While this may be especially true of a historic English county town, with a long established tradition of class segregation, it is likely to be true in some degree of English social life in general.

The Community Attitudes Survey, already cited, suggests as much. Thus, the survey was concerned with discovering the extent to which people acknowledged their residence in an identifiable 'home area', and with the size and character of this area. It found that the higher the socio-economic status of the respondent, the larger is the area identified as a 'home' area. Second, the higher the social status of respondents, the less inclined were they to say that most or all of their relatives or friends were living in their home area, despite the larger geographic size of the area for them. Thus, of socio-economic status group 1 (the highest), 11 per cent said that most or all of their relatives, and 27 per cent most or all of their friends, lived in the same home area. The figures for the socio-economic group 5 were 21 and 43 per cent respectively. Evidence from the same study helps to explain these findings, since the employment of higher status respondents was also more dispersed and they had lower membership in organisations in the home or the local authority area. A picture builds up from the survey data of a differential pattern of social relationships linked to social class, such that the higher the social class, the wider the area of activity and communication and the less dependence on the immediate locality for leisure and work needs. The evidence we have suggests that social status, while related to social and geographical mobility in some degree, also operates independently of the local/non-local division already discussed, to shape the structure and extent of the communication network.

It is evident that communication is likely to occur where there exist common interests, identity and locality. Social class and status is one factor which unites or differentiates, hence promoting or hindering the development of communication and interaction. There are other factors which are also related to place, for example religion and race. The same local area may be shared by populations composed differently in terms of both, and where these differences are salient to the people themselves we are accustomed to find strong tendencies towards segregation. We know this happens where planners for 'community' have attempted to have residential mixing of different income groups (e.g. Heraud[61]) and it has been noted frequently in the case of racial and ethnic difference.

Suttles's[62] study of a Chicago slum area in the early 1960s is a good example of the segmentation of the internal structure of a small area by four different ethnic groups. According to Suttles 'the institutional arrangements in the Addams area demonstrate a constant effort to restrict relations to the safe confines of one's own ethnic section' (p. 59). While the streets might be common territory, the Negroes, Italians, Mexicans and Puerto Ricans largely kept themselves to themselves, using different modes of communication (language, dialect, clothing, grooming and display, dance style, etc.) and having separate channels of communication. In the face of great physical constraints, the separate ethnic groups and, within them, age and sex groups, managed very successfully to establish independent communication networks. If there is a lesson, it is to underline the point with which we began the discussion, the very subsidiary contribution of propinquity and chance contact to the structure of communication flow.

Interpersonal communication in other settings

A number of general factors which influence the flow of communication between people, especially in relatively structured settings, have now been accounted for and we have also looked at the influence of locality and neighbourhood as a setting for communication. Certain questions remain, however, about the flow of communication in modern society — about the diffusion of information, the direction of influence flow, the formation of contact chains and communication relationships relating to particular interests or topics. There are, broadly, four kinds of circumstances which give rise to networks or patterns of intercommunication. One relates to situations of contact, of sharing the same space; another relates to cooperative activity — either for work purposes or for normal social life; a third to communication based on subject matter — thus topics or messages generate communicative networks among those to whom the subject of the message is relevant or interesting; fourth, there are communication networks based on the activities and organisation of social institutions, often widely spread through a large population. Most of the preceding content of this chapter relates to the first two of these. The circumstances surrounding the second two give rise to somewhat different types of problem, hence a separate treatment, despite the fact that certain basic generalisations which have been arrived at also apply in this sphere. There are a number of rich research traditions to be drawn on in examining some of these questions. Some, though not all, of this research has been concerned with mass communication — stimulated by the need to discover what happens to mass media messages after they have been received by the audience member and also by the wish to take account of alternative, society-wide and mainly informal, communication networks which co-exist with the mass media and stand in for them in those exceptional situations where the mass media are withdrawn or cease to be reliable.

Institution-based communication

Certain institutions in society have wide-ranging informal communication networks which act to disseminate and circulate messages related to the concerns of institutions and which are additional to formal channels of communication. The content which flows in these networks relates to the activities which the institution regulates. Examples would include politics, business and economic life, sport or religion. The formal organisations in each institutional area — political parties, religious bodies, trade unions, etc., which are responsible for the 'core' institutionalised activities, 'feed' the informal public networks with content; they have an interest in, or even depend on, the operation of an informal network, but do not actually organise it. Their interest stems from the wish to have extensive influence and from the fact that their activities are, in turn, often guided by messages returning by way of the informal networks into the formal channels. While institutions differ in the extent to which this is true, we can propose a very general model of a communication system which in these circumstances operates successfully. As we have indicated, it is a dual system — a closed, connected and formal internal network with clearly defined communication roles, linked at various points with an open, extensive and informal system which has a lower degree of connectedness and is widely dispersed: there is a connected network within a disconnected one.

What links the internal with the external network? Again, we can suggest a general answer based on the fact that certain participants of the external network act as relay or connecting points. They are most intensively concerned with the institutionalised activities and are strategically located to make contacts in either direction, while remaining members of the wider public. For instance, in the case of religion, there are key lay figures who follow Church affairs, or play a very active part in their local churches. In the case of politics, there are party members and local activitists who do not themselves hold formal political office or have jobs in party organisations. In the field of social welfare, there are voluntary helpers and members of pressure groups. In sport, there are keen fans and members of local clubs. The pattern is a familiar one and we can appreciate in general terms the ways in which such key individuals act as informal organisers and sources of information and influence for the two communication networks. In effect, we should modify our general model to accommodate an intermediary band represented by such key persons. The 'system' is in fact triple rather than dual, taking the shape of concentric rings, with the intermediary section differentiated from the internal formal network by a lower degree of connectedness among its occupants and the lack of any formal role for them in the institution. The intermediaries do have an informal role and the main component of this is an expectation about communication. Thus they are expected by the formal system to transmit centrally originating information and to supply information in return, and expected by members of the relevant public to supply information as well.

The case of politics can be used as a more detailed example, partly because it represents a case where society-wide communication, is, in a democratic society, essential to the working of the institution. Our attention is centred on the party activists who form a small minority of the body of party supporters among an electorate. It has been estimated that in Britain, even at election times, little more than 2 per cent of the general public are actively involved in working to help any political party. On the other hand, there are degrees of participation, ranging from the giving of time to party work and holding voluntary office in a local party organisation to simply being active in some degree in discussion of political matters with other electors. The proportion of members of the public who can be defined as occupying the intermediate sector of our communication model can be variously assessed, depending on our criteria. The defining characteristics would include (*a*) their differential access to political communication content which is centrally originated; (*b*) their acknowledging a role as discussant of politics with others and being looked to as a source of information or opinions on political matters. Where there are centralised mass parties plus an extensive mass communication system, we can expect our group of informal 'communicators' to be divided between those who are very actively participant in a party organisation and receive their most significant information from that source or from specialist political publications and a larger group who rely mainly on mass communication. The former are included in the latter, and it is the group defined in the latter way which is of most relevance to the present discussion. Democratic politics are so organised that local party participants might well be regarded as belonging to the inner closed communication network. Institutions with a less voluntaristic element and a larger degree of formal organisation (e.g. sport, religion, business) would offer a somewhat different case.

In order to shed light on the communication process of a societal institution we focus, therefore, on a category of individuals who have been defined in sociology and political science as 'opinion leaders'. The term was originally coined by Lazarsfeld *et al.*[63], in their study of the 1940 American Presidential election. How many are there, what are their characteristics, what do they do? The original opinion leader study tells us relatively little except that 21 per cent of a sample of American voters, when asked if they had tried to convince anyone of their political ideas recently and if anyone had asked their advice on a political question recently said 'yes' to either or both questions. And this minority was differentially more interested in the election and more exposed to newspaper and radio content about it. It would also seem that such people played an important part in the process of change during the election period. This basic pattern has been confirmed and enlarged in subsequent election campaign studies in the United States and Britain. Thus, of a sample of British voters interviewed during the 1964 general election, 9 per cent were classified as 'opinion leaders' on the basis of a self-assessment about discussing election issues with others and being asked for advice. They were distributed evenly between the main political parties, but they had certain distinguishing characteristics in that they tended to be men, somewhat better educated, interested in the election and motivated to follow the campaign, relatively strong in their partisanship for the party they belonged to, having an above average exposure to political content on the mass media during the campaign (Blumler and McQuail[64], p. 150). This exposure differential was not only a matter of degree. The 'opinion leaders' were particularly likely to follow the election through the press rather than television — a finding connected with the reputation of the press for giving a fuller account of politics than other media. Finally we may note from this study that this minority was differentially inclined to claim to use the political content on television to reinforce their existing views and to use the content 'for ammunition in arguments'.

The study which tells us most about the kinds of people likely to occupy the informal communication role we have been describing and about the process of communication involved, is still perhaps the seminal work of Katz and Lazarsfeld[65], *Personal Influence*. This study took up the theme of *The People's Choice*, without being directly concerned with politics as such, and examined the dynamic of personal influence in a number of different subject areas. One of these areas had to do with public affairs and those who emerged as designated or self-designated leaders in discussion of public affairs were similar to political opinion leaders as we have defined them. These public affairs leaders emerged as somewhat above average in social status, better informed, more exposed to several mass communication sources, especially content relevant to public affairs and more gregarious, in the sense of having a large number of friends and belonging to numerous organisations.

One of the most interesting aspects of this study was the procedure adopted of asking the original sample to name someone they considered expert or influential in public affairs, then to ask these 'experts' a similar question, then to ask the second set of 'experts' to name a third set of 'experts'. Certain relevant findings emerged from this. First, although the original sample was all female, 74 per cent of the 'experts' named were men. Second, if a woman considers herself an opinion leader she is more likely to be able to name another influential than if not, and in turn someone named as an expert is even more likely to name another expert, and so on. Thus half the original sample named an expert, two-thirds of these did likewise and four-fifths of the latter did. The implication would seem to be that 'influentials' move in circles of people with similar attributes of communicative role. It is interesting to note that the social status of each succeeding group of designated 'experts' tends to rise: of the final group only 10 per cent were 'wage-earners' compared to 51 per cent of the original sample. The implication of this, together with other analyses of the same data, is that interpersonal influence in public affairs tends to flow downwards from higher to lower status persons, and from older to younger persons. No such relationship was discovered in other topic areas studied (i.e. marketing, fashion, movies).

The connection between social status and opinion leadership should not however be overstressed in the context of political communication flow, since there are other components of status in interpersonal relations than occupation and evidently people are influenced by friends and day-to-day associates who are likely to be of the same social status. An examination of the part played by discussion in political communication processes affecting a sample of young voters in a British general election (Blumler *et al.*[66]) revealed, for example, that the greater part of political discussion took place with friends rather than with parents. The same study showed some of the reasons underlying political discussion — the majority reason (40 per cent) being for 'self-expression', followed in second place by reasons connected with getting advice and information, third by reasons connected with arguing with, or convincing, others and, finally, with 8 per cent claiming to discuss the election in order to pass on news. While this finding suggests that political discussion is not often a matter of calculated or instrumental transmission to others, it does also suggest that people can see themselves as something more than the mere targets for political propagandists and mass communicators. Informal discussion provides an otherwise rare opportunity to be communicators themselves, if only for 'self-expression'. The lesson should be noted by those who think that people would have 'nothing to say', if given access to the means of communication.

As a postscript to this discussion of opinion leaders, it should perhaps be noted that the original concept of an 'opinion leader' as differentiated from an 'opinion follower', which is implicit in the Katz and Lazarsfeld formulation, has since been modified in the light of a good deal of further evidence. It would seem as if the more appropriate division would be between a minority (of unknown size) who are both givers and receivers of opinion interchangeably and those who are not actively engaged in the discussion of a particular kind of subject matter at all. This revision fits our model in which an informal communication role is located at the boundary of the 'internal' and the 'external' networks. Those who occupy these roles communicate with each other and give or receive information in equal degree. (For modifications of opinion leader theory see Berelson *et al.*[67]; Troldahl[68]; Wright and Cantor[69]; Arndt[70].)

Discussion and diffusion

If we turn to the third type of communication activity noted on p. 125, that arising out of a particular content or subject matter, we find certain distinctive elements in the resulting communication networks and also a variety of types of network. There are different kinds of situation in which content-based communication processes operate. First, there are cases where a particular topic has its own participating public or interest group — gardening, science fiction, fishing, poetry, etc. — topics which may not be linked to any formal social institution. Second, there are cases where diffusion of information is planned and carried out purposefully, for instance the publicising of information by governments about rights and obligations, the advertising of new products, the diffusion of information about innovations in such topics as farming, health, education, etc., an activity which has especial importance in the process of economic development, but which has a place in any society. Third, there are communication processes which act to disseminate particular items of 'news', that is information with a special character of timeliness and relevance (cf. Park[71]; Shibutani[72]). Fourth, there are cases of rumour diffusion, where unverified versions of information circulate, often in widely dispersed populations. These different kinds of situation each have important features in common. They are all 'message-centred' rather than 'participant-centred' — that is, the communication pattern is structured less by the existing relationships between participants than by the characteristic of the content which is in circulation. Next, the structure, or pattern, which forms is only in existence as long as the content is flowing. Finally, it follows that such networks have a rather low degree of formal structure or definition of roles of participants. There is, in fact, a continuum in this respect which is approximated by the order in which the types have been listed. Topic-based discussion circles tend to follow the lines of existing patterns of social contact and to be relatively continuous and stable, while the channels of planned diffusion process tend also to be relatively predictable, since the concept of planning implies this. The social pattern of rumour is the least predictable and the most dependent on the specific subject matter of the rumour and the particular circumstances of its occurrence. The general circumstances under which rumours tend to generate can be stated, but the occurrence of, and degree of participation in, rumour flow is unpredictable.

There is not a great deal to add to what has already been said about informal topic-based communication. It tends to occur where people are already in social contact, in workplaces, homes, pubs or local areas. There tends to be differential participation according to the principles already discussed; some people are more active than others in the exchange of communication about a particular topic, and there are informally established expectations and self-perceptions about the occupancy of such roles. One of the most interesting findings of Katz and Lazarsfeld[73] was that different subject areas involved different circles of participants in discussion. They found this with respect to the areas of marketing, fashion, movies and public affairs. Given this, we should expect to find other separately defined, though overlapping, contact networks based on a range of topics. Katz and Lazarsfeld found, too, that the factors differentiating 'influentials', or the more active transmitters and exchangers, are different in different subject areas. Thus (p. 331): 'marketing leaders are married women with comparatively large families'; 'fashion leaders are concentrated among young women, and among women of high gregariousness'; in the area of public affairs, 'high status women are much more likely to be influential'; for movies it was 'girls' who were most influential. The explanations are not hard to find, but it points up a picture of a complex of overlapping circles of interest, focusing on particular topics, partly contained by and partly crossing, the boundaries of existing social networks.

The planned diffusion of information and innovation is too large a subject to explore in any detail and the research literature is extensive. But again the basic principles of the networks involved are simple enough. Success in diffusion depends on the availability of channels which are already in existence — either institutionally organised, or as established patterns of attention to mass media and other sources of information which have authority and credibility, or as informal social contact patterns. The extent to which a 'target population' participates in the network of channels used by the communicators depends on the degree of social integration, on the interest, relevance and utility of the subject matter and on other facts such as literacy, or possession of broadcast receiving equipment. Typically, diffusion attempts employ multiple channels to maximise the potential contact. It is also apparent from many studies that personal influence and recommendation, and endorsement by existing hierarchies of power and esteem are extremely important for messages to be noticed and believed and, particularly, for them to be acted on. In their study of the adoption of a new drug among doctors, Coleman *et al.*[74] show the rate and speed of adoption to be affected, first, by the degree to which the doctors studied were deeply involved in professional relationships (i.e. an institutional influence) and, second, by their involvement in friendship ties with other colleagues. Those neither deeply involved professionally, nor having colleagues as friends were slowest to adopt the innovation studied.

The diffusion of news items — information of a public character which has wide and immediate interest and relevance — is normally accounted for in modern societies by the mass media. But it is clear that even with news there is a good deal of secondary learning, as a result of information being passed by the initial media contacts to others with whom they are in personal contact. The secondary contact pattern normally coincides with the existing pattern of social relationships — that of family, friends, neighbours or workmates. The speed and extent of secondary diffusion depends, however, on the nature of the news item, and so does the extent to which the contact pattern deviates from the established social networks of the society. In essence, the more relevant and interesting the item to more people, the faster and more extensive the diffusion and the more the contact network departs from the existing pattern. In addition, we can say that under these conditions the higher will be the proportion of a given population aware of an event who will have heard it from personal rather than mass media channels. Greenberg[75] has looked at the diffusion pattern and the source of information in relation to a number of different news events and concludes that the relationship between overall extent of awareness and the proportion hearing from personal contact can be represented by a J-shaped curve. Thus, an item of personal interest, such as the birth of a child, is likely to be known almost entirely as a result of personal contact among friends and relatives, but the proportion knowing of the event is infinitesimal. An item of news which may be important in some sense, such as news of a change of government in a foreign country, is likely to be known by a larger proportion of a population, but almost exclusively by those who have heard it directly through the mass media, since few people would pass on such an item of news. But third, we come to events which are of wide and considerable interest, initially emerging by way of the mass media and then taken up and passed on from person to person. News of the declaration or cessation of war would be instances, or the death of some prominent national or world figure. The most studied case of this kind is that of the assassination of President Kennedy in 1963. Greenberg and Parker[76] report three findings of relevance to our purpose. First, the rate and extent of diffusion of the information was phenomenal — within five hours of the event 99.8 per cent of the American population knew; second, around 50 per cent first heard by word of mouth; third, a fairly high proportion of personal contact sources were strangers, indicating a departure from established communication patterns. As Shibutani[77] writes (p. 21): 'Communication channels are much more than points of contact; they consist of shared understandings concerning who may address whom, about what subject, under what circumstances, with what degree of confidence.' Evidently a report of an event of such general importance as Kennedy's assassination altered the pre-existing channels in this sense, though only temporarily.

Rumour

Rumour as a communication process exhibits some of the characteristic features which have already been described, though it differs in a number of respects. While, by speaking of certain ideas or unverified reports as 'rumours', we equate rumour with content, rumour is better thought of as a process which occurs in certain situations. Thus it is a situation-centred communication process as much as a content-centred one. Second, rumour has the lowest degree of formalisation and institutionalisation of the processes considered in this section. It is characterised by spontaneity, expediency, improvisation. Nevertheless, rumour does also flow through institutionalised channels and in certain settings which are permanently disposed to the production of rumour, such as workplaces, prisons, army camps, schools or other relatively closed institutions, channels of rumour develop a stable existence. As Caplow[78] says of rumours in war 'once channels are established diffusion occurs over a relatively small number of well-defined routes'. A third characteristic of rumour is its lack of linearity: it cannot be represented by a message chain or network. Rumour, unlike information, is acted upon by those who participate in the diffusion process. Shibutani stresses the element of *construction* in the rumour process and defines it as 'a recurrent form of communication through which men caught in an ambiguous situation attempt to construct a meaningful interpretation of it by pooling their intellectual resources' (p. 17).

Our immediate interest is in the flow of rumour, who participates, what precipitates it, what kind of relationships are involved, how the process terminates. There is a good deal of agreement on the conditions which precipitate rumour. It tends to flourish in situations which are ambiguous or problematic, or where there is tension, unrest, anxiety; according to Shibutani it is the situation rather than the significance of the messages passed which is the key to rumour. In addition to there being a problematic situation, rumour is also associated with the failure of the existing news channels or their inadequacy in some respect. Thus, natural disasters create situations of anxiety and uncertainty and are often accompanied by a breakdown of communication channels. Shibutani cites the San Francisco earthquake, the Halifax explosion of 1917 and Hiroshima after the bomb as instances. The case of inadequacy of news channels is represented either in war conditions generally or in closed institutions and bureaucracies — hospitals, barracks, etc., where there is both a practice of secrecy and the occurrence of events of great importance to participants. Third, inadequacy may be taking the form of lack of credibility — as in the case of the Soviet Union, in the past at least. Inkeles and Bauer[79] discovered from their interviews with former Soviet citizens that word of mouth closely followed newspapers as the most important source of information, and for some sections of the population, notably the urban élite with access to presumably better personal sources, word of mouth contact was regarded as the more reliable source, regardless of attitude to the regime. Rumour is thus both an alternative to and a substitute for other processes.

Anyone who shares a situation and perceives it as problematic may become a participant in the flow of rumour, and to this extent participation is not closely related to existing patterns of social relationship. The new situation, if it is extreme enough, transcends prior relationships. More often than not, however, certain aspects of previous social structure do intrude to affect the flow of rumour, except perhaps in the most extreme crisis situations. Thus, Festinger *et al.*[80], in their experimental study of rumour flow in a housing project, found that rumour tended to circulate among those most affected by the subject matter of the rumour, and that those with friendships in the project were likely to be more involved than others. The communicative acts involved in rumour are not simply acts of transmission and reception, since, of its nature, rumour generates attempts at verification and reinterpretation of the subject matter. While there seems to be no empirical evidence to go by, it seems also plausible that just as there is a minority of influentials in the circulation of opinion, so there are certain key individuals more prone to participate in rumour than others. Particular situations may determine who these people are, but there is also likely to be proneness to circulate rumours going with personality and location in a social structure. As we have implied, the rumour process and the communication network it brings into being are ephemeral — they are unlikely to survive the period of uncertainty. The availability of hard news, the resolution of anxiety in a situation, will kill the rumour process. We discussed earlier the possible manipulable uses of the grapevine in formal organisations. Rumour in less formal situations or in large populations may also be used as a communicative device, either to assist in control or as a weapon in psychological warfare. Propaganda machines in wartime situations have attempted to use the rumour process in planned ways to affect morale or to mislead a population. Such planned uses of the rumour process require, however, an intimate knowledge of the whole situation and access through key individuals who will initiate the rumour process. Conversely, it is often an aim of authorities to control rumour (Shibutani[81], p. 202) as for instance, in England in the Second World War where defence regulations made it an offence to spread alarm and despondency. The main conclusion to be drawn from the general characteristics of the rumour process as we have outlined them is that it is extremely difficult to manipulate, to control or to suppress, that it has the character of a 'natural event'.

Conclusion

This review of the structural factors which affect and differentiate communication processes may have given an erroneous impression of discreteness. Implicit in the discussion, however, is a view of society as a complex of overlapping and connected networks and chains of contact, based variously on particular activities or topics, or environments, or interdependence. The whole complex is further shaped by the variable of culture and by the distribution of power and status. Any attempt by individuals or organised groups to use the communication structure or act within it must come to terms with this situation. For the individual, it might be a matter of simply making friends, or getting support for a cause, or redress for a grievance; for collectivities, it might be a problem of educating, or transmitting information or mobilising people to some end. Whatever the case, the intention to communicate has to be negotiated past a series of barriers and take account of discontinuities in channels of communication. Each institutionalised or normal activity in society tends to be served by its appropriate set of pathways. Most communicative activities tend to take place within the 'usual channels' and present no problems, since the necessary structural conditions will be met. It is when some new communication effort is being made, as it continually has to be in a changing society, that the 'usual channels' appear not facilitating but restrictive. We become aware how strongly defined and limiting the customary pathways of contact actually are. Thus the proponent of some political or social innovation will have great difficulty in getting the attention of, let alone convincing, large numbers, even with resources to use new media of communication. Effective channels to people cannot that easily be 'opened' and people attend to 'new' messages only under a limiting set of conditions and usually with low probabilities of any desired response.

The case of 'modernising' communication in developing countries provides another example, and a much clearer and more extreme one, of the limits which are set by culture and social structure to communication. The problem has usually been expressed in terms of a dualistic social structure (cf. Lerner[82]) the one part traditional and based on old values and relationships, the other 'modern' and based on the values of equality, success, impersonality, rationality and so on. In such societies, this duality is matched by the co-existence of two communication systems, one based on interpersonal contact and traditional symbols, another serving the new economic and social processes of the society. The significance of the former is much more pronounced than is the comparable system in developed societies, partly because many more people are excluded from the newer systems, partly because a great deal of power is still exercised through it, as it affects people in their daily lives. The typical problem of the moderniser has been to penetrate and use the traditional and interpersonal system which normally exerts great control over thinking and action. Communication in favour of new ways can easily be transmitted through the modern communication systems of education, government, or mass media, but will either mainly reach the system that has been 'modernised' or fail to influence the culture and way of life of others who are reached.

The apparent ease of communicating by way of new technologies to almost anyone chosen is quite misleading; without massive support from other power and authority structures, these attempts to transmit messages are ineffective. In a lesser degree, the same is true in developed countries of such would-be communicators as commercial advertisers, political campaigners, educators, in fact almost all collective communication enterprises. If we take the individual and his wish to communicate, it takes little thought to appreciate that the same is true in principle for him. The availability of telephone, mail, private car do not secure communication access either to neighbours, or to large groups of other individuals, or to those at the centres of power. The channels cannot be so easily 'opened' nor can the norms defining new communication links be readily invented. The question of communication effectiveness is a large one but some discussion of it logically follows at this point.

Communication as an influence process 5

Change is of the essence of communication in that after communication things are not the same as they were before for the participants or for the relationship between them (see above p. 24). However, changes which result from communication cannot be properly equated with influence. There are varying degrees of intention or lack of it, and there is a continuum of types of effect from communication, ranging from the most deliberate and unambiguous to the most unpredictable and casual consequences. At one end of the continuum one might find, for instance, the order in military drill, at the other some unanticipated and unplanned imitative act or form of 'contagion', to borrow a term from Lippitt[1]. In this chapter we are concerned with communication which is either intended to achieve an effect or which can be expected, or observed, to produce such an effect. Our discussion relates, in principle, to any effect, whether planned or not, which is explicable in terms of the actions of a communicator.

There has been much research on, and discussion of, the process of communication effects and it is not easy to find a single focus, or a single path through the labyrinth of theory and evidence on this question. However, our interest in social process and in communication as involving a social relationship inclines us to use a framework based on the concept of power. The use of the term 'influence' implies the use of power to gain the compliance of another, in situations where communication is the main instrument, channel or medium through which power resources are deployed. To give priority to such a framework is to neglect others. For instance, communication effects (and hence influence) could be treated as part of a learning process, or as the outcome of an information-processing activity by a receiver, or as some form of functional adjustment guided by the needs of a receiver. Something will be said about the third of these, since we cannot entirely leave aside the conditions under which communication occurs, but, for the most part, alternative paradigms will have to be ignored. The advantage of power as a focus is that it obliges us to consider the dynamics of the relationship between sender and receiver. It helps us to avoid the mechanistic thinking which learning theory often involves and it is less one-sided than approaches based primarily on the needs of communication receivers.

The concepts of power and influence

Influence may mean either to produce compliance in another, or simply greater similarity in thought or behaviour between a sender and a receiver. Communication, in one sense, means establishing greater commonality between the participants in a relationship, and it is with this aspect of communication that we are concerned. Following Weber, we can define power in general terms as 'the probability that one actor within a social relationship will be in a position to carry out his own will despite resistance'. While this is too strong a version of the concept to apply to communication, three elements of the definition are relevant: the idea of a relationship, the idea of achieving some control over another, and the probabilistic nature of the outcome. The outcome is not determined, it is a matter of expectation about the future and it is variable in occurrence. The element in Weber's definition of power which is absent from the concept of influence by way of communication is the element of coercion or force. Influence, even in the most extreme form of persuasion, can only be effective with the compliance of the recipient. Perhaps the best characterisation of influence as a concept distinct from power has been made by Parsons[2] who treats it as 'a generalised mechanism by which attitudes and opinions are determined', particularly 'in the process of social interaction in its intentional forms'. In the same context he refers to influence as 'symbolic means of persuasion'. It is 'a means of persuasion. It is bringing about a decision on *alter's* part to act in a certain way because it is felt to be a "good thing" for *him* . . . not because of the obligations he would violate through noncompliance.' Parsons stresses the *normative* basis for the effectiveness of influence conceived in this way: 'common belongingness in a *Gemeinschaft* type of solidarity is the primary "basis" of mutual influence, and is for influence systems the equivalent of gold for monetary, or force for power systems'. As we use the term, influence is thus an outcome of the co-orientation of the sender and receiver of communication.

In their analysis of power and influence in groups, Cartwright and Zander[3] offer a formulation and some ideas which are more specifically relevant to communication. They take the basic concept of a power relationship and propose that 'one person has power over another if he can perform an act that will result in a change in the other person' (p. 216). They go on to say that the capacity to influence another depends on two components: certain 'properties' of the agent which they call 'resources of power' and certain needs or values of the person who is influenced, which they call the 'motive bases of power'. They argue that an 'influential act establishes a relationship between a resource' of an agent and a 'motive base' of the person to be influenced. This conception will serve us reasonably well in the absence of a full analysis of the concept of social power. In our discussion, the relevant process of influence is the communication between a sender and receiver which may have a predictable effect on the latter, depending on a number of variables in the relationship and on the context or situation in which the communication occurs.

Certain other frameworks for the study of social influence can be briefly mentioned, since they have the advantage of extending discussion beyond the level of interpersonal contact. A little more can first be said of Parsons's concept of influence. He confines his attention to the intentional use of influence to elicit a desired response from others and treats it as comparable with money and political power as a means of obtaining ends through social interaction. He suggests that an actor can seek to gain compliance from another either by affecting the intentions of this other or by manipulating his situation in a way favourable to himself. For the most part, communication is appropriate to the first and can be employed positively by rational argument or negatively by activating some commitments on the part of the recipient of influence. In this version, influence is reduced to the single category of persuasion, which is clearly much too restricted for our purposes, although the model is useful for comparing communication with other forms of the exercise of power, especially at the level of a whole society.

In another approach to this problem, Kelman[4] has sought to explicate three basic processes of social influence, with particular reference to opinion change and to communication. He was particularly concerned with qualitative differences between measured changes of opinion which might not otherwise be distinguishable, and termed the three processes as 'compliance', 'identification' and 'internalisation'. Compliance refers to the acceptance of influence in the expectation of receiving a desired response from the other, in other words for some reward or to avoid some punishment. Identification occurs 'when an individual adopts behaviour derived from another person or a group because this behaviour is associated with a satisfying self-defining relationship to this person or group'. With identification, as with compliance, change or influence is tied to the external source and 'dependent on social support'. By contrast, 'internalisation' refers to change which 'is congruent' with the 'value system' of the person who accepts influence: the 'individual adopts [the position of a communicator] because he finds it useful for the solution of a problem or because it is congenial to his own orientation, or because it is demanded by his own values'. The examples cited by Kelman suggest that change adopted on rational grounds, especially under the influence of an expert, is most likely, although not exclusively, to represent *internalisation* as an influence process. The outcome is least dependent, among the three processes described, on the continued relationship and on surveillance by the source of influence. Each of the three processes is characterised, according to Kelman, by certain particular antecedent and consequent conditions, touching the basis for accepting influence, the basis of power of the influencing agent, the likely permanence of effects and other matters. It is worth noting that 'compliance' as a process of influence is, of the three, the least likely to occur as a 'pure' communication effect, since it is so much dependent on the social situation. For example, the motorist who obeys the signals of a policeman directing traffic is accepting influence on the basis of compliance rather than just rationally responding to the signalled message. The same signals or directions given by an ordinary member of the public are likely to be ignored, even in similar traffic conditions. The point of the example is that the motorist responds to authority symbolised in the person of the policeman with power to punish, rather than to the message alone. What we normally understand as persuasion seems closest to the process which Kelman calls 'internalisation', where message and response are rationally calculated in terms of the merits of the case and the information available at the time. The approaches of Parsons and Kelman provide a view of influence as the outcome of a particular kind of relationship between communicator and receiver which is affected by the situation in which both are placed. What we need, in order to take the analysis of influence somewhat further, is a more complete typology of the different kinds of relationship which mediate the exercise of communicative power.

Types of influence through communication

The sheer variety of communicative events has already been illustrated and we can expect some parallel, if not equal, diversity in the forms taken by the process of influence through communication. Our intention is to offer a reasonably unified account of the main types of influence, drawing inevitably on rather eclectic materials, although most derive from social psychological investigations of communication. There are several different and variable elements to be taken account of in social communication and these can be combined in different ways. In addition, the view of the influence process which we choose to adopt will be affected by the priority we attach to the following elements: (*a*) the situation and context in which communication occurs; (*b*) communicator or message characteristics; (*c*) receiver characteristics; (*d*) sub-processes such as attention-giving, comprehension, acceptance; (*e*) the different kinds of effect which may be involved. The context or situation may vary, for example, according to whether it is voluntaristic, as with the mass media, or in formally defined complementary role situations as in a school. The communicator may vary in the degree of prestige or credibility attributed to him. Content may vary according to whether the topic is very close to, and significant for, the receiver, or according to style and type of appeal employed. Receivers of messages will differ according to their predisposition to the source or to the message, or generally in 'persuasibility' (see Janis and Hovland[5]), aside from relevant factors such as ability or interest. The fact that influence can produce a variety of different outcomes is clearly a complicating factor since there are good reasons for thinking that changes of a cognitive kind, emotional responses, overt behaviour, or attitude change are, in each case, the outcome of qualitatively different processes.

While there can be no single type of influence process, there are, nevertheless, a limited number of basic 'mechanisms' involved, in the sense that communication effects are achieved on the basis of a social relationship between sender and receiver and, while each relationship is in some sense unique, such social relationships do lend themselves to typification. The problem is to find the correct basis for establishing a typology. In the light of what has already been said about the nature of influence and about the importance of the communication relationship, a relevant typology must take account of some element in the sender which is likely to produce effects and some motive or orientation on the part of the recipient which is relevant to the sender characteristic. Different types of influence process are distinguished by a particular concurrence of such elements. The problem of finding an economic typology or classification system is not, however, easily solved and the literature on the subject provides no best solution. Reducing the problem to its essentials, we have the choice of focusing either on properties of the source of influence, or on characteristics of the recipient, or on variables in the situation, and in particular the level of social organisation at which the influence process is operating (interpersonal, group, organisational or societal). It is hardly possible to suggest a framework which gives equal weight to these three variable components of the communication process.

We have, nevertheless, chosen as a starting point an analysis which seems to contribute to an understanding of the basic dynamics of communication as a process of influence and to have a wide range of application. This is the discussion by French and Raven[6] of the bases of social power, which proposes five main types of power relationship between a communicating 'agent' and the recipient. Here the focus is on an interpersonal relationship, in which both agent and recipient are individuals, or where the recipient is an individual although the agent might be a role, norm, group or part of a group. It should also be noted that the theory 'focuses on the primary changes in a system which are produced directly by social influence', while acknowledging the interdependence of any system 'with other parts of the life space'. In addition, the theory is not only concerned with intentional acts of influence but takes account of influence which results from 'passive' acts of an agent — for instance, the physical presence of a policeman exerting a restraining influence on others. The analysis does not specifically mention communication as the means of influence and is not a communication theory; nevertheless, the main assumptions and terms in which the theory is stated are very apposite to the purpose of studying influence exerted by way of communication. French and Raven remind us that, while aiming to distinguish five bases of power 'which seem especially common and important', one could rarely say with certainty that in a given empirical case power is limited to only one source. To classify basic types of social power is not to classify instances of communication influence.

The five bases of power or influence, that is, properties of the agent, or communicator, which give a potentiality for influence are as follows: reward power; coercive power; legitimate power; referent power; expert power.

1. *Reward* power is defined as 'power whose basis is the ability to reward', the primary reference being to the promise or offer of material advantages — in particular money or position. To translate this to a situation of communication influence, the reward would have to be conceived in terms of satisfactions gratifying to the recipient.
2. *Coercive* power is based on the expectation on the part of the recipient that he will be punished by the agent (communicator) if he 'fails to conform to the influence attempt'.

The distinction from reward power is mainly in terms of there being negative rather than positive sanctions involved. French and Raven find it important, nevertheless, to see these as distinct types of the exercise of power, in particular because reward power tends to increase the attraction between giver and receiver of influence, while coercive power will have the reverse effect, hence there are quite different long-term implications for the relationship between the participants.

3. *Referent* power is based on an identification on the part of the recipient with the agent, identification being defined as 'a feeling of oneness' or 'a desire for such an identity'. French and Raven note the relevance here of the reference group concept and that of 'prestige suggestion'. A prestigious person or group may be valued by someone who then seeks to be associated or identified with such a source by adopting attitudes or beliefs of the source. In numerous communication situations we can find examples of this process: the adoption of habits of speech and styles of dress from mass media heroes, the influence process of a parallel kind between friends, within peer groups, between teachers and pupils, leaders and followers, etc.

4. *Legitimate* power, that is, influence based on the mutual understanding that someone has a *right* to expect compliance from another. Such an understanding may be embodied in a role relationship, as between teacher and pupil, parent and child, etc., but may also exist on the basis of mutual obligation. 'In all cases, the notion of legitimacy involves some sort of code or standard, accepted by the individual, by virtue of which the external agent can assert his power.' Again we can think of many examples where communications are influential because of this underlying aspect of the relationship: the political message addressed to supporters; the moral exhortation within a church membership; the guidance process within a family; the advice of a teacher to a pupil, and so on.

5. *Expert* power, influence based on an attribution of

superior knowledge to the agent, normally has effects on the cognitive structure of the recipient. The stranger who accepts directions from a local resident, the person who acquires information from a newspaper, the student who learns from his textbook, are all being influenced by communication on the basis of expert power. It is worth noting that such power is very much determined by the situation and the institutional context, since, by definition, the recipient cannot normally evaluate the correctness of the information. The process of effect relies on a definition of expert status in a given situation and for a given subject area which is acceptable to the recipient.

This typology of the bases of power seems to identify, order and, in part, explain the main 'mechanisms' of communicative influence, and it is generally consistent with our view of communication as involving a social relationship. Although the five terms describing the different types of social power refer primarily to attributes of the agent of influence, each implies a particular kind of co-orientation on the part of another. Thus, reward or coercion calls for a calculative orientation; legitimate influence is based on a normatively regulated submission; referent power depends on identification with the communicator; expert power on the trust and credence of the receiver. The separate bases of power are ineffective without the appropriate complementary orientation on the part of the recipient. Influence through communication is the outcome of one or more of these basic forms of power relationship. The typology is general enough to accommodate a wide range of different cases of influence, although we should not expect a given instance of communication influence to have a uniquely correct location. As Collins and Raven[7] (p. 183) comment, in a different account of essentially the same typology, 'it is seldom that only one source of power is operative at a given time. Usually various combinations of power are involved in the influence situation and ... they operate in a non-additive, interactive, relationship.'

Conditions affecting the acceptance of influence

Influence as a function of the needs of a receiver

The functional approach to communication influence is based on the view that response to communication, and attitude change in particular, can best be accounted for in terms of the varying needs of the receiver. This view is not inconsistent with the typology discussed above, but it substitutes the notion of 'disposition to be influenced' for that of communication, or communicator, 'power to influence'. It also involves the adoption of the receiver's rather than the sender's perspective on the relationship between them. One proponent of this view is Daniel Katz[8], who expresses it in opposition to dominant modes of thinking about communication effects. According to his analysis, we are generally offered two mutually inconsistent and unspecific versions of how people are influenced, which both equally fail to account for the available evidence about effects and lack of effects. One of these versions is based on an 'irrational model of man' which represents people as prey to any form of powerful suggestion. The other is based on a rational model of man using his critical and reasoning faculty to arrive at opinions and beliefs. Katz suggests that we look, instead, at the motivational basis of attitudes and assume these to have a varying utility for people. If this is so, then communication effects can be understood in terms of the varying needs of those who attend to messages. He proposes that the main 'functions which attitudes perform for the personality can be grouped according to their motivational basis under our headings: the instrumental, adjustive or utilitarian; the ego-defensive; the value-expressive; the knowledge function'. His concern here is exclusively with 'psychological motivations', that is, with needs of the individual personality.

The 'adjustment function' is explained in terms of the maximisation of rewards and the minimisation of penalties. The motivation in this case is essentially utilitarian and calculative:

> Attitudes and habits are formed towards specific objects, people, and symbols as they satisfy needs. The closer these objects are to actual need satisfaction and the more clearly they are perceived as relevant to need satisfaction, the greater are the probabilities of positive attitude formation.

The implication for communication influence process is that people will be influenced in the direction of maximising their satisfactions and instrumental needs, the messages received in communication are *used* by, and are *useful to*, recipients and their effects are determined by the degree of utility. The ego-defensive function refers to the tendency people have to try and maintain a favourable and bearable view of themselves and a consistency between this view and the views of others:

> the mechanisms by which the individual protects his ego from his own unacceptable impulses and from the knowledge of threatening forces from without, and the methods by which he reduces his anxieties created by such problems are known as mechanisms of ego-defense.

In communication terms, this implies a highly selective approach to messages from others and from the environment, reinterpreting or misperceiving some which might be damaging to the self, or failing to notice them; responding differentially to those which are most helpful in maintaining a consistent and acceptable self-image. The value-expressive function is of a similar kind: 'value-expressive attitudes give clarity to the self-image but also mold that self-image closer to the heart's desire'. The process of socialisation and self-development depends very much on this tendency at the level of the individual psychology. It has rather the same implications for communication influence as the function previously mentioned, in that it must lead to a selective attention and response to messages, but, in addition, it implies a process of identification as essential to influence. Finally, the 'knowledge function' refers to people's needs to 'give meaning to what would otherwise be an unorganised and chaotic universe'. This again has wide relevance for communication and perhaps especially for mass communication. It does not, as Katz stresses, imply a universal thirst for knowledge, but simply relates to the need, which all experience, to understand events which impinge directly on their lives and to have some coherent and stable frame of reference for ordering experience.

The framework which Katz puts forward has a different focus from the French and Raven typology, but in some respects it extends its scope. We can regard it as stating some of the conditions under which one or other of the types of social power will be operative and as indicating the limits of such power. Thus, instrumental motivation is relevant to communicator power based on reward or coercion, in that the latter will work in situations where receivers are predisposed, in their own interest, to accept influence. Similarly, motives concerned with knowledge relate mainly to expert power and value-expressive functions to referent power. The ego-defensive motivation for holding attitudes and beliefs is understandably without a corresponding basis in communicative power, since it implies an independence, even solipsism, on the part of a recipient. In these circumstances, there is little or no chance of calculable direction by the communicator. It would be misleading, nevertheless, to suggest that the adoption of the viewpoint recommended by Katz does not alter the perspective which has already been put forward. In essence, the change of perspective may be summed up as involving a shift from viewing influence as the outcome of a relationship between sender and receiver to viewing it as stemming from the relationship between *message* and receiver. The communicator, or source, only figures marginally, or as a special case, in the Katz view of influence. For example, a person may be motivated to conform to the wishes or views of a highly valued other, like parent or lover, and in such cases message and source cannot be separated. But, for the most part, the functional approach implies a view of influence as residing in the message, as being 'topic-bound', to use Janis and Hovland's[9] term: effects occur where the specific topic and the message about it are relevant to some interest or orientation of the receiver.

Another type of functional explanation of influence, which takes us somewhat further away from the concept of power, is offered by the various versions of balance or congruence theory which were briefly discussed in Chapter 3 (pp. 40—2). These theories hold that an individual seeks to organise his outlook by cognitive processes in systematic ways, such that overall consistency will be maintained and psychological tension and discomfort will be avoided. Communication influence can be accounted for in terms of the need to maintain a balance among cognitive elements, since messages will be responded to according to their relationship to the existing outlook of the receiver. The approach is intellectually persuasive as a general view of human personality, but attempts to confirm dissonance theory in communication research have been mainly negative or ambiguous in their outcome (Lin[10]; McGuire[11]) and, from our point of view, the range of application to instances of communication influence is too narrow. Dissonance reduction is only one aspect of response to communication and we know that in practice people can sustain a high degree of inconsistency in their attitudes and beliefs without apparent discomfort. As an example of this, we can cite the evidence of Butler and Stokes[12] on the structure of opinion on various political issues in Britain. They showed a marked tendency for people to hold views which seem mutually inconsistent and scarcely consistent with their choice of political party.

In the sociology of mass communication there is a related approach to the explanation of mass communication effects, related in the sense of depending mainly on a functional line of argument. This is the 'uses and gratifications' research tradition, which largely shares the assumptions just outlined. It is assumed that needs arising out of social circumstances and psychological dispositions largely determine or shape both the pattern of use of mass media and response to media content (see McQuail[13] and McQuail *et al.*[14]). The orientation of the audience member towards the message or source is guided, in this view, by an expectation that content can help solve these needs. It follows that the process of media effects is likely to be mediated through these expectations and that to understand or predict mass communication effects we should take account of the motives which the audience member has for attending to particular sorts of content. The emphasis is thus on perceiver-determination of communication influence. Some ways in which this process might work are obvious enough, especially where informational effects are concerned: learning effects are most likely, for instance, where receivers are motivated to acquire information. However, the approach has much wider implications for effects, although so far it has been applied more to explaining patterns of audience attention to mass media rather than measured effects on audiences. Indeed, it is almost a tenet of the school of thought associated with 'uses' research that it is arbitrary and artificial to separate out a category of behavioural 'effects' from other phenomena of response and interpretation on the part of audience members. That is, effects only have meaning as they are defined and interpreted by those who experience them.

While the strength of this latter position should be acknowledged, it is also reasonable to suppose that we can look at the influence of communication, as defined in this chapter, and take account of audience motivations and needs as setting the conditions under which particular kinds of influence occur. Some of the main kinds of audience motivation or need which have been established in 'uses and gratifications' research are directly relevant to the process of communication influence on behaviour, beliefs, attitudes, states of mind and relationships with others. We can offer a number of hypothetical statements about how such a need-guided process of influence can occur, based on a reading of work in this field, but without particular citations. The need to identify with a reference group or valued other can lead to patterns of media attention conforming to others and the adoption of behaviour or cultural traits promoted by the media content. This happens all the time with children in relation to their peer groups, but it also occurs among adults in the adoption of fashions, life-styles or even opinions. A second example has to do with the need for security or reassurance which has been shown to underly some quite different kinds of mass media use. Motivation of this kind is likely to increase the effectiveness of media messages and the power of a communicator to induce compliance, in the form either of imitative behaviour or changes of attitudes and opinions. This may be especially relevant to those in situations of isolation, or conflict, or emotional deprivation, and have a bearing on the possible effects of mass media content which portrays violence (see Halloran *et al.*[15]). A third example concerns the motivation to use media content for interaction with others, either as subject matter for conversation or to help 'feed' the informal role of informant, giver of advice, discussant or opinion leader. Those, usually more gregarious, persons who use mass media for such reasons are likely to be most directly open to certain kinds of influence from the media. These are only three among a number of established motives, uses or needs, but the discussion should have helped to demonstrate that any given motivation has some distinct implications for consequent communication effects.

At the same time, these examples have probably also shown how complex and ambiguous are the links between motive, attention and effect. In the circumstances, it is not so surprising that studies concerned directly with the effects of mass communication have not so far made much use of this approach (but see Blumler and Katz[16]). An exception is the study of political communication by Blumler and McQuail[17], in which a systematic attempt was made to identify and measure the main types of motivation of electors for following politics on television during the 1964 general election in Britain and to relate types of motivation to types of communication effect. The study had been prompted by the near failure of earlier work to find any effects from a very large amount of election campaign communication (e.g. Trenaman and McQuail[18]). The main motives for following election broadcasts in 1964 could be reduced to a small number of categories: the wish to be generally informed, the wish for reinforcement of existing loyalties, the search for guidance or advice in coming to a voting decision, the interest in judging the quality of leaders, and the spectator interest in the election 'race'. While the allocation of survey respondents to these categories of motivation was accomplished with some degree of reliability and validity, they are not all mutually exclusive and even where they are, as with 'reinforcement' and 'guidance', the distinction is not independent of other relevant factors. In the outcome, it was found possible to connect the amount of motivation with certain kinds of communication effect, but not to relate specific motives with specific kinds of influence. This failure may have been due to the fact that the motives mentioned do overlap with each other, or it may be attributable simply to the complexity of a communication event like an election campaign in which it is hard to isolate a single element in the whole effects 'equation'. As a contribution to a model or schema of the process of political communication, the study of audience motivation is, nevertheless, of value, and it is possible that in certain conditions we would find audience motivation to be a clear determinant of effects in political campaigns.

So far as consistency with the French and Raven typology is concerned, much the same remarks apply to the uses and gratifications tradition as to the functional approach described above. To some extent, the various functions attributed by their audiences to mass media use can be connected with the main types of social power, although it must also be said that some of them cannot fit this typology because they do not presuppose a relationship between sender and receiver. That is, a number of motives for attending to mass media involve no orientation to the source or the communicator, but have significance only in the personal world of the audience member. This is especially true of motives to do with diversion or escape, or with 'social utility', or with motives which have been described as concerned with 'personal reference' (McQuail *et al.*[19]).

Social support in the influence process

During several decades of empirical research on the effects of communication in a variety of contexts, more and more evidence has accumulated to suggest that the key sociological variable in the influence process is the presence or absence of support for the acceptance of influence from known and trusted others, or from the norms and definitions available in the relevant group or institutional setting. Convergence on this basic proposition has been noted in two otherwise independent traditions of research on communication (Katz[20]; Katz *et al.*[21]). The two traditions are concerned, respectively, with the effects of mass communications and with the diffusion of innovations. In both fields it has been found that influence is more likely to be accepted from someone who is personally known and that 'external' sources of communication, to be effective, require institutional sanction and interpersonal confirmation. Some of this research has been discussed in the previous chapter, though not directly from the point of view of influence and effect. The main relevant tradition of mass communication research in the United States begins with the study, by Lazarsfeld *et al.*[22], of the Presidential election of 1940. A panel study designed to establish the contribution of various sources to political change over time led to the conclusion that discussion with others was more likely to lead to change than were mass media sources. A study specifically designed to test the effectiveness of personal influence subsequently confirmed this proposition and firmly established the hypothesis of a 'two-step flow' of communication, that: 'ideas often flow from radio and print *to* the opinion leaders and *from* them to the less active sections of the population' (Katz and Lazarsfeld[23], p. 309). People are more likely to act on information and advice from those they know personally, partly because of greater trust, partly because a personal contact can exert some informal pressure to follow, partly because argument and discussion are possible and persuasion can be a matter of two-way exchange, partly because a suggestion from a known other within one's circle of social contacts carries a guarantee of conformity to group norms. Personal influence can be clearly seen as an exercise in social power, based on a relationship between giver and receiver. Despite modifications, the basic theoretical underpinning of the two-step flow hypothesis has resisted challenge, and it is consistent with our knowledge of social structure to accept that in some circumstances there will be those who act as 'gatekeepers', key sources of information, controllers of the channels of communication for particular flows of information and influence.

The research evidence on the diffusion of innovations supports this general position very firmly. Diffusion studies undertaken by anthropologists and students of communication have been concerned for many years with the adoption over time of new practices and ideas, whether cultural items or technical innovations. In one aspect, diffusion is always a matter of communication, but the question of influence by way of communication arises specifically where there are attempts to promote the adoption of new ideas, practices, or techniques. Diffusion is usually understood as involving adoption or acceptance — that is, a stage beyond the acquisition of information about an innovation; the problem with planned diffusion is not to purvey information but to induce adoption, especially adoption which is sustained over time. Katz *et al.*[24] stress the importance of interpersonal relations as a major channel of influence, especially as a determinant of adoption. They note, for instance, that recent work by rural sociologists on adoption suggests that 'for the initial "awareness" stage of receiving information, the mass media are obviously more efficient than interpersonal relations, but the reverse is true for the stage of "acceptance"'. There is now a good deal of agreement about the basic process of communication involved when diffusion occurs, based on the assumption that adoption of innovations occurs as an outcome of competition between two forces, one in favour of the adoption and another resistant, whether this stems from tradition, or vested interest, or merely inertia. A small minority, who tend to have distinctive characteristics (Rogers[25]; Rogers and Shoemaker[26]), act independently on new information and try innovatory practices together with a small proportion of other 'early adopters' under their influence. There is usually a relatively long 'trial' period before the innovation spreads further; then, if it is successful, a rapid spread among the majority of the relevant population, leaving a small proportion unaffected. The rapid spread takes place largely on the basis of personal recommendation and group sanction, while the 'laggards', as in the case of the drug diffusion study already cited (Coleman[27]) tend to differ in a number of respects, especially in being relatively more socially isolated. Diffusion as such is thus rarely a simple communication process but a larger process of social influence in which a characteristic pattern of communication channels is involved.

Communication 'effects' and the influence process

There has been a great amount of research on the effects of

communication, both in small group situations and in relation to mass communication, and the reviews of the literature are themselves voluminous. The most useful include McGuire[28] on persuasion and attitude change, Collins and Raven[29] on group communication effects, and Weiss[30] on mass media. To provide even a summary of summaries would be a large task. However, it will help to show the relevance of the preceding discussion if we take a few of the most striking generalisations of past research and fit them to the typology of influence which has been offered (see also pp. 193–6 below).

The first general point to be considered about effects is the finding that the greater the monopoly of the communication source over the recipient, the greater the effect, or change in the direction favoured by the source. This is true not only of mass propaganda in societies where opposed views are censored, or where a dominant political economic system produces a similar result, but also in the sphere of the family or the school where the same principles are at work. Thus, monopoly refers principally to the exclusion of alternative or contradictory messages and the repetition of consistent messages. Repetition, even without monopoly, is known to be conducive to achieving effects in an intended direction. Except in the extreme case of the isolated and brainwashed prisoner, the condition of monopoly is never fully obtained and sustained. Nevertheless, in most cases of communication influence, we find that a dominant definition of the situation and a consistent and unchallenged message are present in varying degrees, and the more this is so the greater the influence of the message. In an interesting re-examination of the question of mass media influence, Noelle-Neumann[31] has suggested that we should not only conceive of monopoly conditions in political or commercial terms, but take account also of the 'consistency effect' in media content resulting from the operation of similar journalistic practices and the application of a limited set of news values (see below, p. 189). The type of power relationship which favours the monopoly condition, or tends to go with it, varies with circumstances, but we can account in general for the success of monopoly by the presence of power based either on reward or on coercion. The extreme case of monopoly occurs in total societies or institutions, where the sender can deploy rewards or punishments to induce compliance, something which may occur in families, mental hospitals or prisons as well as in total societies. To a lesser extent, the power relationship based on the accepted legitimacy of the source tends to go with monopoly of communication, in that in some spheres legitimate authorities are the only source of messages.

A second major generalisation is that communication effects are greatest where the message is in line with the existing opinions, beliefs and dispositions of the receiver. Thus Berelson and Steiner[32] say that 'people respond to persuasive communication in line with their predispositions and change or resist change accordingly'. The point has also been frequently made (for instance by Klapper[33]) that mass communication effects seem to take the form of reinforcement rather than change or conversion to new ideas. Most of the direct evidence for this view is of a rather negative kind, in that most people seem unchanged after, if not resistant to, persuasive communication. The supportive evidence relates to the high degree of selectivity which people exhibit in attending to, or in avoiding, messages. This selectivity is guided by the pre-existing interests and dispositions of the receiver, with the result that messages are more likely to be supportive of, than discrepant from, existing views. The theoretical support for this generalisation comes mainly from the functional and congruence arguments already discussed. The type of power relationship most relevant to reinforcement effects of communication is that based on reward, in that the message and the relationship to the source are both offering rewards gratifying to the receiver and enhancing his self-esteem by confirming the rightness of his position.

A third area of generalisation has to do with the kinds of content or the topics on which communications are most likely to be influential. The most important point to make can be cited again from Berelson and Steiner[34] (p. 542) who conclude that 'mass communication can be effective in producing a shift on unfamiliar, lightly felt, peripheral issues – those that do not matter much or are not tied to audience predispositions'. Much the same has been found to be true of communication with groups in experimental situations (Collins and Raven[35]). This is both a corollary of the preceding point, in that peripheral matters are ones on which there is, by definition, no formed predisposition, and something else besides. Thus it has been found, especially in mass communication research, that the issues and behaviours on which communication can be influential are those not deeply rooted in the personality and past behaviour patterns. New issues, opinions about distant matters and those which cannot be checked from personal experience are most susceptible to communication effects. By contrast, such things as political loyalties and beliefs, views about race and racial groups, religious or national loyalties are stable over time and resistant to influence.

There are wide ramifications to this point, since it reflects the variable of ego-involvement which has already been mentioned as well as the variability of available information, and also the presence or absence of group support. Thus new or distant issues are also ones over which a given communication source is likely to have some monopoly of information and to be outside a check from personal experience or lacking a definition in terms of group norms and standards. To give an example from some research carried out in the Soviet Union among readers of the trade union paper *Trud*, it was found that trust in the objectivity of the newspaper and, by implication, its power to influence, was related to the 'distance' of the topic from the experience of the reader. Thus, 45 per cent of the sample of readers interviewed claimed to trust reports on international life and events abroad, 34 per cent trusted reports on the position of the economy and only 25 per cent on relations between supervisors and employees. A tendency in line with this generalisation was invoked by Blumler and McQuail[36] to explain their finding that it was the less politically interested electors who were influenced by television presentations in favour of the political party (the Liberal Party) which was least well known and whose reputation was less anchored in deeply held attitudes. To connect this with our typology of the bases of influence, we can suggest that the situations described are also likely to be characterised by the existence of expert power which is not cross-cut by the presence of negative sanctions. The further from experience the subject matter, the more likely is expertise to be acknowledged, and the 'further from the self' the topic at issue, the less relevant will be questions of reward or self-reinforcement. There will also be less tendency in such cases to doubt the legitimacy of the source of influence.

The fourth general finding to be noted has to do with the character of the source. In a variety of communication situations, it has been found that the greater the prestige and credibility attributed by the receiver to the source of a message, the greater the likelihood of successful influence. This is a matter of commonsense as well as being well supported by research evidence, and needs little explanation. We should note, however, that several different elements are involved in this general formulation, and it has a complex relationship with our typology of influence. A number of different, but related, aspects of communicators have been found to be associated with influence. One is expertise on the subject, as perceived by the receiver, and this may be mixed with judgments about status and authoritativeness made by someone who cannot judge specific expertise. Another is status as a general characteristic unrelated to a specific message. Another is the believed objectivity and reliability of the source, in the sense that the receiver perceives a communicator as having no ulterior or partisan motive or an intention to persuade. This has been found as a variable in experiments on persuasion, for example by Walster and Festinger[37], who observed greater effects from messages which were supposedly overheard unintentionally by the receiver. Finally, there are the factors of source likeability and similarity to the recipient. There is evidence that people accept influence from those they like and also from those they perceive as similar to themselves (Byrne[38]). The considerable variety of power relationships implied by this discussion will be apparent. However, the dominant type of influence would seem to be that based on referent power, with identification as the most salient process in such cases of influence. At the same time, certain findings about source prestige and communication effect also indicate the occurrence of influence based on possible rewards or coercion, or on expert power, and also legitimate power, since the concept of an 'acknowledged authority' on a subject is involved in some of the findings of research on this point.

A final matter which has been much commented on in communication research is the great importance of the social context, group, or reference group in mediating influence and affecting whether influence is or is not accepted. Enough has been said already about this phenomenon for it to need little more comment. It should be emphasised, however, that the finding applies about equally, though in somewhat different ways, to situations of mass communication and to small group contexts, where there is much experimental evidence, dating back many years, to show that the behaviour and attitudes of group members are strongly influenced according to group norms and standards. Again, the types of power base for such influence are diverse, since the evidence we have could be the outcome of any of the following: the capacity of interpersonal and intra-group relationships to confer rewards or apply sanctions; the tendency of groups to legitimate in terms of their own norms; the identification with the group or with salient members of it, which members normally exhibit. Thus, the exercise of influence in group-related situations may be based on reward, coercion, legitimacy or deference.

Conclusion

This chapter has been concerned in general with underlining one key feature of communication as a process of influence. Influence is not just a matter of learning, or understanding, or acquiring information, or imitating, or reacting, or gaining attention. All these may be, and often are, elements in the whole process, but the central and universal feature of communication influence is the voluntary compliance of the receiver to a sender. The relationship between them is a power relationship, and the varying types of power base we have discussed provide the key to analysing and understanding the forms which this power relationship can take. The forms of compliance are diverse, and social situations are usually too complex to find a one-to-one relationship between a type of power and a given case of influence. Our purpose has been to give some order to the diversity and to sketch the outline of a framework for studying and interrelating the different kinds of communication influence.

Mass communication 6

The invention of new means of multiple reproduction and dissemination of messages — printing press, photography, wireless telegraphy, etc. — and the development of social institutions based on the use of these techniques have added another dimension to the social process of communication. It is not the techniques themselves which make any essential difference to communication process, but rather the particular uses to which they have been put, the new kinds of social relationship which have been made possible and become institutionalised, the forms of social organisation and production developed. The examples of social process which have been described up to this point have all been open to analysis in terms of some 'unit act' of communication, an interaction between a given receiver and sender and an interpersonal relationship which provides a framework for the communicative act. Even where communicative process may involve a complex network of channels and a hierarchy of positions, the 'building blocks' from which such processes are constructed are communication relationships between people. The fiction becomes too difficult to uphold in the case of mass communication and too often there is no discrete relationship between 'sender' and 'receiver' to be analysed. The frame of reference and concepts which have been used so far are consequently less useful.

Characteristics of mass communication

For this reason we need to begin with a characterisation of

the typical features of mass communication, locating the main areas of difference from an interpersonal communication process. First, there is a basic difference of participant, in that the actors in mass communication often are collectivities rather than individuals and the behaviour we have to analyse has a collective character. In its developed forms, mass communication is complex and large in scale, involving the linking of organised groups of producers with aggregates of people who constitute audiences and are treated as collectivities by mass communicators, even if they do not regard themselves as such. The means of mass communication are so called partly because they are designed for mass reproduction and partly because they are appropriate to communicating with a 'mass' — an internally undifferentiated aggregate of people, united by a common interest in a particular message or kind of message and sharing certain other common features at the same time and for related reasons.

The collectivity at the source, or sending end, of mass communication is of a different character from the audience, normally being organised as a work group, with an internally differentiated structure of relationships, with its own organised internal network of communication, some degree of shared norms and values, and a shared location within which face to face interaction can take place. Thus not only are sender and receiver not individuals, they are not the same kind of collectivity, and the relationship between them must be affected by this difference. The most striking feature of the difference is the degree of control and cohesion. The sending organisation is in a position to have a developed view of what it is seeking to achieve, of its audience and of its rights and obligations, while the audience, though treated as a whole, is much less likely to have any collective perception of itself, any organised set of expectations or view of its rights. The typical communication relationship is discussed in more detail below, but we can see already that the relationship is an asymmetrical and unbalanced one, with the advantage tending to lie with the communicator, as long as certain preconditions for gaining the attention of an audience are assured. The audience lacks representation and the capacity to respond, not only because the technology is unavailable for direct response, but also because the social conditions for having a collective reply are missing.

The second obvious point of difference between mass communication and interpersonal communication is the interposition of a complex technology of a particular kind. As we have noted this technology of production and dissemination has been designed to facilitate communication in one direction. The newspaper and magazine press and broadcasting have relatively little feedback capacity. For this purpose they rely on individual response by mail, telephone or personal contact, and especially 'audience research', which is normally a form of market research. The mediation of contact through the technology of mass communication has other consequences, however. It extends the distance between sender and receiver who might otherwise have been in closer personal contact and establishes links between those who would otherwise be too physically or socially distant to be 'in touch' with each other. This 'distance' has several aspects, among them the mystery which attaches to the machine and the technology — a mystery from which the communicator benefits by association — adding still more to the imbalance of the relationship. There is at least one more point to note in this respect: the technology of mass communication is expensive as well as arcane, and access to it is generally open only to those who can buy it or achieve the use of it. In some societies access can be 'bought' for individuals by the society or on some communal basis, but it remains generally a scarce resource rather than a free good, subject to the forces of whatever market and power system operate in a given society.

A third area of difference has to do with typical features of the relationship between sender and receiver in the mass communication process. The relationship cannot, in the circumstances, be genuinely interactive. The participants are distanced from each other physically and often socially and, as we have noted, only one party to the relationship can initiate. Several consequences flow from this basic circumstance. The communicative event, as it occurs, lacks the 'negotiability' of interpersonal contact, which makes such communication more open and less predictable. At the same time, the communication relationship in mass communication is not fixed or invariable. The mass communicator and the audience member can, and often do, have a view of each other which they construct for themselves, modify and give meaning to. But they do this in rather an autistic way, without much reference to the other and tend to deal in stereotypes, the communicator with a stereotype of the audience and the audience member with stereotyped views of what to expect from mass media. At the same time both parties are unusually free to define the situation and the meaning of content differently. Expectations are not necessarily complementary or consistent, and the meaning of content is more open to 'misinterpretation' (from the sender's point of view) than is the case either in informal interpersonal communication or more formal institutionalised communication. The result is only partly due to the lack of facilities for 'correcting' errors and control by the sender; it is also due to the fact that the receiver is a 'consumer' who has 'bought' the message, treats it as his property and is free to make of it what he wants.

Fourth, the typical content of mass communication differs from that carried in interpersonal channels, aside from the fact that it is, to an extent, manufactured and multiplied. Because the media comprise a relatively open system, messages are public in the sense of being open to reception by all and about matters in the public sphere — such as events of wide relevance, issues on which public opinion should form or persons playing a recognised public role.

In practice, the media are an important means for defining matters as public rather than private or purely for 'expert' decision. This happens both intentionally and unintentionally. For instance, investigative journalism often involves an attempt to 'make public' details of private lives or things which closed organisations try to keep either secret or within the sphere of expert assessment. It can also happen that chance disclosures bring areas of private life into public discussion.

A model of mass communication

To see the process of mass communication as a whole rather than as a communication relationship we can make use of the conceptual model proposed by Westley and MacLean[1] which has already been briefly described (pp. 27—8). In outline it is represented in Fig. 2.

This model illustrates a number of distinctive features of the sequence of events in mass communication and the relationship between elements in the process, in particular the three main elements of communicator, channel and audience. We can also look at the process from the perspective of any of these and it is somewhat different in each case. The main implication of the model is to show mass media organisations and the people who work in them as occupying an intermediary position between the 'audience' on the one hand and, on the other, either the events of the world or the views and interpretations of events in the world which some people (advocates) wish to convey to the audience (or part of it). The intermediary position is characterised by the authors of the model as a 'channel' role or, following White[2], as a 'gatekeeper' role. The intermediary position thus has a dual character which is described by Westley and MacLean as either 'purposive' or 'non-purposive', the former when it involves conveying messages from an 'advocate' with a particular audience or public in mind, the latter when it is a

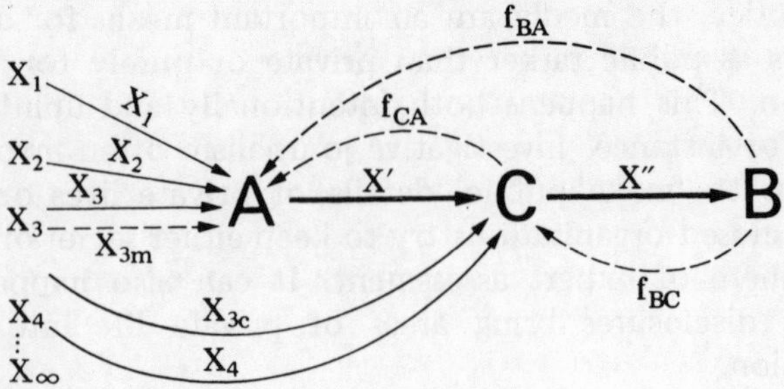

A: the would-be communicator or 'advocate'.
B: the audience member.
C: the mass communication organisation and its agents who control the channel.
X: any event or object in the environment of A, B, or C which is a subject of communication.
f: feedback.

This model illustrates how the messages C transmits to B (X″) represent his selections from both messages to him from A's (X′) and C's selections and abstractions from Xs in his own sensory field (X_{3c}, X_4), which may or may not be Xs in A's field. Feedback not only moves from B to A (f_{BA}) and from B to C (f_{BC}) but also from C to A (f_{CA}). Clearly, in the mass communication situation, a large number of Cs receive from a very large number of As and transmit to a vastly large number of Bs, who simultaneously receive from other Cs.

Source. Westley and MacLean, 1957.

Fig. 2. A model of mass communication

matter of conveying the unplanned events of the world to an audience.

This is an important distinction which is not well enough expressed in terms of degrees of purposiveness, since it is also a matter of degrees of control and filtering by the communicator organisations. In the extreme case, for instance a television broadcast to the nation by an American president, the media do no more than provide the technical and institutional facilities; at the other extreme the message is produced entirely within and by the organisation, as in the editorial column of a newspaper. Elliott[3] (p. 156), in a discussion of the producer role, suggests that there is a continuum of direct access and communicator control: 'Proceeding along the continuum the greater the scope of the television producer's role the more limited the access available for the society as source to the society as audience.' Elliott tends to stress the very limited opportunity for direct communication, by way of mass communication, especially television, while Westley and MacLean tend to emphasise the neutrality and intermediary character of the mass communication filter in a self-adjusting system of information transfer. The model does, nevertheless, clearly imply a selecting and editing activity as essential to the process of mass communication, and this again differentiates it from most other forms of the communication process, where contact is unmediated. The process of selecting has a dual aspect. First it is a matter of choosing among the objects of the world to 'report' or convey to an audience and choosing among potential 'communicators' or advocates. It is also a matter of interpreting the needs and interests of potential audience members. By so doing, the mass media give rise to a pattern of audience expectations and turn the audience aggregate into something qualitatively different — usually a number of distinct publics or sub-audiences which share certain interests or locations and have some more or less shadowy identity and group character.

If we look at the process from the point of view of the receiver, we would, in the terms of this model, see the mass media as extending our environment, adding to the experience which can be acquired from sensory contact, *making available* information from which to select freely according to our needs. The media are supplementary to direct experience, though in many cases they act to confirm what we learn directly about the objects of the external world. Thus the events and objects of the world and the messages of the mass media provide a set of impressions which are not sharply differentiated from each other, except perhaps in certain areas of knowledge (physically or socially remote events) where the media have a near monopoly of our opportunities of knowing. The process of attending to mass media, in this view, takes on the general character of a continuous 'scanning' process rather than of the experience of 'being in touch' or 'in communication' with an identifiable source. This description is obviously subject to the continuum of purposiveness or direct access discussed above – in that mass media do at times provide the experience of a direct communication relationship with a given individual.

The process of mass communication as a whole can now be viewed, in summary terms, in any of three possible ways. From the media point of view, the process is one of selecting communicators and messages with a view to meeting communication needs of a chosen audience or public. From the would-be communicator's point of view it is a matter of gaining access to means of transmission in order to reach a chosen audience. From the audience point of view it is a matter of selecting what is useful from a range of messages made available to them. Since the media organisations have the final say on what gets 'carried' on media channels, and hence on access and what is available, perhaps their view should be regarded as the most appropriate for characterising the process as a whole.

Whether one accepts this or not, it is difficult to avoid the implication that mass communication can scarcely be regarded as a single process. In part, this implied fragmentation is a result of the scale and complexity of the media operation, since there is bound to be a division of labour in any large scale industrial activity. Thus there are specialists in the production of messages, in the technical aspects of distribution, in the matter of interpreting audience needs and interests and in 'marketing' the product. But the breakdown of the single concept version of mass communication (except for the most general and abstracted purposes) has more to do with the differences of perspective described above and the resulting differences in the communication model needed to cope with this diversity. For the communicator wishing to persuade, or to convey information and experience to a particular audience, the basic communication model as a linear relationship of source to receiver is appropriate. For the audience member, a model of selective attention to, and perception of, an environment is nearer to the facts. For the media organisation, the process is less one of communication than of cultural production for a particular market.

Elliott[4] has already drawn attention to the inadequacy of conventional communication models for handling problems of mass communication and to their misleading character. Following his analysis of television documentary production, he writes:

> Our model of the mass communication process consists of three separate systems, society as source, mass communicators and society as audience. Each of these systems takes from the other what is necessary for its own needs. The mass communicators draw on society for material suitable for their own purposes, the audience is left largely on its own to respond to the material put before it. Each system has its own set of interests and its own ways of bringing influence to bear on the others. This model is in direct contrast to those which link the different parts of the communication process directly, conceptualising it as a process of influence or communication flow (p. 164).

He goes on to suggest that the model can be clarified 'by substituting the term "spectator" for audience', thus reflecting the point made above about the different model appropriate for the audience perspective on the mass communication process.

To continue with a discussion of mass communication we need to abandon the single model approach, and look instead at the separate areas of (*a*) production, selection and transmission of messages; and (*b*) audience attention, attitudes and 'consumption'.

Production of mass communication

When we speak of the production of mass communication we are thinking of the work of those whom Elliott calls 'mass communicators', people who might be defined as occupying roles in formal mass communication organisations which involve a direct influence over the content of mass media. Thus, we are thinking in terms of a group of employees of a large industry, who loosely constitute a profession. A number of questions about them and their work are of particular relevance to our present purpose, which is to assess the communicative character of the mass communication process. We are interested, first of all, in who these communicators are, the people who have a privileged access to the sender role or source position. Second, we are interested in how they view their role as communicators. Who do they think they are addressing and how do they conceive their audience? Third, we are interested in how the work of the formal media organisation and the constraints of an industrial and bureaucratic setting affect the production of messages (media content).

We can only answer the first question in very general terms and explain our interest in the question. Thus, we are interested because the personal values and social background of 'communicators' is likely to have some effect on two of their most important activities: selecting content and controlling access; and interpreting the needs and interests of the audience. The scope for selective judgment according to personal values is limited, but it is bound to be greater in organisations which Tunstall[5] classifies, following Perrow[6], as 'non-routine bureaucracies'. We have some evidence from studies of editorial processes of newspapers of the large scope for subjective judgment (e.g. Gieber[7]). We know, too, that one way out of the difficulty of remoteness from the audience is to address an imaginary audience which is like oneself or of the same social milieu (Gans[8]). Hence to know something of the social characteristics of the communicators is to know something about content.

Who are the communicators and how do they define their role?

Of course, the mass media communicators, even in one society, are a heterogeneous group if we think only of the gap which must separate the editor of *The Times* from a reporter on a provincial weekly newspaper. The composition of this occupational group also varies from one society to another. Some features of the profession of journalism in Britain have been charted by Tunstall[9] and these suggest a few general points of interest. First, it is an intermediate or indeterminate profession, without a definite career hierarchy and with some open boundaries with other occupations. Second, it is mainly middle or lower-middle class in composition, usually with a stratification into two levels, a better educated minority who monopolise higher status jobs on national media and a majority without much status or prospects. Third, it is a profession which reflects the character of the social stratification of the society and whose members also tend to reflect dominant political and social values. Gans goes so far as to suggest that the freedom of news broadcasters in the United States stems from the fact that such men are 'safe', in that they subscribe to the basic values of the society even if they represent the liberal wing of such values. In this particular respect, the situation is thus little different in principle from the Soviet Union where the mass communicators are also safe in the same sense, because they voluntarily adhere to the purposes and values of the Soviet state and need little formal control by censorship. The difference between the two societies stems from there being different sets of values to be upheld.

Although the underlying conformity of professional communicators to the basic values of their society is a plausible hypothesis and one which is more than trivial, more detailed study of particular groups of mass communicators has shown there to be important variations in the way they regard their role and consequently in their behaviour as communicators, aside from differences which arise from social status and personal values. For present purposes, perhaps the most significant point to emerge from such work is that the orientation of mass communicators is shaped by the structure and culture of the work organisation which provides an appropriate socialisation experience to various alternative role positions. The way in which a mass communicator sees his role, and in particular his relationship to an audience, is the outcome of the ethos of the organisation, the options it makes available and his own past and future career. The result is a considerable variety, and yet also an underlying similarity of basic choices open to mass communicators in quite different organisational settings.

As a first example, Burns's[10] study of the BBC begins with the observation that professional communicators in the BBC have a basically defensive attitude towards the public they are supposed to serve, a response which is also found in other occupations 'which exist to provide direct services to customers, an audience or a clientele'. The expected deference to the client has an alienative effect on members of the occupation, hence they 'tend to carry with them a countervailing, and ordinarily concealed, posture of invidious hostility'. Burns distinguishes three main forms of adaptation to this situation: one a 'responsible' or 'Platonist' attitude which involves adopting the traditional BBC role of upholding cultural standards and supporting national institutions, of being responsible; second, an attitude which he terms 'pragmatist' — the wish to meet public demand, or giving the audience what it wants; third, a 'professional' attitude ('television for television's sake'), which involves a primary orientation to one's colleagues and the standards of the profession. The communicators studied by Burns opted for one or other of these modes of adaptation and, along with them, a correlative form of relationship to the audience. The first involves adopting a position of superiority, an immunity to certain forms of criticism, a degree of protection by the organisation, an assumption of the right to decide for the audience what is good for it. The second, pragmatist, view involves the desire to please the audience, as far as audience research allows, and seeks justification from 'good' viewing figures, whatever these may actually mean. The third approach involves some distain both for audience figures and for the traditional role of the Corporation; all that really matters is the exercise of one's own professional skill and judgment and the approbation of fellow professionals. Each of these alternatives involves an insulation, in varying degrees, from contact with the audience in any real sense, and a very limited version of communication in the sense of the transmission of 'ordered meaning'. It is for this reason that Burns speaks of the 'world of autistic activity and belief which producers, programme departments, and broadcasting as a whole can create around itself'. In another case study of BBC producers, Blumler[11] noted the appearance of two quite different approaches to election current affairs reporting which fits the classification of Burns. He found producers to have either a 'sacerdotal' approach or a 'pragmatic' approach, the former based on the assumption of a public service duty to report certain events in a serious or comprehensive way, whatever their 'news interest', the latter holding that coverage of an election should be governed only by standards of what is lively, entertaining and having news value. Each approach involves a different kind of relationship with the audience and a different view of what mass communication should be concerned with.

Tunstall[12], in a study of specialist journalists in the British press, distinguishes three different journalistic roles and three different goals of the media organisation which influence the orientation of a journalist. The three roles are employee, newsgatherer, and competitor-colleague. Put very simply, in the first of these roles the journalist is oriented to his employer and the goals formally set by the organisation; in the second he is concerned with his *sources*, those on whom he relies for his working material, whether it is the police, or politicians, or business firms, or whatever; in the third, he is oriented to his fellow professionals and concerned with their judgment and his standing in relation to them. The precise implications for his orientation to an audience depend, however, on what the goals of the organisation actually are. As he makes clear, these are not merely concerned with communication, but consist, broadly, of three different goals: one concerned with revenue from an audience, another with revenue from advertising, a third with 'non-revenue goals'. The first two may be self-explanatory, and of the third Tunstall explains that it refers to any other objective 'such as gaining political influence, furthering cultural or educational objectives or merely increasing general prestige'. To make the point clearer, we can note that of the journalists studied, those concerned with non-revenue goals were exemplified by foreign correspondents (i.e. prestigious, but not big audience-pullers); those concerned with audience revenue include sport and crime reporters; those concerned with advertising revenue goals include fashion and motoring correspondents. Tunstall's basic point is that the study of mass media communicators must take account of this variety of goals and roles. Our main interest stems from the clear demonstration that mass communicators frequently are not in the business of communicating, and where they are, they are not necessarily communicating primarily to the audience as normally conceived, but to very special audiences which might consist of employers, or fellow journalists, or potential advertisers, or members of other institutions. It would be difficult, in the light of this, to represent the process of mass communication by any simple communication model and our earlier point is underlined.

A final example, from a different sphere of communication, will help to reinforce the main line of argument. It is taken from Muriel Cantor's[13] study of Hollywood television producers. As with Tunstall, she stresses the variety of organisational goals in this branch of the media industry and suggests that there are three basic alternative foci of orientation for 'mass communicators' in this context, one concerned with occupational crafts, another with pleasing the network bureaucracy and a third with the audience. She finds a correspondence between these different goals and three rather different kinds of television producer. One she calls the 'film-makers', who opt for an orientation to the craft. These are mainly younger, university trained, with an ambition some day to become major independent film-makers. They have no quarrel with the goals of their employers, the network bureaucracies, but their concern is with the profession and not the audience. A second group are termed 'writer-producers'. These are a mainly middle-aged group, who are interested in communication to an audience and see this goal as thwarted by the interests of their employers. The writer-producer 'sees one of his responsibilities as informing the viewing audience of the social realities of the world in which they live' (pp. 202—3). His commitment is to writing and to his message and he tends to feel that the audience is underestimated by the network planners. Finally, there are the 'old-time producers' — in reality an older generation with less education and few ideas or illusions. They pitch their work to a mass audience which they see as small town and unsophisticated and have no general quarrel with the network. They 'see themselves as businessmen producing entertainment as a product', their 'fundamental aspirations are the same as the network executives and the studio heads — to be successful'. The correspondence with the other cases cited is not exact, but the same general picture emerges, of the mass communicator role as a matter of choice between communicating to an audience, or pleasing an employer, or exercising the skills of the trade.

It would seem that to be a mass communicator involves

having a greater degree of freedom of definition of the communicator role than the basic linear communication model seems to allow for, or even than the Westley—MacLean model suggests. This is not just a matter of division of labour, since the basic choices that have been described have been taken up by people doing essentially the same job. The same activity is the source of different satisfactions to different people. To some, it offers the interest of practising the various arts and skills of producing symbols, and the interesting implication of the work described is that the interest in *form* seems not to be connected particularly with an interest in effect, except the effect of a favourable reaction from significant others or reference group members. To those who are interested in the effect on the audience, whether in qualitative or quantitative terms, message form would seem to be subordinate. The situation is complicated by the fact that media organisations have alternative goals, sometimes available within the same organisation, sometimes not. While the continued attention of an audience is a necessary condition for the continuance of any media organisation, this can be achieved by more than one path and can mean several different things, among which the communication of meaning to this audience is only one.

Communicators' view of their audience

The point has already been made that mass communicators, in the nature of things, experience some difficulty in establishing a relationship with their anonymous and distant audience. The previous discussion has also suggested that not all mass communicators have a central interest in overcoming this difficulty. On the other hand, there must be some element of role-complementarity between communicator and audience member and however autistic the 'act of communication' may tend to become within a large media organisation, some reference to the audience is essential, if only to allow planning, calculation and allocation of resources in what is normally a rational, bureaucratic structure. There is reason to believe, and some concrete evidence (e.g. Martell and McCall[14]), that media organisations and forms of mass communication which survive over time manage to maintain a close correspondence between their own content and the salient characteristics (in terms of values, beliefs, social position) of their main audience group. Thus we might say that 'successful' mass communication must be open to influence from its audience. The relationship between mass communication and mass audience is clearly a two-way relationship, however devious and latent the means by which this relationship is accomplished. Our concern here is with some of the more discoverable mechanisms by which mass communicators establish an image of who their audience is and act accordingly.

One solution to the problem has already been mentioned: communicators can make for themselves an image of the audience to whom they are addressing their messages, an audience which might consist of people like themselves, as Gans[15] suggests, and as is implicit in Gieber's[16] account of the subjectivity of newsmen. Bauer[17] comments on this phenomenon that 'communications are seldom directed towards a single manifest audience. Secondary audiences or reference groups, usually internalised and often imaginary, are important targets of communication and may at times play a decisive part in the flow of communication.' Bauer finds this tendency to reflect Cooley's concept of the 'imaginary interlocutor', the partner of imaginary conversations that we all engage in, in the development of the self. Pool and Shulman[18] shed an interesting light on this process by research which shows that newspaper writers, when they do have an image of an audience at the time of writing, think in terms either of people they wish to please and 'reward' or those they would like to 'punish' — that is either of supporters or critics:

> For most of our respondents the act of writing seemed to provide one of two alternative kinds of gratification. For some, writing provided the opportunity to bestow pleasure on readers, who would

> reward them for it by admiration and affection. For others the gratification came from awareness of the weapons of words . . . and the damage that it can do to the 'bad guys'.

Clearly there are numerous alternative conceptualisations of an audience, and the more intent the mass communicator is on 'real communication' the sharper and more consistent the image of the audience and the more overt the process of formulating such an image. There are two other main ways in which the problem of having an audience reference point can be solved. One is by audience research, which can describe previous audiences and likely future audiences in terms of social composition. But to rely on what such research normally provides is often to rely on a stereotype of a social group, with a certain income level and life-style. This is hardly likely to provide a satisfactory basis for a genuine communicative intent and it may encourage a manipulative and routinised approach to the task of communication. Finally, there is the institutional solution, the adoption of an image of the audience which is consistent with the ethos and self-definition of the media organisation and its task. To judge from Burns's[19] account, the BBC offers such an image, which is derived from its traditions and its role in the national life, and some BBC employees adopt this. *The Times* offers a similar example, to judge from a former advertising slogan: 'Top People Take *The Times*'. The Soviet media, in general, have worked according to a definition of what the audience ought to be like and have created an image which is consistent with the ideal of the good citizen. Examples could no doubt be multiplied and all imply a degree of insulation from 'reality', a lack of interest in knowing what the audience is really like, some element of wish fulfilment and, at times, the intention of shaping the audience to conform with the communicator's view of it. C. W. Mills[20] (p. 314) wrote of the media in mass society that they give us our identities and aspirations, provide new models of conduct for us: 'The media tell the man in the mass who he is — they give him identity; they tell him what he wants to be – they give him aspirations.' This is to turn our formulation the other way round and to suggest that the media do not search for a true representation of the audience they address, but manufacture an image according to their own interests and then supply this as a readymade self-image which the audience adopts. Certainly Mills exaggerates and tends to equate aspirations with achievement, but at the same time he vividly characterises a tendency which the more insulated and 'autistic' mass communicators do exhibit.

Routines of production

A last aspect of mass communication production which needs discussion concerns the consequences which flow from following what Elliott[21] (p. 166) describes as 'the accepted production routines within established organisational systems'. His main point is that the possibility for genuine communication is limited by the constraints of working in what is essentially an industrial and bureaucratic organisation. There is a good deal of evidence, extending over a long period of time, that what emerges as content from mass media bears the mark not only of the intentions of its 'creators' but also of the demands of a mass production process. Thus Berelson and Salter[22] explained the bias and distortion in the presentation of ethnic minorities in American magazine fiction in terms of the convenience of drawing on stock characters and known formulas in producing this kind of cheap fiction for a large heterogeneous audience. More recently, Hartmann and Husband[23] have explained the tendency for British news media to present race in terms of 'problems' and 'conflict' as a result of pressure to conform to dominant news values. There are several main elements in the situation and the way the process works. First, there is the need for continuous production: the media have not only to provide an unending supply of film, television, radio and print material to fill established schedules, they have the added difficulty of needing to provide a succession of supposedly new and unique products. Evidently the task is impossible and only *appearance* of novelty can be attained. Second, the media have to meet expectations which they have themselves created over time and to depart from these, to provide something really unexpected, would risk the loss of their customers. Third, there are limitations imposed by a time schedule and shortages of time and resources. Media products are expected to appear on time, often very frequently. There can be no parallel in another manufacturing industry to such problems on this scale. The resource problem arises particularly in relation to news where reporters and technical equipment have to be present for a news event to be reported. There is thus a tension between the need to report a news event, which is by definition unexpected, and the need to plan for and anticipate the occurrence of such events and their location.

The solutions found to these various problems account in large part for the effects of the production process on what is actually presented as content over the media. Media organisations have to prepare as much content as possible well in advance, which may mean either 'saving up' news, prerecording television and radio material, relying on series and serials and repeats, having articles and stories in reserve, using illustrative material from files and libraries of past production. Where possible, the media have to anticipate what is 'news' and where it will occur and at times even 'manufacture' news or keep old news fresh as long as possible. The constraint of audience expectation involves the use of stereotypes and stock formulas, the rigid adherence to timetables and formats which have been 'promised' implicitly, if not advertised in advance. It also restricts any effort to depart from established routines. It is a matter, not of choice, but of necessity to develop routines and procedures which ease the production process, prevent too much costly duplication of effort, enable the inescapable deadlines to be met. In the production of a television documentary series which has been so well described by Elliott[24] as a single case study, we can see some of the consequences of production routines at work. In particular, we see the very limited nature of the field from which source material is drawn, limited to the ideas of the production team, the personal contacts they have, the illustrative material conveniently available; limited also by the known 'experts' who happen to be available, by the 'conventional wisdom' on the subject matter. It is also clear that content is often subordinated to forms of presentation, decided on through considerations of what is likely to keep or lose audience *attention* rather than what is likely to convey anything meaningful to the audience.

Perhaps the evidence which most strikingly confirms the hypothesis of content determination by the exigencies under which media organisations work comes from the study by Halloran *et al.*[25] of the reporting of a public demonstration in London in 1968. Essentially what this showed was that an event was largely 'created', in its main dimensions, by press reporting and then given major news media coverage in terms not of what actually happened, but in terms of an *anticipated* version of it. The result was not only to inflate the significance of the event and perhaps change it, but also to produce a misperception of what actually occurred. The early study by Lang and Lang[26] of the television coverage of MacArthur's return from Korea is a classic account of this particular effect. The point to emphasise is the great pressure which mass communicators are under to have control over the 'reality' which they reflect or report to their audiences. Of course, ultimate control is achieved by being able to 'make' the reality. The extreme case of fiction is rarely attained, but the news communicators must occasionally envy the control which writers of fiction have over the supply of material. In the circumstances of media production, the tension is always there between the predictable and the unpredictable and between standardisation and individual creation (Elliott[27], p. 11).

The news genre

Little has so far been said about the content of mass communication, the message which is passed from communicator to receiver, although much has already been implied in discussing its production. If it is produced in a routine way, under conditions which promote standardisation, then it is no surprise to discover that the output of mass communication tends to be a standardised product, predictable in form and meaning, suitable for easy recognition and comprehension. The mass media have often been castigated for lack of originality and creativity, though perhaps without much understanding of their (partly self-created) problems. The amount of repetition of basic themes and plots, the recurrence of images and myths, the survival of certain forms of expression and their extension across different cultures is certainly very striking, although it cannot only be explained in terms of production needs. It has also to do with the needs of its 'consumers' or audiences. Before turning to the receiving end of the mass communication process a final comment on one major content item in mass communication can be made: 'news'. It happens also to be a form of content largely developed by the mass media, whereas most other staple content commodities were taken over from elsewhere.

Park[28] offered some reflections on the nature of news which are still apposite. Its main characteristics, in his view, include its unsystematic character, being composed of a series of unrelated items of information which it does not seek to relate to each other or explain; its reference to the present moment rather than past or future, and its consequent transient and ephemeral quality; its concern with the unusual or unexpected — 'even the most trivial happening, it seems, provided it represents a departure from the customary ritual and routine of everyday life is likely to be reported'; finally, what makes news is 'news interest' and news interest or news value is relative and open to subjective judgment rather than objective determination. All these points are important, though perhaps the last two have attracted most attention from students of mass communication. On the unexpectedness of news, Park goes on to say that

> it is the not wholly unexpected that gets into the news. The events that have made news in the past, as in the present, are actually the expected things . . . it is on the whole the accidents and incidents that the public is prepared for . . . the things that one fears and the things that one hopes that make news.

This point, together with the question of news values, has been elaborated since, especially with a view to explaining the rather consistent patterns of news reporting and the similarity of standards of what is news which develops in the news media of the world. Some part of an explanation has already been suggested in the tendency of mass communicators to anticipate events and then describe them selectively in terms of certain stock images. This does not explain as much as can be explained, and at least one impressive effort has been made to propose a general theory of the factors that determine, for foreign news at least, the relative news value of different events (Galtung and Ruge[29]). The proposal is an elaborate one, but we record their isolation of three main factors which contribute to 'newsworthiness': having to do with élites (people or nations); being open to 'personification'; being essentially negative (i.e. bad news). Whatever the predictive value of the hypothesis of Galtung and Ruge, they demonstrate cogently that consistent distortions are built into the selection of events for news coverage and into their ultimate presentation. They support the view that news does not record reality as it happens but is a somewhat arbitrary, culturally patterned, version of this 'reality' which meets the expectations of audiences and fits the production and distribution requirements of mass media systems.

Audience reception of mass communication

The questions which we have been following through in this

chapter have to do, first, with differences between mass communication process and interpersonal communication and, second, with whether it is appropriate to represent it as a single process at all. The question has even been raised (by Elliott[30]) as to whether mass communication is communication at all. We have three kinds of evidence about audiences for mass communication which might shed some light on these questions. One is evidence about the size and composition of the aggregates who attend to particular media or items of content. Another tells us something about audience response and about the reasons which people have for attending to mass communication and the satisfactions which are derived from the experience. Third, we have some evidence about the effects of mass communication. However, the evidence is relatively sparse, given the sheer quantity of mass communication that occurs. And, although it gives some support to the doubts which have been aired, it is inconclusive.

The audience as market

If we try to assess the audience experience in the light of the research on listeners, viewers and readers, we are likely to be influenced by the form in which these data are normally collected and reported. Audience research, as usually conducted, is a form of market research and hence represents the audience as a market — a body of consumers of a particular product. We do not normally regard the recipients of communication in other contexts in this way: the people we talk to are not 'consumers' of our words, children are not a market for their lessons, employees of an organisation are not consumers of organisational messages, nor are voters a market for the appeals of political leaders. There is an inbuilt bias towards a certain view of the mass communication process, a view which reflects not only the forms of research, but the main features of mass media structures. This bias lends support to the view that the audience is not engaging in communication, but in a form of behaviour which is characterised simply by giving attention to, or buying the products of, mass media organisations, which happen to come in the form of messages.

In examining the data of typical audience research, we are struck by the consistency of patterns over time in the attention given to particular sources and types of content. Despite the apparent regularity and predictability, the suspicion is bound to arise that the behaviour being measured does have a diversity of meanings which are not differentiated by the form in which evidence has been collected. To give some examples which can all be documented from evidence, though they are also quite recognisable from daily experience, 'being in the audience for mass communication', as it would be measured by audience research, covers the following different situations: visiting a cinema in order to go out with a friend; having a radio on to create an appropriate mood for some other activity or as background to a boring task; sitting in front of a television set as a substitute for doing nothing, just to fill in time; watching or reading something to satisfy someone else's expectation or to establish an image of oneself which one might like to present; leaving a radio on to suggest that someone is at home; taking one's children to a cinema. The examples could be multiplied and many would be trivial, but they illustrate the point that attending to, or buying, or being in the presence of, media messages can have a diversity of meanings and involve very differently defined social situations. The media, in short, have many different uses in social life beyond the acquisition of ordered meaning or sharing in experience by way of communication. To say this, however, is not to conclude that mass communication is never communication. It is only sometimes communication.

Audience uses of media content

There is by now a long tradition of 'functional' inquiries into audience behaviour which rests on the observation that media messages are *used by* their audiences and are not simply experienced by them (see above, p. 155). It is a tradition which lays a good deal of stress on the freedom of the audience member to act *on* the message, to interpret it and incorporate it into his own daily life. It focuses on the different ways in which members of an audience solve problems, meet their needs with the help of mass communication. This is the 'uses and gratification' approach discussed in chapter 5; in chapter 2 we discussed alternative ways of viewing communication in terms of a continuum from conditioning to spontaneous action. Uses and gratifications studies can be found at various points on such a continuum, though not at either extreme. Thus some investigators have used functional language explicitly to describe and account for mass media use. Rosengren and Windahl[31], for example, have looked at the relationship between attending to certain kinds of mass media material and taking part in other kinds of direct interpersonal interaction, proposing specifically that the fewer the opportunities for such interaction the higher will be the reliance on such mass media content.

Media use may be considered as a 'functional alternative', or as 'parasocial interaction'[32]. It is an activity which meets individual needs which cannot be as easily satisfied by the opportunities available. In this context, the idea of a 'need' has been described by Fearing[33] as referring to the fact 'that the individual seeks experience beyond that furnished by his immediate environment'. The needs the mass media may satisfy, either as substitutes or as the 'first-choice' way, have been variously described and listed. They include needs for information, for escape, for release from tension and anxiety, for security and reassurance, for companionship, for aiding social interaction with others, for maintaining a mood, for giving a framework to daily routine, and so on (McQuail[34], p. 74). In an attempt to establish an overall framework or taxonomy of audience uses of mass communication (or 'media person interactions') McQuail *et al.*[35] have suggested four main types of relationship with media content as having to do with diversion, personal relationships, personal identity, and surveillance, or maintaining an overall view of the immediate environment. This particular version of the relationship of audience member to communicator does not presuppose a functional or deterministic perspective, nor does it exclude the possibility of there being communicative relationships in the proper sense between sender and receiver. Both this formulation and the uses and gratifications approach as a whole do tend to stress, however, first, the wide range of uses to which media content may be put by its audience; second, the fact that the same content may have different uses; and, third, the relative freedom of the individual audience member to interpret the experience of receiving communication. This freedom may be conceived in terms of an independent audience-content system which has as its dynamic the needs of audience members in interaction with gratifications inherent in the content. In such a view, the mass communicator is no more than the original supplier of a useful commodity, and the audience member is no more in a relationship to him than the user of a car is in a relationship with the car manufacturer. Alternatively, the freedom can be conceived of as the genuine free choice which a person has to receive communications from whatever source he wants and interpret the message in whatever aspect he wants. In looking at mass communication from either perspective there is scope for handling real communication relationships as well as acts of consumption, though the overall bias of the uses and gratifications approach is towards the latter view (see McQuail and Gurevitch[36]).

The effects of mass communication

Numerous investigations have by now seemed to indicate that the direct effects of mass communication on attitudes and behaviour are either non-existent, very small, or beyond measurement by current techniques. (For reviews of research, see McGuire[37]; Weiss[38]; McQuail[39]; Halloran[40, 41]; Klapper[42]; Berelson and Steiner[43].) Occasionally, case studies have found evidence of effects under certain conditions (Halloran *et al.*[44]; Blumler and McQuail[45]; Lang and Lang[46]), but the proved direct effects seem not to match the intentions or expectations of mass communicators and investigators, given the massive investment in time and attention. Some explanation has already been given for this fact in the last chapter in terms of variable conditions and the varying basis of communicative power. But the bald fact of limited effectiveness as persuasion lends some support to the argument that mass media do not communicate, either because the mass communicators are not seriously in the business of 'changing' people, or because the audience is not, for reasons already discussed, oriented to mass communication as receivers of meaningful messages.

Nevertheless, there are ways of interpreting the accumulated evidence in less simplistic terms. It has already been suggested that at least some of the time there is an element of communicative intent on the part of mass communicators and that at times audience members are also orientated to content and source as would-be receivers of communication. For instance Blumler and McQuail's[47] study of communication during a political campaign shows very clear evidence that people look to the mass media to provide essential information and ideas which enable them to fulfil political roles, and that for the most part their expectations are fulfilled. The problem in obtaining or interpreting evidence about effects in general lies partly in the inappropriateness of many formulations of the process of mass communication, a failure to acknowledge that this is a subtle and complex process, a matter of bargaining, interaction and exchange, just as much as a conversation is between two people. We would not say that a conversation or a lecture had 'failed' as communication if the participants held approximately the same opinions and attitudes after the event as before. We tend to apply double standards without good reason. There has also been a tendency to look only at short term effects and ignore those which occur in the long term. There has, especially, been a tendency to ignore the obvious, for instance the fact that people in societies which are penetrated by mass media know and have opinions about many matters beyond their direct experience because of their access to mass media. In the light of this, to suppose that the mass media do not have effects is clearly absurd. There is a growing body of opinion and a good deal of evidence that the effects of the mass media are much more to be found in the provision of what Lippman[48] called the 'pictures in our heads', the frames of reference and the cognitive detail about the world. To cite one specific example, the research of Hartmann and Husband[49], while showing that mass media probably do not directly affect attitudes to coloured people in Britain, suggested fairly conclusively that the mass media are the source of a quite uniformly held and specific 'definition of the situation'. This definition tends to override personal experience and gives people the information and ideas with which to compose their own attitudes:

> The mass media, by making available particular kinds of information, and by the range of perspectives they present, by what they emphasise and what they play down, may help to influence public consciousness in the sense of influencing what is widely known and what is not, and what is thought important (pp. 115–16).

Much could be said along these lines in many other areas of knowledge, opinion and belief about the consequences of processes of mass communication. The media of mass communication communicate not only to individuals — they communicate to groups and institutions and to societies as a whole and they communicate from one society to another. It is a collective process of communication which cannot be understood solely in terms of individual senders and individual receivers. The suspicions voiced at the outset and followed through in this chapter have as much to do with this fundamental point as with the 'autism' of communicators or audience.

Mass communication and society

In an earlier chapter, we discussed the social distribution of the means of communication, and the relationship between the stratification system of a society and its communication process. As a general rule, the higher the social status, the greater the social and economic power, the greater access to and control over the processes of communication. Processes of communication are horizontal and vertical and we have seen examples of both. Where they are vertical the direction of flow tends to be predominantly downward, with those having more social power being able to initiate more communication than they receive. As normally organised, mass communication is almost wholly vertical and hence, according to this rule, tending to convey the messages of the more powerful to the less powerful. It is consequently regarded in all societies as a power asset or resource, a property which is advantageous to groups and interests which own or control the media. As a result, there is both competition for access according to an agreed set of rules and criteria (economic, ideological, legal, evaluative) and also a variety of mechanisms of control and accountability established to protect power holders and the recipients. A mass communication relationship is inevitably in some measure a power relationship, though a relatively weak one, since influence can only be exerted by persuasive, normative or utilitarian means and not by the use of force. The relative weakness of mass communication stems largely from the voluntary character of reception — without attention from an audience there can be no power and attention cannot easily be compelled. A mass media system can only approach compulsion by establishing a monopoly and relying on certain necessary functions of mass media in a society to induce attention. The normal case of media—audience relationship is more balanced, closer to a market relationship in which consumer satisfaction is required.

Nevertheless the mass communication process is more likely to sustain rather than challenge the existing power structure of a society and it does not take a conspiracy theory to account for this. Mass communication process has become a major institution in industrialised societies. The media institution must coexist with other institutions and broadly respect the prevailing consensus of beliefs in the population as a whole and the interests of power-holding or vocal groups. Where societies are characterised by internal conflicts, it is possible for segments of the media to take sides, but the more common circumstance is to find the dominant mass media standing aside from such conflict. This seems to have happened in Europe and North America, with the rise of television, a medium which is especially likely to be centralised, subject to public, if not governmental, control, and compelled to a degree of neutrality not required of the press. It is this enforced (though often widely welcomed) neutrality which gives broadcasting its tendency to respect if not actively support the existing order, and its disinclination to promote radical change. If the tendency has begun with broadcasting, it seems to have spread slowly to the less formally constrained press (Seymour-Ure[50]). Within an established neutrality, it is inevitable that the terms of discussion tend to be decided (though never wholly) by the established élites of power in a society (who are not necessarily in agreement among themselves). However independent and resistant the audience, however much media content is filtered through institutional and interpersonal channels, in the long run the major communicative effects of the media will tend to favour dominant social values and the interests of power holding groups.

Conclusion

Of all the instances of communication process which have been discussed in this book, developed mass communication systems are the largest in scale, most complicated and least easy to define or characterise in a unitary way. Mass communication is many things at the same time and it differs from one societal setting to another and alters as historical circumstances alter. While there is something approaching an institutionalised ideal type of a mass media system, this type embodies a diversity of uses and meaning for those involved.

Communication and society: a review of principal themes 7

Contrasting models of communication

Underlying many of the differences of approach and interpretation which have been encountered in this book is a single fundamental division of emphasis which, in turn, has deep roots in the human sciences. We tend either to view the social world that we apprehend as a symbolic environment which is structured primarily by the giving of the definitions and meanings which govern behaviour, or as primarily a world of things, events, people and ideas which have an objective existence and a direct constraining power over us. In the former view, communication is seen as the process which develops, disseminates and maintains the dominant meaning systems and in the second view communication is the mechanism which connects, by information, various social activities with each other and with their environment. In the one case, communication is more likely to be studied in its expressive forms and in the latter as a network or set of channels through which messages flow in measurable ways. The two approaches do not exclude each other, since a 'symbolic' view also presupposes processes of message flow and exchange, but in practice it has been difficult to give equal weight to both in selecting matters for attention in the study of communication and in the development of communication theory.

An eloquent description of what is essentially the same division has been given by Carey[1] in seeking to argue for 'a cultural approach to communication'. Drawing on the work of John Dewey, he distinguishes two alternative conceptions of communication, which he labels a 'transmission' view and a 'ritual' view. He writes: 'the transmission view of communication is the commonest in our culture and . . . is defined by such terms as sending, transmitting, or giving information to others. It is formed off a metaphor of geography or transportation. . . . The centre of this idea of communication is the transmission of signals or messages over distance for the purpose of control.' In the alternative, 'ritual', view, 'communication is linked to such terms as sharing, participation, association, fellowship and the possession of a common faith. . . . A ritual view is not directed towards the extension of messages in space, but the maintenance of society in time; not the act of imparting information, but the representation of shared beliefs.' Carey illustrates the difference by comparing two conceptions of the newspaper. According to a transmission view, a newspaper is a device for disseminating news and knowledge over large distances with different kinds of probable effect. A ritual view sees reading a newspaper as a process by which little new is learned, but a particular view of the world is received and confirmed. News is essentially drama, not information — a replaying of recurrent conflicts in which we can all vicariously participate.

This account has already indicated the main consequences of taking one rather than the other view, but there are other associated tendencies which are included in the following summary tabulation of differences.

Symbolic-ritual view of communication	*Mechanistic-transmission view of communication*
bias towards:	bias towards:
Language, modes, forms	Channels, networks
Content	Means, technology
Meaning and interpretation	Causes and effects

Expressive use	Instrumental use
Interaction and exchange	One-directional flow
Sharing, participation	Control, management
Ambiguity	Non-ambiguity
The static	The dynamic
Lateral flow	Vertical flow
Descriptive method	Measurement and quantification
Open systems	Closed systems
Storage of information	Transmission of information
Ideas	Behaviour
The indexical	The cognitive

These oppositions give some idea of why the two conceptions, although logically reconcilable, are difficult to combine in their application because they draw on different world views, involve different priorities and direct attention to various aspects of the potential field of enquiry as well as requiring different kinds of method. The world view of the 'culturalist' is one which supposes our world to be man-made, in the sense that we know of it through definitions and impressions developed in social life and potentially open to some measure of resistance, redefinition and personal renegotiation of the dominant meanings we encounter. We are not necessarily less constrained according to such a view, but the strategies for increasing freedom are different from those available according to the 'mechanistic-transmission' view. In the latter case, the world is also made by man, but in the more literal sense that man has constructed a physical environment, struggled with nature and erected human organisational forms for maintaining and extending control of the material environment. The way to increase freedom is to intensify the struggle by more and more efficient activity with communication as a major human and technological resource in the endeavour. There are echoes in this presentation of the opposition between 'traditional' and 'modern' societal forms, between collectivism and individualism, stability and change, community and technocracy and many more. There is no cause to evaluate the two broad conceptions and it is more than a gesture in the direction of consensus to say that no adequate science of communication could neglect either version. A purely mechanistic approach to communication would fail and has largely failed already, but a study of communication only directed to the elucidation of cultural meaning would be equally inadequate to the task, even if it might be less arid.

If the contents of this book are reviewed in rather a few words, according to the dichotomy presented, the following summary points might be made. First, the opposite poles of theory (p. 36—9), 'Passive' and 'Active' very broadly correspond to the mechanistic and cultural positions respectively, although there arises a verbal confusion, since the 'transmission' view is in one respect more dynamic and active in its approach to communication than the 'ritual' view. The point, however, is that in the former view, only the senders are active and the ritual view emphasises the receivers as acting in and on their symbolic environment. Second, and rather obviously, a ritual view gives much emphasis to ways of communicating and, especially, has a place for communication of an 'indexical' rather than cognitive kind, thus all forms of paralanguage which are not usually consciously deployed for instrumental purposes. Third, a ritual view of the structure of communication process gives more weight to the cultural context and setting and to the discontinuities and barriers which may nullify efforts at persuasive communication. Finally, in respect of mass communication, an example has already been given from Carey of what the alternatives imply for news and, in general, a ritual view orients us much more to the messages and meanings than to effects; to the sub-cultural variations within the audience rather than their similarities; and to a view of mass media as a somewhat enclosed world with its own culture rather than an open system acting as neutral carrier of 'new information' from one part of society to another.

Power and solidarity

The significance of the relationship between communication and power was stressed at the start of the book and has been touched upon at numerous points. The general notion that communication is a power resource and even a necessary condition of the exercise of power needs little argument. As we have seen, there are different kinds of power relationship and different kinds of influence. Of the latter, some may be considered as *sender-determined*, in the sense that influence will depend on the ultimate sanction of force or material reward or penalty. In such cases communication is a substitute for other kinds of power and may be used as a reminder of the realities of a power relationship, although more often as a means for achieving voluntary compliance through propaganda and the establishment of legitimacy. Second, there is a type of power which is *receiver-determined*, in the sense that the relationship is voluntary and governed by an expectation of rewards and by a self-assessment of what is 'functional' for the receiver, or in his or her own interest. Often communication may itself be rewarding, when it pleases, informs, interests or amuses. Third, there is a *relationship-determined* kind of influence which depends on a stable commitment of 'receiver' to 'giver' of influence, based on personal attraction, respect or moral belief. Such influence is communicative in the sense that the qualities and values associated with the source of influence are often of a symbolic kind and the continuity of the relationship depends on a continued sharing and interaction.

Before considering how this typology is reflected in the variety of contexts treated in this book, the concept of 'solidarity' can be introduced as the *lateral* dimension of relationships which cuts across the *vertical* dimension of power. Solidaristic relations imply equality and similarity, power relations asymmetry and some divergence of interest. If one refers back to the theme discussed above, the ritual view involves more emphasis on solidarity and the transmission view, on power, although power and solidarity are not logically in opposition. The substantive discussion until now has referred, at different points, to three main levels of social life: that of informal association in groups and local communities; organisational and institutional life; and of the complete society.

What can be said of power, solidarity and communication at the first of these levels? In general, communication will be more solidaristic in purpose and effect. It is a process of developing, expressing and sharing common outlooks which are a basis for, and a sign of membership of, the group or association. While the question of leadership and status differences does arise in group contexts, the emphasis is generally on equality of rights and mutuality of benefits. According to the three-way division described above, power will depend very much on the relationship, since membership of a group will carry some kinds of commitment to comply with others. The power dimension is more apparent in the patterns of differentiation between groups. As we have seen, there are cultural and life-style differences between groups which are strongly marked by variation in linguistic usage and by other indexical codes — behaviour, gesture, appearance, etc. In sum, at the primary level of social life there is no necessary opposition between the lateral and vertical dimensions of communication. They tend to be kept apart, perhaps because solidarity is more comfortable and reminders of power can be avoided.

At the 'intermediary' level of organisation and institution communication patterns and processes reflect the opposition between power and solidarity more sharply. Thus work organisations usually exhibit two types of relatively independent network, one following the chain of command from top to bottom, with most flow downwards and the other being cross-cutting informal channels based on similarities of function or status and on propinquity. A communication 'map' of an organisation would thus show up the different kinds of relationship which are involved and a measure of flows in the network so mapped would offer some guide to the degree of conflict or co-operation in the organisation. Two of the types of power relationship described above will be equally in evidence — that which is sender-determined, in the formal structure, and that which is relationship-determined in the informal, lateral, flows. In institutional spheres which have no fixed organisational boundaries the situation is less clear, but the patterns and balance between power-related and solidarity-related communication would depend on the degree to which involvement is voluntary — as for instance in a political party or movement; or involuntary, as in the welfare apparatus. In the first (voluntary) case, power is exercised and accepted by agreement, while in the latter there is likely to be a predominance of sender-related, vertical, power, with little feedback and also little solidaristic communication between the 'clients' of welfare institutions.

On the society-wide level, one can point to no single or dominant pattern and there is obviously a wide range of options dependent on the nature of state and society and on which of the society-wide networks is at issue. The case of mass media offers some possibilities for making general observations, even if interpretations of how mass media exercise power diverge widely. There is some agreement that mass media *can* exercise power, mainly of a 'top-down' kind, in a variety of ways: by direct propaganda or instruction; by offering definitions of situations, issues and actors which are favourable to certain interests; by the 'legitimation' of existing institutions and arrangements; or by direct motivation of some individuals to action. By implication the media can have negative consequences for power holders, if some of these processes do not operate. There is also ground for arguing that the media can exercise power in a reverse direction — on behalf of the societal base, or of an opposition, by controlling and limiting the freedom of action of power-holders. There is also agreement that the media can contribute to social integration and solidarity, by providing common objects of attention and interest for everyone, encouraging a more or less common view of society and of the world, disseminating a culture which is shared throughout the society and by providing similar models of behaviour. Whether any of these things happen, and to what degree, and in whose interest, are matters of dispute, not easily settled by reference to evidence.

A sender-determined view of media power does find many supporters, particularly when the senders are identified with a dominant class which owns or controls most of the mass media. However, it is countered by a receiver-determined view, also with some support in evidence, that sees the media as voluntarily chosen with messages selectively attended to, or interpreted, according to a chosen interest. The type of power exercise which depends on a relationship between sender and receiver seems at first sight less in evidence in the case of mass communication, since such relationships are typically calculative rather than normative and there is inevitably a physical and social distance between most communicators and their audience. However, there are possibilities for influence through mass media, on grounds of attractiveness and authority and also via processes of identification and involvement[2]. There are some situations in mass communication where normative relations do play a part, for instance with the political or religious press.

The integrative function of the media has been widely discussed[3], but has not been easy to demonstrate, except on *prima facie* grounds. Thus the local and community press in its stated purpose and content does often serve to express and protect local and community interests and identity, to work for consensus and for 'the good of the town'. Second, the media seem to provide a good deal of the common 'coin of exchange' for informal conversation on a society-wide basis, which contributes to some measure of integration. The part played by the media in incorporating foreign immigrants into a new culture and society can also be noted in this connection. Third, studies of news suggest that there is a generally patriotic line of reporting of international events, reflecting, at the national level, the consensual process which occurs at the local level. Fourth, it is possible that the repetitive themes of the most widely diffused medium, television, help to cultivate shared views of the world amongst its heaviest viewers. Finally, there is evidence that the media tend to offer a largely consensual view of society, contributing to social harmony rather than conflict.

While some of these points are certainly relevant to a view of solidarity in the sense of national and community consensus in the face of an outside world, they may also be turned around and taken as evidence of the subtle exercise of power from above, through the concealment of real conflicts of interest and of the inequality of benefit from current social arrangements. Thus needs for solidarity (a sense of belonging) can be manipulated for sectional ends. For evidence of 'genuine' solidarity achieved through mass media, one would probably have to concentrate on those areas where normative relationships, or distinctive subculture and minority identity, are the basis for the giving and receiving of messages. Such situations are, almost by definition, relatively marginal or untypical. However, one might also see the media as having society-wide solidarity functions (effects) at critical times — under conditions of national danger or arousal. Again, such situations are, by definition, untypical and the effort to make them normal and continuous (as with some totalitarian or manipulative regimes) turns the natural process of forging of solidarity into an instrument of control from above.

Dynamics and patterns of communication

This heading covers two or three related issues which have surfaced in the discussion and which have not yet been dealt with in a summarising way. First of all there is the question of whether communication should be considered as either cause or effect of social organisation. Inevitably, in a book on communication, the approach is communication-centred, but it still allows the question of degree and direction of determination to be considered. There is obviously a variety of possible answers and several gradations of position may be taken up, depending on the level of social organisation involved, the kind of communication process in question and one's chosen theory of society. In discussing the formation of networks, the various influences on the initiation and continuation of communication seemed reducible to three basic factors: *subject matter*; *people*; and *situation*. Thus, certain message flows are topic- or message-based and survive as the topic survives as a matter of discussion; some depend on relationships between people formed out of the sharing of activities, needs, situations, places or characteristics; some arise from situations alone, as when the search for information or the tendency to communicate is stimulated by crisis, uncertainty or sudden change. This particular trichotomy helps in elucidating the question of cause and effect posed above.

At the informal and group level it would seem that most communication is, by definition, person-based, thus secondary to pre-formed relationships. Nevertheless, it is also likely that for many groups the sense of belonging has to be fed by discussion of shared topics and objects of common interest and that without this additive the shared activity of some groups would be insufficient to maintain their structure and boundaries. Similarly, without the experience of a shared external situation and the need to react to this by communication, the group identity and purpose would be weaker. It should also be acknowledged that a common situation can lead to group formation through an intermediate process of intercommunication, thus giving communication a definite causal role as a necessary condition of group formation. At the organisational level, it is clear that formally constituted organisations are invariably the cause of the initiation of most of the networks or flows which have been discussed in this context. Yet it is worth noting that the differently based patterns in organisations may still be important for each other. Thus topic-based informal communication has a positive or a negative effect on the formal channels which derive from the co-operation of people in work tasks.

At the level of the whole society, taking mass communication as the chief example, the question of cause and effect has already been partly discussed, although not settled. It is possible to argue, however, that mass communication does have a causal role in social life. For instance, audiences are formed for particular types of content, channels, 'stars' or organisations (such as a newspaper). These audiences are often loose aggregates of dissimilar, scattered and unorganised individuals, with little constancy over time, but sometimes, as with regular newspaper readership groups they have more stability and identity and cannot be dismissed as without significance. In some cases publics form around issues and are sustained, despite physical separation of members and lack of formal organisation, by mass media, which provide a forum for debate and means of interconnection. Such publics are different from the 'mass' which might follow a particular star by having a longer term purpose and often a political or normative goal. While political movements and aspirations can exist without mass media and media are rarely the primary cause of the formation of a public in this sense, some claim can be made that they are a necessary condition for a genuine public — that is, a society-wide collective movement based on ideas and active in the public sphere.

While these examples of mass communication as an originator of social phenomena seem to belong to the message- or topic-centred category, rather than being people- or situation-centred, it might be necessary to admit a new category — that of 'medium-centred' communication networks, since it is clear that particular media do attract audiences regardless of specific content, shared characteristics of people or their situations. This circumstance does open possibilities for communication (media) determination which are otherwise hard to place in the framework outlined above. As yet, however, the effects of such media determination have been little more than a redistribution of available time between different activities. A key element of the mass communication process, unlike most of the others considered, is in fact the process of *attention giving* as a general form of behaviour, detached, for the most part, from specific subject-matter. It is now a very large occupier of time which is hard to account for on grounds of situation or personal characteristics, or the objects of attention, since these do not account for much variance of behaviour. It is also a historically quite new phenomenon that people should spend so much time attending in a relatively uninvolved way to some 'distant', but at the same time familiar, messages about people and events. The significance is hard to assess, but there is no doubt that this attention-giving (in practice the time 'spent' by the audience) has become a valued commodity for commercial and political reasons and that a central dynamic of the media industry is to maximise a share of audience attention by whatever devices are legal and effective. As a consequence, the notion of communication as the transmission of information has certainly to be modified, although it is not clear that the achieved condition of habitual attention without involvement corresponds very closely to the conception of ritual communication described above as the alternative. That also presupposes at least some element of active participation.

Communication in an information society

While little support is offered in this book for any simple version of determination by way of communication technology, since communication itself is nearly always a product of its social context, the possibility has not been ruled out that means and forms of communication make some contribution of their own to social processes. At the present time a number of changes are occurring in society which seem to depend in some degree on developments in communication technology. While the direction and pace of change is very hard to ascertain, the very fact that many people believe communication technology to be a main cause of change and have given the name 'information society' to what is emerging, strengthens the case for taking seriously the centrality of communication. Unlike earlier occasions in human history when communication seems to have stimulated change, it is now the actual changes in the means of transferring information rather than the messages carried which are likely to be more important.

The main characteristics of the information society seem to be a shift from employment in manufacturing to service industries and in manufacturing from 'first' to 'third' world locations, computerisation of many work tasks and mechanical processes and more importance for information and expertise as power resources. Changes in work are also associated with new electronic technologies, resulting in more leisure time (not always freely chosen) and physical dispersal of work with replacement of physical by telecommunication links. These trends have been under way for some time and cannot simply be claimed as a consequence of new information technology, although this must play an enabling and accelerating role. The diffusion of the technology has also helped to extend the arena of change from work and the public sphere to the home and the interpersonal sphere.

The most relevant features of the changing situation for

the communication processes that we have been considering seem to be the potential abundance of audiovisual channels and materials as a result of cable and satellites, the introduction of computer-based videotext services with interactive possibilities and the spread of individual video-recording facilities which virtually establishes a new mass medium as well as freeing people from the constraints of time and place with past film and television reception. Account should also be taken of the spread of home computers and the further diffusion of an old medium, the telephone. There has been much speculation about the consequences of these changes and the most important ones have been spelt out in characterising the coming 'information society'. A few potentially negative consequences can be added. One is the danger of information 'overload', leading to waste, inefficiency and confusion. Another concerns the greater potential for central control as a result of the recording and storing of private or confidential data on computers and its accessibility to authority. The potential for new forms of inequality based on the distribution of new communication equipment, software and skills has already been mentioned. One can add the tendency to 'internationalisation' as posing a threat to cultural identity and having implications for economic dependency.

In Chapter 2 (pp. 36—9), the differentiation between the active and passive mode for sender and receiver was used to identify types of communication situation and the same device can be used to help assess the possible significance of what is happening as technologies of communication change. Here a cross-classification of sender and receiver in their active or passive roles gives four basic types of communication pattern, much as described before, but with different labels supplied (Fig. 3).

The entry labelled 'address/dissemination' covers the situation of 'one to many' communication which has been the dominant mode of institutionalised public communica-

		SENDER	
		Active	Passive
RECEIVER	Active:	Exchange/ Interaction	Search
	Passive:	Address/ Dissemination	Time-filling/ Surveillance

Fig. 3. Four types of communication pattern

tion for a good many centuries. It covers the cases of preaching, lecturing, political address and much 'purposive' mass communication of a persuasive or informational kind. In practice, many of the other kinds of mass communication in which a large audience is reached without an opportunity to respond are covered by this mode and the development of radio and television altered the balance of public communication in the direction of one-way, non-interactional dissemination.

The 'exchange' type is most characteristic of interpersonal contexts, but occurs also in work organisations and in areas of public institutional life where participation and involvement are necessary components, as with political and social movements. Communication technologies, until recently, have played an ambiguous role in respect of social interaction and exchange. Print technology (books and newspapers in particular) contributed to the emergence of separate publics within the wider society by disseminating ideas for debate, offering 'platforms' for views, providing focal points and channels within social movements and organisations. However, they did not greatly aid interaction and encouraged rather passive and detached relationships. While wireless telegraphy had obvious interactive potential, the main forms of radio and television were developed in ways more likely to encourage 'spectatorship' rather than interaction. Only the telephone really contributed, and to a degree rarely acknowledged by social theorists, to interaction at all levels of social life.

The two remaining modes of communication labelled as 'search' and 'time-filling' are certainly not new, but both have been influenced by technological development. The purposeful scanning of potential sources of information or interest is as old as record-keeping and the main contribution of printing and, later, audio-visual media was to extend the quantity and range of stored sources and increase the possibility of access. Such access was largely a private good and it has become much more open and public. Such storage and access have a price and they are thus dependent on levels of private and public wealth. The 'time-filling' mode of relationship between a passive sender and a passive receiver is also not new, but modern mass media have made it their own, in an era of free time and almost unlimited multiple transmission of messages for diversion.

This account maps and characterises in a summary way the distribution of types of communication relationship and information flow at the present time, but the question which remains is, How will the new technologies alter this map? The precise answer will have to await the future historian, but certain predictions are in order, in the interests of theory-building. First, there will be a shift from the 'address' and 'time-filling' mode to the 'search' mode. The new technology reduces dependence on organised distributors and decision-makers and widens the range of what is stored and accessible, at relatively low cost. A side effect of this is likely to be a fragmentation of current large audiences for media and content types into functionally more specific taste/demand aggregates. The extent of this movement will depend, not only on the diffusion of the new hardware but on the form of organisation of the production and distribution of the new software — the content, thus, on institutional developments which are much harder to predict. In effect, if the new technological changes are accomplished within the current framework they are likely to be more apparent than real and management of supply and limited access will remain, even if in disguised forms.

Second, there will be an increase in exchange/interaction modes. The computer technology makes this possible and, given the past success of postal and telephone services and the advantages offered by the addition of pictures, word display and the print-out of graphic and written messages, it is hard to see why the new media should not eventually develop extensively in private as well as in work and public contexts. The main limiting factor is cost, but the flexibility and multi-functionality of new communication systems, apart from anything else, should make this less of an obstacle in the long term. Less predictable is whether 'exchange' and 'interaction' communication types will actually increase overall or whether there will simply be a redistribution between the current and the newer media. Again, the answer depends on social-institutional changes which are largely independent of technology.

Third, while the 'time-filling' mode of communication is likely to remain and will have some potential for growth, as more time is available, the nature of the relationship between 'passive' receiver and 'passive' sender, which happens to be an electronic machine system, may well change. What is new is the capacity for all uses of time to be registered and recorded and 'passive' machines may be 'actively' storing all uses. As long as this is done without particular intention it has no consequence, but when it becomes a purposeful function of new media systems then it opens the way at least to surveillance and control. There is as yet little reason for elevating this to the status of a prediction at the present time, but it is unlikely that such a simple way of achieving an end so greatly prized by information providers and managers and by authorities will be totally neglected. It is certainly a significant threshold when one crosses from fearful dreams of a totally controlled society to the stage of practicality of such control based on effortless intelligence-gathering.

It is much too early for either optimism or pessimism about the 'information society' if and when it arrives. More important than the pattern of distribution of communication modes will be the content which flows in the new channels and the institutional frameworks within which they operate. Both are relatively unknown, but neither are outside the scope of individual and collective choice. We have some indications of what are the available options, but we also need a set of values to help in exercising that choice.

Current directions in communication theory and research 8

The aim of this chapter is to supplement the view of communication as a field of study, originally set down in 1974, with comments on later developments and current trends. These comments are unavoidably brief, selective and biased. The nature of the bias is, however, much the same as that of the first edition so that what follows should show some continuity and consistency with its predecessor and be more than an arbitrary collection of remarks and references chosen from a field which is too large to deal with at all adequately. The purpose is mainly informative — to fill some gaps, indicate developments, give new references and record changes in some aspects of the subject. The perspective adopted remains sociological, but there has been some tendency for 'communication science' to develop as a more integrated field of study which crosses the boundaries of existing established 'disciplines' and is thus not easily contained as simply a sub-field of sociology.

Communication theory and social theory

When the first edition was written, the neglect of communication within sociology was noted. That remains largely true of the formal 'dividing up' of the subject for purposes of organising or indexing sociological work. Nevertheless, communication problems do seem very high on the agenda of debate about how to analyse and understand society, although the agenda is often obscured by diversity of terminology and by disciplinary standard-bearing. Three main debates have dominated the history of sociology and thus of social theory: over the question of hereditary-biological or social determination; over the conflict and consensus views of society; and over behavioural-positivist and symbolic-voluntarist conceptions of social process. There are other relevant terms and distinctions and there is a loose connection between the three sets of oppositions, with biological, consensual and positivist on the one side and social, conflictual and symbolic on the other.

The purpose here is not to analyse the opposition further, but to point to communication as a key element in the debate. In particular, a communication perspective is implicit in the second grouping of positions. The view that nurture (socialisation) rather than nature shapes behaviour is based on the fact that we learn from our social surroundings and adapt to them; they provide us with the means to form an identity, with definitions of our situation, meanings, guidance, capacities and appropriate tasks. The view that society is an arena of struggle between the powerful and the subordinated, rather than a co-operative enterprise to solve common problems in the most effective way, presupposes a ubiquitous, continuous and largely successful effort to conceal the 'true' character of social life, since the consensus view of society is apparently dominant and often taken for granted.

Central to the conflict–consensus debate is a difference of view about reality and a struggle to define it, thus centrally a communication process. The positivist–symbolicist debate is even more openly a contest between theorists who put considerable weight on the idea of an observable, verifiable, material reality and those who stress the contingent nature of reality and the variability of perception and definition. They stress the compelling evidence that social reality is 'constructed', the possibility of redefinition and negotiation and the rewriting indeed of what 'positivism' takes for inescapable fact. The reference here is to schools of symbolic interactionism, phenomenology and ethnomethodology which were discussed in Chapter 2.

While all this could have been written in 1974, there are signs that a symbolic or communicative perspective has become more firmly established within sociology. For example, Giddens' influential book, *New Rules of Sociological Method*, sets down some of the guiding principles of an interpretative sociology, which views society as the outcome of human action and perception, rather than a given, externally constraining, framework of fact[1]. While there is much evidence of the maturing of interpretative sociology, there is also evidence of life in the old debate, indicated by the revival of 'sociobiology'[2]. While this poses a sharp challenge to symbolic interactionism and phenomenology, it has its advocates among communication scholars[3]. This is some testimony to the flexibility of a communication approach, although some might interpret it as a sign of theoretical flabbiness or emptiness. Thus it does seem reconcilable with highly mechanistic, systemic and deterministic versions of social life as well as with those which stress openness and voluntariness.

Some aspects of this divide have been discussed in Chapters 1 and 7 and, as pointed out there, the choice for students of communication is largely one between attention to channels and structures or to codes and meanings. If the former is chosen, positivism and functionalism are likely to be underpinned, if the latter, openness and negotiability. Despite the resurgence of sociobiology, the dominant influence among students of communication at the time of writing does seem (even allowing for some bias of view) to be in the direction of conceiving society as a set of meanings maintained and distributed in a certain way so as to uphold an established pattern of social organisation and division of power. This general social-theoretical perspective is illustrated in comments which follow in this chapter.

Continuities in organisational and interpersonal communication research

There are a number of areas where one can only record continuity of direction and indicate more recent publications, even though the volume of activity may have risen notably. One such area is that of *organisational* communication, treated above as a case of 'communication in formal settings'. The practical value of work in this sphere ensures a continuous demand and also a continuity of direction, since the basic problems of organisations do not change quickly or fundamentally. There is, however, some evidence of more integrated treatment, for instance in the books by Rogers and Rogers[4], Porter and Roberts[5] and Redding[6]. While the broad issues are the same, there seems to be more attention than previously to communication across the boundaries of formal organisations, the interface between organisation and the wider public, the problems of information overload and the need to restrict as well as facilitate information flow, and the diversity of communication roles in the communication network of an organisation – e.g. the 'liaison role', the 'gatekeeper' or the 'opinion leader'. Another development has been in the application of evaluation to communication flows in organisation, with the emergence of the idea of a 'communication audit' as well as a financial or production audit[7].

In respect of studies of *paralanguage* and non-verbal communication generally, there has been much more detailed research and analysis (e.g. Wiemann and Harrison[8] and Argyle[9]), with a lot of attention being paid to the relation between verbal and non-verbal behaviour, to the encoding skills employed in nonverbal behaviour at the interpersonal level and to individual differences and those based on gender (Eakin and Eakin[10]). The study of nonverbal interaction is not easy to separate from that of *interpersonal* communication in general, which has involved a similar range of questions during the last decade. How do people negotiate encounters with others? How do they seek to present themselves? What rules govern interpersonal relationships and where do they come from? How are such matters as opening and closing and 'turn-taking' in conversations to be handled? How do relationships develop? The new sources are numerous, but the work of Miller[11], Roloff and Berger[12], Weitz[13], and Allen and Guy[14] are useful guides to recent research.

Principally at issue here is the availability of certain strategies for communication with others and the distribution of skills in their application. The motive for research in these matters has partly been the wish to apply the results in therapy for those diagnosed as having problems in relationships, partly the intrinsic interest of the theoretical and methodological puzzles of such research in what are somewhat uncharted waters for social scientists. The availability of film and video as tools of record and observation has played some part in stimulating such work (Berkowitz[15] and Roloff[16]).

While the sources of an interest in interpersonal communication, verbal or nonverbal, are diverse, there is no doubt that, in the last decade, the work of Goffman has continued to be very influential. Perhaps the key concept in this connection is that of 'framing'[17]. According to Goffman, much of social life, as we experience it, is a series of frames of socially defined situations which we learn to recognise and interpret, but also to change and reinterpret to our advantage. Thus, situations are social events which have built-in cues as to their meaning and what is expected of us. These can be conceived of as frameworks (of meaning) in our heads and are in varying degrees open to challenge, adaptation or replacement by self-chosen frameworks. We are continually engaged in a series of symbolic activities of this kind — decoding, manipulating, inventing the frameworks appropriate to social events. This approach was not invented by Goffman and has its roots in symbolic interactionism, but Goffman has almost made it his own by virtue of his voluminous recording and illustration of the practices involved and by his clever codification of apparently trivial detail.

There is a link between this work and yet another approach to communication — that based on the analogy between social life and drama[18]. Thus, we can consider communicational interaction as a series of performances, the playing of roles according to plans or 'scripts' (Schank[19]) and often having an element of play. Important in this conception of social behaviour, which is clearly inconsistent with traditional positivist social science, is, first of all, the stress on the 'view from below' and, second, a prevailing doubt about the reality of what we encounter and about the notion of fixed meanings. Much communication between persons may be seen as a 'try-on', or a form of concealment, or almost anything but what it seems to be; so much so as to make us doubt most of what we see and of what people tell us, with alarming implications for empirical social research of the traditional kind which often relies on accounts given in answers to survey questions. One question which has attracted attention in this connection is the source of our repertory of frames. Davis and Baran[20] suggest that many components of scripts and styles upon which we draw in everyday life are now derived more from mass media than from direct personal experience.

Mass communication

More will be said of mass media under later but, in the light of the enormous volume of work during the last decade on mass media, it is appropriate to mention some of the main developments and additions at this point. The contours of the field of study have not greatly shifted and the main debates are not very different, but there is a good deal more evidence to cope with, especially perhaps in relation to media production organisations and to news. In fact, most of the organisational studies also relate to news and, in this connection, of particular note are: Gans on American newsmakers[21]; Tuchman on the making of news[22]; Golding and Elliott on television news in four countries[23]; Tracey[24] and Schlesinger[25] on British television news; Chibnall on source-reporter relationships[26]; the Glasgow Media Group on British television news content[27] and Johnstone *et al.* on the values and attitudes of news reporters[28]. More wholistic studies of media organisations have been offered by Burns[29] (for the BBC) and Engwall, dealing with newspaper organisations[30]. A number of useful synthesising frameworks have been developed, for instance by Elliott[31] and by Hirsch[32]. The conclusions defy summary, but one important theme is that news should be viewed as a particular cultural form, rooted in the news-gathering and news-processing activity and the work culture of its makers rather than an objective reflection of reality. Much has also been written about the concept of objectivity and of particular interest has been a study by Schudson of the emergence of 'objective reporting' in the history of North American newspapers[33].

The study of the media audience has claimed its share of attention, with a continuing flow of research in the tradition of 'uses and gratifications'[34]. Conceptual work on the audience and on the factors which shape its recruitment has not made a great deal of progress, despite the vast industry engaged in the task of audience research. However, one study by Goodhardt which demonstrated the very low degree of selectivity of the mass television audience has created some controversy[35]. For the American television audience, Comstock *et al.*[36] have performed a very good accounting task and it is quite likely that new media distribution forms (especially cable and video) will generate both changes of behaviour and research in the immediate future. One conceptual development, which is not unconnected with the growing media abundance[37], involves the notion of the 'taste culture', first sketched by Gans[38] and recently elaborated by Lewis[39], to help deal with the emergence of audiences for particular kinds of content which are otherwise not identifiable in terms of their social characteristics and certainly not easy to place in a hierarchy of class, education or culture. The actual development of taste cultures is associated with conditions of 'post-industrial' societies and the obsolescence of conceptions of mass or elite culture. At the same time, they represent what earlier theorists might have seen as an aspect of mass society, since taste cultures often correspond with markets — aggregates of potential consumers and target groups for advertisers. Hence, they lack any clear social identity or roots in community and society.

Attention to the question of power and effects of mass media has shown no tendency to lessen since 1974, a year which was itself something of a watershed, since it was about the time of the publication of Noelle-Neumann's seminal article 'Return to the concept of powerful mass media'[40]. Since then, her further work in promoting the theory of a 'spiral of silence' has been reflective of the terms of the debate about media power[41]. According to the theory, a normal human 'fear of isolation' leads to a tendency for individuals to remain silent in face of what they perceive, correctly or not, to be the dominant orthodoxies of public opinion, with the result that the latter receive even wider currency and more dominance. The theory is relevant to mass media because they are likely to be a major source of impressions or beliefs about the direction of majority opinion. Implicit in the theory is the notion that media journalists may have a disproportionate power to shape opinion, especially when they offer a consistent view of the world and set of opinions. That media journalism does often tend to exhibit a certain consistent bias has been argued by critics from both the political right and left, and more or less objective studies of newsmaking have given some grounds for supposing that production of news and information is subject to constraints which make homogeneity and predictability more likely than internal diversity and inconsistency of subject matter and direction.

In mapping the main development of the debate about media effects, a framework of approaches recently suggested by Lang and Lang[42] is of particular value. It is worth recalling that these students of media power since the 1950s have consistently argued that this power is considerable and has often been demonstrated by research, notwithstanding the 'myth' of media powerlessness which has at times been promulgated. They suggest four main strategies for research into the effects of mass media on opinion which can serve equally as a guide to the main current directions of research. The first is by way of a *study of the audience*, with an emphasis on the mediation of effects through motives, needs and expectations which are brought by members of the audience to the experience and also on the identification of potentially susceptible sub-groups within the total audience. A certain amount of work on political communication, following the lines of Blumler and McQuail's 'uses and gratifications' study of a political campaign[43] has continued and the general notion that a campaign designed to influence must also be a reciprocal and interactive process has gained ground[44]. The 'audience centered' approach has also been prominent in more recent work on media and children[45], well represented in the collection of research papers edited by Brown[46] and the longitudinal study of television and adolescent development reported by Hedinsson[47].

The second strategy is called by Lang and Lang *the search for correspondences* and refers to that kind of assessment which draws on the correlation over time between tendencies in the media and tendencies in society and public. While correlational evidence has always been notoriously suspect, it may be the only source of knowledge about broad historical changes in culture and society on the one hand and developments in scale and kind of media activity on the other. The empirical work adduced by Noelle-Neumann to support the theory of the spiral of silence belongs to this heading[48]. Another good example is Robinson's demonstration of a correlation between newspaper editorial endorsements and the direction of voting by readers over a period of 16 years[49]. Perhaps the work which fits closest to the underlying idea of this strategy is that associated with the idea of 'cultural indicators'[50]. The core proposition here is that cultural change in general reflects or is reflected in social structural change and that we can study social change by way of media content which is the most accessible and analysable manifestation of culture at our disposal. To do so, one develops 'cultural indicators', which are symbolic reflections of what is happening in society and can take many guises — themes, images, styles, forms and more. Gerbner has pioneered a related form of 'cultivation analysis' which was first designed to test the view that television content, as the most pervasive and consistent message system about social reality, has shaped the perception of that reality over time for those who rely most heavily on the medium and in ways which deviate systematically from other more objective indicators of reality[51]. The claim to have demonstrated that this is so has been contested[52], but the theory as such has not been dismissed as implausible and still gains some circumstantial support. In connection with this strategy, one should refer also to one of the most flourishing branches of enquiry in recent years, that concerned with media 'agenda-setting'[53]. Here, the argument is that the pervasive and respected character of mass media gives them a considerable authority in the writing of the terms of public debate — thus they indicate by inclusion or omission what subjects are more or less important for public opinion. This belongs to the 'correspondence' category because the main source of evidence has usually been the degree of correspondence between coverage of issues in mass media and the order and amount of attention paid to the same issues by the public. Whether such a process of agenda *setting* actually occurs remains a matter of debate, but the research goes on[54].

The third strategy is named *concern with refraction* and deals with the equally broad proposition, not unrelated to the foregoing, that the mass media provide the sets of images, ideas, definitions and priorities which limit or shape what people think and know (see p. 195 above). The adoption of this approach gives prominence to the question of what version of the world and what norms and values are actually being offered by the mass media. The answers to such questions require detailed content analysis, sensitive to implicit as well as to explicit meaning and it is in the development of such content analysis that we see most signs of this strategy as well as in inquiries into the nature of the ideology or consciousness which characterises the majority media. Examples include work on news[55] and studies of the world portrayed in television drama and entertainment[56].

The fourth strategy is called *the study of outcomes* and relates to effects which come from media because they are essential channels of communication and are believed to be effective. Thus the adaptation of other actors and institutions to a widespread definition of the situation may in turn be a cause of important effects on institutions and on society. There are a good many examples of such effects in the behaviour of political parties and other organisations and there have been interesting case studies of some less obvious processes of effect. One such has explored the relationship between mass communication and terrorism, showing the ways in which violence is used to gain attention for political causes[57]. Another example derives from the experience of the new left and student radical movement in the United States during the 1960s, which found itself reliant on the media for recognition, but in turn very dependent on them and inclined to adapt tactics and message, being eventually saddled with the image and definition given by the media[58].

Before leaving the topic of media effects, it is worth noting that the study of persuasion and of public information campaigns seems also to have gained some renewed currency in the recent past, to judge from the flow of publications reporting new research and theory[59].

Ways of communicating

The study of language of all kinds and in a variety of contexts has experienced considerable growth. As we have seen there has been a lot of attention to paralanguages — those concerned with gesture, expression, dress and display, especially in the context of interpersonal communication. The literature dealing with body language and kinesics is now too extensive to summarise, but useful recent sources include the following: Wiemann and Harrison[60], Davis and Skupien[61], Harper[62] and Knapp[63]. Here, however, we direct attention mainly to advances in one particular form of 'discourse analysis'[64], that which deals with texts of various kinds, especially those which are found in pictorial, auditory or written form and intended to be 'read' in more or less public contexts. While this seems to refer mainly to mass media content, there are many other possibilities — public documents, speeches, rituals, public imagery and symbols. The growth of interest in such matters has several causes, including the redirection of literature study towards more systematic methods and more 'socially relevant' concerns, the growth of cultural studies as a field in its own right and the pressure to find ways of analysing the ever-more ubiquitous products of the audio-visual media which are not easily dealt with by traditional methods. The intellectual resources which have been brought to the new tasks are diverse, but a good deal is owed to the development of structuralism and of semiology — the general science of signs[65]. Both provide principles and guides to methods for uncovering the underlying meaning systems of a given category of text. They assume such categories to have their own 'language' of images, symbols and metaphors which can be deciphered in terms of the wider cultural context in which they are found. The essential claim is that a deep and systematic analysis can reveal more of the hidden meaning which is 'built into' cultural products, to a certain degree independently of the overt intentions of the authors and of the interpretations of 'readers'. Armed with clues as to the hidden meaning, so it is argued, one can give a better account of the function of a text in culture and society.

The relevant literature is voluminous and there is much internal division according to method and social theory. Of particular interest are those attempts to develop methods of analysis for non-written texts and the following are some examples: Leymore on advertising[66], Glasgow Media Group on television news[67], Barthes[68] and Hall[69] on photography, Fiske and Hartley on television drama[70] and Metz on film[71]. Traditional content analysis has not ignored such cultural products but has been most adapted to written texts and to surface meanings. While the very volume of research using structuralist and semiotic method has begun to yield some qualitative results, there has been no clear theoretical breakthrough in the direction of discovering a general method of analysis and thus no escape from detailed, intelligent interpretation, taking some account of the purpose of a text and the context of its reception. Thus, cultural texts retain a core of uniqueness and of ambiguity which sets a limit to what a 'science of signs' can deliver. In the light of this, progress has been of more practical than theoretical interest (by uncovering possible 'bias'), somewhat paradoxically, given the somewhat arcane image and reality of structuralism.

Work on language and texts does not all belong to the structuralist–semiological category, since much has also been contributed by sociolinguistics and there has been a move towards establishing a field of 'political linguistics', concerned to explore the main modes and functions of political discourse[72]. There seems to have been little progress in systematic codification of the language of public space and architecture, in which recurrent symbols play such a part. A relevant work of interest, however, is the *Dictionary of Visual Language*, by Thompson and Davenport[73].

Power and equality

A guiding thread of the treatment of communication in this book has been the link between communication and power and thus an attention to equality and inequality. While developments since 1975 do not seem dramatic, the theme does help to classify a good deal of new research. The ideology, if not always the practice, of modern democratic societies places great stress on increasing equality of access to a range of communication 'goods' including information of all kinds as well as the scientific and artistic culture of the society, participation in circles of discussion and influence in neighbourhoods, work and politics and the means of self-expression. Cultural policies are usually formulated to help achieve such ends and much attention is paid to the public means for achieving them by way of mass media, libraries, museums and schools. The relevant literature is thus anything which bears on the facilitation and flow of communication, on reducing barriers, enlarging skills, providing the means for satisfactory expression and participation.

An especially useful contribution to discussion of these matters has been the work of Thunberg *et al.*[74], who deal with communication in family, school, work and politics as well as mass media, from the point of view of increasing equality. Their central concern is with the development of a 'communication potential' which can contribute to the realisation of certain basic values for individuals, including a feeling of self-esteem, a sense of belonging with society and the ability to exert some influence on their surroundings. The book charts the obstacles to developing equal communication potential and posits the notion of a virtuous 'spiral of interaction' in the different contexts named which could help to maximise, although never equalise, the communication potential. The book has a good deal to say about difficulties, but it gives concrete expression to a normative version of why and how communication should be studied.

A good deal of the discussion about equality has concerned mass communication, but there has been a continued attention to early socialisation and to communication within families. The work of Bernstein described above (pp. 74–6) has continued to exert influence and provoke debate, but it is not the only contribution. Another approach deserving notice is that of Chaffee and McLeod on the difference between what they call 'socio-oriented' and 'concept-oriented' family communication types[75]. In the former pattern, which has affinities with the 'restricted code' of Bernstein, the emphasis is on harmony and family solidarity, while in the latter it is on discussion, argument, ideas and greater equality. The two patterns are not mutually exclusive, but the relative strength of one over the other seems to have consequences for communication in later life, including use of mass media. Of course, the communication climate so depicted does have a relationship with social class position, but this is not so strong as in the case of Bernstein's typology.

The most voluminous work on power and equality in the field of mass communication has concerned the long-standing debate over whether or not the mass media extend and reinforce the power of a ruling class or other dominant interest.

Notable here has been the growth of a school of political-economic analysis which seeks to establish connections between developments in the commercial and market structure of media and the content of what they produce[76]. Otherwise, the main thrust has been towards the analysis of media 'bias' in respect of a number of different minorities, or disadvantaged groups, including immigrants[77], trade unionists[78], welfare claimants[79], deviants[80] and youth[81]. The evidence collected suggests that such groups are often treated in news accounts in ways which are tendentious, through patterns of selective attention and omission, assumption-making and unfavourable association. Important are the notions of 'dominant discourse' and 'preferred reading', the latter a process by which the audience is led towards interpretations favourable to established authority[82].

Such work extends beyond the analysis of news, to deal with other kinds of cultural production. An influential proposition was that of Parkin[83], who suggested that alternative meanings systems are deployed in the encoding and decoding of public communication. He names one of these as 'dominant', another as 'subordinate' and the third 'radical'. Hall has renamed these as codes, calling the second 'negotiated' and the third 'oppositional'. The first implies that messages are sent and received according to a dominant consensus and thus confirm the power relations that exist. The second refers to the relaying of messages according to the objective journalistic mode which allows some distancing from, and neutralisation of, power relations. The third refers either to the possibility of minority expression, if necessary against the tide of the dominant consensus or to the 'reading' of public communication according to the viewpoint of a deviant, resistant sub-culture or simply an alternative world-view.

There are quite a few other developments to mention. Edelman has written of the penetration of power into all forms of public communication — in myths, symbols and stereotypes[84]. Mueller has analysed mechanisms of legitimation and domination by the use of political language and has developed the notion of 'distorted communication' — the deliberate manipulation of language and control of communication channels in order to maintain power[85]. In this version, the opposite of distortion would be communication that is open, free, participant, critical, interactive, with encouragement for wide access and the development of skills. There are many themes, but one which merits note has to do with the view that the 'public sphere' has been in decline, under the impact of commercial forces making for consumerism and individualisation and a concomitant privatisation and detachment from broader concerns of the society. The work of Sennett[86] and of Gouldner[87] is relevant here, pointing in various ways to the decline of public debate, discussion and partisanship, which were once the mark of a democratic society. This echoes an older theme in the critique of mass society[88], but it is acquiring a new relevance with the advent of an 'information society'. If old debts are to be paid, mention should be made of the Frankfurt School[89] and the work of Habermas, whose concept of 'communicative competence' has linked linguistic, political and sociological analysis and involves ideas similar to those associated with the concept of distorted communication[90].

A separate entry is clearly in order for the explosion of research and theory concerned with gender and communication. The study of communication has become quite closely involved with the question of women's inequality. The matters studied in this connection include: the image (often subordinate and stereotyped) of women in media content; differences between the sexes in all kinds of communication behaviour; the potential role-socializing influence of mass media and the exploitation of women, especially in pornography. The opportunities, or lack of them, for women to work in media was also studied as was the possibility of developing alternative, feminist, forms of culture. A few relevant authors are Tuchman[91], Millum[92], Ferguson[93], Butler and Paisley[94], Baher[95], and Gallagher[96].

The work carried out in relation to women and communication has affinities with research on other out-groups or minorities and the study of popular culture has developed within the field of 'cultural studies', with particular attention to forms of culture which would once have been treated as either non-cultural or even pathological. In relation to the theme of power and equality, there is a particular effort to examine popular culture from the point of view of the more marginal or oppressed groups, including the young, the blacks, the poor and the educationally deprived. For these, styles of dress and choice of music can be ways of self-expression and opposition (Hall and Jefferson[97]; Hebdige[98]). The work involved is often ethnographic in method and critical in its purpose and offers possibilities for understanding modes of communication beyond what is offered by normal methods of textual analysis.

Remaining comments in respect of power and equality are somewhat disconnected, although not necessarily unimportant. One line of research has been concerned with 'knowledge gaps' — the structured inequality in the distribution of information[99]. Inequalities are mostly those related to education and social class differences and research has been concerned with the extent of inequalities (the size of the 'gaps') and with the contribution of mass media to opening or closing of gaps. In principle, mass media which are informative and accessible to all should help to close gaps originally caused by differences of educational experience. There is evidence that this occurs, but an advantage remains with those with most 'communication potential' and new gaps open as old ones are closed. If there are gaps between social groups within societies, there are even wider ones on a global scale which are also systematic and resistant to modification. The inequalities are those between the more developed and less developed societies. The former tend to control or occupy most of the channels of international communication, with the result that not only are they better served by relevant information, but they are in a position to supply the less developed world with information and ideas which tend to be more in the interests of the senders than of the receivers. This imbalance of flow has given rise to the concept of a new cultural imperialism to replace former economic and political colonialism, but with some comparable effects. The nature and scale of the problem has been well described and documented (e.g. in McBride[100], Tunstall[101], Boyd-Barrett[102], McPhail[103], Lent and Gifford[104]), but solutions seem distant or politically unacceptable.

There has long been a political, professional and intellectual debate over the application of electronic technology to minority and local needs, in the interests of balancing the power of large-scale and centralised mass media. The research tradition has not been strong, since researchers have also been drawn by the pull of big media, but there has been some work on access and participation[105] and the coming of new media, with the promise of abundance of channels and interactive potential has stimulated thought and research. The key question is how the uses of the new media will be defined and how their potential will be exploited — as extensions of existing mass distribution systems or for greater participation and minority provision. While the new media seem to offer chances for closing information gaps, the achievement of this will depend on how resources and skills are distributed. There is no great reason to expect any redistribution in favour of those who have less power and lower communication potential.

Convergence in communication science

The heading is pre-emptive and only partly defensible, since the idea of a 'communication science' rests, as yet, on somewhat shaky foundations. Nevertheless, there are a number of common themes in the disparate kinds of work which have been reviewed and this commonality seems to grow rather than diminish as the subject develops as an academic activity. For the most part these themes have now been set out in reviewing recent work. One concerns the mode of communication, the symbolising process and the vehicle for carrying meaning, whether as language, code, myth, ritual or sign-system. There is a growing similarity of concept and terminology in previously separate spheres of research, spanning literature, sociology, psychology and information science. The theme of power and equality, just discussed, has a reach across disparate contexts of research and levels of social organisation. The pervasiveness of latent or open conflict in all kinds of relationships is the simple cause of this and there is an essential similarity between the exercise of power through communication in families, work organisations, politics and elsewhere. A third theme, related to this, has to do with the effectiveness of communication for achieving some end and there seems to be a perhaps renewed growth of interest in this aspect of communication, not only in mass communication, but also in interpersonal relations and in work organisations[106]. A fourth sign of convergence is to be seen in the attention to *cognitive* aspects of communication. In research on interpersonal relations this shows up in the significance attached to 'social cognitions'[107] in intrapersonal communication to the idea of 'mental maps'[108]. In the case of mass communication, it can be observed in a new interest in comprehension, in the concept of agenda-setting and in research knowledge gaps and 'cultivation', in work on information-seeking and processing[109]. All of these are rooted in a view of communication as a primarily informative process with effects first on what we know or think we know and only secondly on how we feel or behave. Finally, in all kinds of situations, we are being reminded that all communication is an inter-active process, involving relationships and interdependence. Even mass communication is no longer very often typified as a purely one-way process and its effects are seen to depend on co-orientation and exchange. This is very much the case of political communication, but it is no less marked in research on communication for development. The decade of the 1970s saw the overturning of a 'dominant paradigm' of communication from 'outside' and 'above' in favour of a view of communication as a complex network of interactive relationships[110] whose understanding is a necessary condition of 'successful' communication.

The case for convergence as a reality is quite a strong one. There is less emphasis on the difference between one type of language and another, one medium and another, or one level or context of communication and another. There is also a tendency towards a common set of themes, concepts, methods and vocabulary among different kinds of communication researchers. A closing word on the subject of convergence in communication science can refer to the part played by model-building as a way of mapping common concerns and joining the separate areas of communication study (McQuail and Windahl[111]).

References and further reading

Chapter 1 Communication process and society

1. F. E. X. Dance, 'The concept of communication', *Journal of Communication*, 20, 1970, 201–10.
2. E. Sapir, 'Communication', *International Encyclopedia of the Social Sciences*, 1st edn, Macmillan, 1930.
3. D. Lerner, *The Passing of Traditional Society*, Free Press, 1958.
4. H. Innis, *The Bias of Communication*, University of Toronto Press, 1951.
5. M. McLuhan, *The Gutenberg Galaxy*, University of Toronto Press, 1962.
6. G. Gerbner, 'Mass media and human communication theory' in D. McQuail, ed., *Sociology of Mass Communications*, Penguin, 1972, pp. 35–58.
7. A. Gouldner, *The Dialectic of Ideology and Technology*, Macmillan, 1976.
8. E. Durkheim, *The Division of Labour in Society*, Free Press, 1933.
9. J. Carey, 'The communication revolution and the professional communicator', in P. Halmos, ed., *The Sociology of Mass Media Communicators*, Sociological Review Monographs, 1969, pp. 23–38.

Chapter 2 Theories of communication

1. G. A. Miller, 'What is information measurement?', *American Psychologist*, 8, 1953.

2. N. Lin, *The Study of Human Communication*, Bobbs-Merrill, 1973.
3. C. W. Morris, *Signs, Language and Behavior*, Prentice-Hall, 1946.
4. M. Weber, *The Theory of Social and Economic Organization*, ed. T. Parsons, Free Press of Glencoe, 1947.
5. C. E. Shannon and W. Weaver, *The Mathematical Theory of Communication*, University of Illinois Press, 1949.
6. N. Wiener, *Cybernetics*, Wiley, 1948.
7. W. Schramm, 'The nature of communication between humans', in W. Schramm and D. F. Roberts, eds., *The Process and Effects of Mass Communication*, rev. edn, University of Illinois Press, 1971, pp. 3–53.
8. M. DeFleur, *Theories of Mass Communication*, 2nd edn, McKay, 1970.
9. K. W. Deutsch, *The Nerves of Government*, Free Press of Glencoe, 1963.
10. T. Newcomb, 'An approach to the study of communicative acts', *Psychological Review*, 60, 1953, 393–404.
11. K. Lewin, 'Channels of group life', *Human Relations*, 1, 1947, 143–53.
12. M. DeFleur and O. Larsen, *The Flow of Information*, Harper & Row, 1958.
13. J. Galtung and M. H. Ruge, 'The structure of foreign news', *Journal of International Peace Research*, 1, 1965, 64–90; reprinted in *Media Sociology*, ed. J. Tunstall, Constable, 1970.
14. B. H. Westley and M. S. MacLean, 'A conceptual model for communications research', *Journalism Quarterly*, 34, 1957, 31–8.
15. G. Gerbner, 'Towards a general model of communication', *AudioVisual Communication Review*, 4, 1956, 171–99.
16. M. W. Riley and J. W. Riley, 'Mass communication and the social system', in R. K. Merton *et al*, eds., *Sociology Today*, Basic Books, 1959.

17. D. C. Barnlund, 'A transactional model of communication', in Sereno and Mortenson, eds., *Foundations of Communication Theory*, Harper & Row, 1970.
18. F. E. X. Dance, 'A helical model of communication', in Dance, ed., *Human Communication Theory*, Holt, Rinehart & Winston, 1967; reprinted in Sereno and Mortenson, op. cit., 1970, pp. 103–7.
19. T. R. Nilsen, 'On defining communication', in Sereno and Mortenson, op. cit., pp. 15–24.
20. Westley and MacLean, op. cit., 1957.
21. C. R. Wright, 'Functional analysis and mass communication', *Public Opinion Quarterly*, 24, 1960, 605–20.
22. M. DeFleur, op. cit., 1970.
23. D. McQuail and M. Gurevitch, 'Explaining audience behavior', in J. G. Blumler and E. Katz, eds., *The Uses of Mass Communications, Sage Annual Review of Communication*, 3, 1974, pp. 287–301.
24. C. Hull, *Principles of Behavior*, Appleton-Century Crofts, 1943.
25. E. L. Thorndike, *The Fundamentals of Learning*, Teachers' College, New York, 1932.
26. E. C. Tolman, 'Theories of learning', in F. A. Moss, ed., *Comparative Psychology*, Prentice-Hall, 1934.
27. B. F. Skinner, *Verbal Behavior*, Methuen, 1959.
28. T. Newcomb, op. cit., 1953.
29. A. H. Maslow, 'The expressive component in behavior', *Psychological Review*, 56, 1949, 261–73.
30. N. Wiener, *The Human Use of Human Beings*, Houghton-Mifflin, 1954.
31. F. C. Frick, 'Information theory', in S. Koch, ed., *Psychology: a study of a science*, McGraw-Hill, 2, 1959, 611–36.
32. Ibid.
33. F. Heider, 'Attitudes and cognitive information', *Journal of Psychology*, 21, 1946, 107–12.
34. T. Newcomb, op. cit.

35. T. Newcomb, 'Individual systems of orientation', in Koch, op. cit., 1959.
36. R. R. Zajonc, 'The concepts of balance, congruence and dissonance', *Public Opinion Quarterly*, 24, 1960, 280–96.
37. L. A. Festinger, *A Theory of Cognitive Dissonance*, Row Peterson, 1957.
38. Zajonc, op. cit.
39. T. Parsons, *The Social System*, Free Press of Glencoe, 1951.
40. G. H. Mead, *Mind, Self and Society*, University of Chicago Press, 1934.
41. H. Blumer, *Symbolic Interactionism*, Prentice-Hall, 1969.
42. A. Strauss, *Selected Papers on Social Psychology*, ed., Strauss, Free Press of Glencoe; quotations from third impression, 1965.
43. H. R. Wagner, ed., *Alfred Schutz on Phenomenology and Social Relations; Selected writings*, University of Chicago Press, 1970.
44. A. Schutz, *Phenomenology of the Social World*, Heinemann, 1972.
45. Wagner, op. cit.
46. Ibid.
47. E. Goffman, *Relations in Public*, Allen Lane, The Penguin Press, 1971.

Chapter 3 Ways of communicating

1. F. P. Dinneen, *An Introduction to General Linguistics*, Holt, Rinehart, 1967.
2. F. de Saussure, *Course in General Linguistics*, trans. W. Baskin, McGraw-Hill, 1966; first published, 1916.
3. R. Firth, *Symbols, Public and Private*, Allen & Unwin, 1973.
4. C. S. Peirce, *Collected Papers*, eds., C. Harteshorne and

P. Weiss, Harvard University Press, Vols II & V, 1931–35.
5. J. Gumperz, 'The speech community', in *International Encyclopedia of the Social Sciences*, 2nd edn, Macmillan, 1968.
6. W. F. Cottrell, *The Railroader*, Stanford University Press, 1940, ch. 7.
7. E. H. Sutherland, *The Professional Thief*, University of Chicago Press, 1956, glossary.
8. H. S. Becker, *Outsiders*, Free Press of Glencoe, 1963.
9. D. C. Miller and W. H. Form, *Industrial Sociology*, Harper & Row, 1962.
10. J. Goody and I. Watt, 'The consequences of literacy', *Comparative Studies in Society and History*, 5, 1962–63; reprinted in Giglioli, ed., *Language and Social Context*, Penguin, 1972.
11. A. Beteille, *Castes, Old and New*, Asia Publishing House, 1969.
12. D. Hymes, 'Toward ethnographies of communication', *American Anthropologist*, 66, No. 6, 1964, 12–25.
13. B. Whorf, *Language, Thought and Reality: selected writings*, Wiley, 1956.
14. Gumperz, op. cit.
15. R. Brown and A. Gilman, 'The pronouns of power and solidarity', in *Style in Language*, ed., T. A. Sebeok, MIT Press, 1960; reprinted in Giglioli, op. cit., 1972.
16. L. Schatzman and A. Strauss, 'Social class and modes of communication', *American Journal of Sociology*, 60, 1954, 329–38.
17. B. Bernstein, *Class, Codes and Control*, Paladin, 1973.
18. W. Labov, 'The logic of nonstandard English', in Giglioli, op. cit., 1972.
19. W. P. Robinson, *Language and Social Behaviour*, Penguin, 1972.
20. J. Laver and S. Hutcheson, eds., *Communication in Face to Face Interaction*, Penguin, 1972.
21. D. Abercrombie, 'Paralanguage', *British Journal of Dis-

orders of Communication, 3, 1968, 55—9; reprinted in Laver and Hutcheson, op. cit.

22. R. P. Harrison and M. L. Knapp, Introduction to special issue on non-verbal communication of *Journal of Communication*, 22, 1972.
23. M. Argyle and A. Kendon, 'The experimental analysis of social performance', in L. Berkovitz, ed., *Advances in Experimental Social Psychology*, Academic Press, 1967.
24. Laver and Hutcheson, op. cit.
25. R. Birdwhistell, *Kinesics and Context*, University of Pennsylvania Press, 1970.
26. R. Birdwhistell, 'Paralanguage twenty-five years after Sapir', in H. G. Brosin, ed., *Lectures in Experimental Psychiatry*, Pittsburgh University Press, 1961, pp. 43—63; reprinted in Laver and Hutcheson, op. cit.
27. W. LaBarre, 'The cultural basis of emotions and gestures', *Journal of Personality*, 16, 1947, 46—68.
28. E. T. Hall, *The Silent Language*, Doubleday, 1959.
29. R. Sommer, *Personal Space*, Prentice-Hall, 1969.
30. E. T. Hall, 'Silent assumptions in social communication', in Laver and Hutcheson, op. cit., pp. 274—88.
31. G. D. Suttle, *The Social Order of the Slum*, University of Chicago Press, 1968.
32. Firth, op. cit.
33. E. Durkheim, *Elementary Forms of Religious Life*, Paris, Alcan, 1912.
34. D. Diringer, *Writing*, Thames & Hudson, 1962.
35. M. McLuhan, *The Gutenberg Galaxy*, Routledge, 1962.
36. J. Frank, *The Beginnings of English Newspapers 1620—60*, Harvard University Press, 1961.
37. R. Williams, *The Long Revolution*, Chatto & Windus, 1961.
38. H. Menzel, 'Quasi-mass communication: a neglected area', *Public Opinion Quarterly*, 35, 1971, 406—9.

Chapter 4 The structure of communication process

1. G. C. Homans, *The Human Group*, Routledge, 1951.
2. B. Berelson and G. A. Steiner, *Human Behavior*, Harcourt, Brace, 1964.
3. L. A. Festinger, S. Schachter and K. Back, *Social Pressures in Informal Groups*, Stanford University Press, 1950.
4. K. W. Deutsch, 'Group', in *International Encyclopedia of the Social Sciences*, 2nd edn, Macmillan, 1968.
5. A. P. Hare, *Handbook of Small Group Research*, Free Press of Glencoe, 1962.
6. T. Mills, *The Sociology of Small Groups*, Prentice-Hall, 1967.
7. Deutsch, op. cit.
8. Homans, op. cit.
9. F. W. Whyte, *Street Corner Society*, Chicago University Press, 1956.
10. Homans, op. cit.
11. R. F. Bales *et al.*, 'Channels of communication in small groups', *American Sociological Review*, 16, 1951, 461–8.
12. Homans, op. cit.
13. Whyte, op. cit.
14. Homans, op. cit.
15. M. Weber, 'Bureaucracy', in H. H. Gerth and C. W. Mills, eds., *From Max Weber*, Routledge, 1948, pp. 196–244.
16. M. Argyle, *The Social Psychology of Work*, Allen Lane, 1972.
17. C. R. Walker and R. Guest, *The Man on the Assembly Line*, Harvard University Press, 1952.
18. J. H. Goldthorpe *et al.*, *The Affluent Worker*, Cambridge University Press, 1968.
19. H. H. Kelley, 'Communication in experimentally created hierarchies', *Human Relations*, 4, 1951, 39–56.
20. A. Etzioni, *Modern Organizations*, Prentice-Hall, 1964.

21. A. Bavelas, 'Communication patterns in task-oriented groups', in H. D. Lerner and D. Lerner, eds., *The Policy Sciences*, Stanford University Press, 1951.
22. H. J. Leavitt and R. A. H. Mueller, 'Some effects of feedback on communication', *Human Relations*, 4, 1951, 401–10.
23. R. F. Bales *et al.*, 'Structure and dynamics of small groups: a review of four variables', in J. B. Gittler, ed., *Review of Sociology*, Wiley, 1957, pp. 391–422.
24. R. L. Simpson, 'Vertical and horizontal communication in formal organizations', *Administrative Science Quarterly*, 4, 1959–60, 188–96.
25. T. Burns, 'The direction of activity and communication in a departmental executive group', *Human Relations*, 7, 1954, 73–97.
26. N. H. Berkovitz and W. Benniss, 'Interaction patterns in formal service oriented organizations', *Administrative Science Quarterly*, 6, 1961–62.
27. P. M. Blau, *The Dynamics of Bureaucracy*, Chicago University Press, 1955.
28. Burns, op. cit.
29. K. Davis, 'Management communication and the grapevine', *Harvard Business Review*, Sept./Oct., 1953.
30. E. Jacobson and S. Seashore, 'Communication practises in complex organizations', *Journal of Social Issues*, 7, 1951, 28–40.
31. Festinger *et al.*, op. cit.
32. P. M. Blau and W. Scott, *Complex Organizations*, Routledge, 1963.
33. C. I. Barnard, 'Functions and pathology of status systems in formal organizations', in W. F. Whyte, ed., *Industry and Society*, McGraw-Hill, 1946.
34. H. L. Wilensky, *Organizational Intelligence*, Basic Books, 1969.
35. R. W. Revans, 'The morale and effectiveness of general hospitals', in G. McLachlan, ed., *Problems and Progress*

in Medical Care, Oxford University Press, 1964.
36. Wilensky, op. cit.
37. Burns, op. cit.
38. Kelley, op. cit.
39. W. R. Rosengren, 'Communication organization and conduct in the therapeutic setting', *Administrative Science Quarterly*, 9, 1964–65, 70–90.
40. E. E. Mishler and A. Tropp, 'Status and interaction in a psychiatric hospital', *Human Relations*, 9, 1956, 187–204.
41. J. A. Barnes, 'Class and community in a Norwegian island parish', *Human Relations*, 7, 1954.
42. E. Bott, *Family and Social Network*, Routledge, 1957.
43. R. Frankenburg, *Communities in Britain*, Penguin, 1966.
44. J. Boissevain, *Friends of Friends*, Blackwell, 1974.
45. Bott, op. cit.
46. Frankenburg, op. cit.
47. Festinger *et al.*, op. cit.
48. F. Lenz-Romeiss, *The City*, Praeger, 1973.
49. C. Rosser and C. C. Harris, *The Family and Social Change*, Routledge, 1965.
50. C. Bell, *Middle Class Families*, Routledge, 1968.
51. Royal Commission on Local Government, *Research Studies, No. 9: Community Attitudes Survey, England*, HMSO, 1969.
52. J. Mogey and R. N. Morris, *The Sociology of Housing*, Routledge, 1965.
53. J. Mogey, *Family and Neighbourhood*, Routledge, 1957.
54. Bell, op. cit.
55. H. J. Gans, *The Levittowners*, Allen Lane, 1967.
56. W. Watson, 'Social mobility and social class in industrial communities', in Gluckman, ed., *Closed Systems and Open Minds*, Aldine, 1964.
57. J. Seeley, R. Sim and E. Loosly, *Crestwood Heights*, Basic Books, 1956.
58. Gans, op. cit.

59. R. K. Merton, 'Personal influence', in *Social Theory and Social Structure*, Free Press of Glencoe, 1957.
60. M. Stacey, *Tradition and Change*, Oxford University Press, 1960.
61. B. Heraud, 'Social class in new towns', *Urban Studies*, 5, 1968.
62. G. D. Suttles, *The Social Order of the Slum*, Chicago University Press, 1968.
63. P. F. Lazarsfeld, B. Berelson and H. Gaudet, *The People's Choice*, Columbia University Press, 1944.
64. J. G. Blumler and D. McQuail, *Television in Politics*, Faber, 1968.
65. E. Katz and P. F. Lazarsfeld, *Personal Influence*, Free Press of Glencoe, 1956.
66. J. G. Blumler, T. Nossiter and D. McQuail, *Political Communication and the Young Voter*, SSRC Reports, 1975 and 1976.
67. B. Berelson, P. F. Lazarsfeld and W. N. McPhee, *Voting*, Chicago University Press, 1954.
68. V. C. Troldahl, 'A field test of a modified "two-step flow of communication model"', *Public Opinion Quarterly*, **30**, 1966, 609–23.
69. C. R. Wright and M. Cantor, 'The opinion seeker and avoider: steps beyond the opinion leader concept', *Pacific Sociological Review*, **10**, 1967, 33–43.
70. J. Arndt, 'A test of the two-step flow in the diffusion of a new product', *Journalism Quarterly*, **45**, 1968, 457–65.
71. R. Park, 'News as a form of knowledge', in R. H. Turner, ed., *On Social Control and Collective*, Chicago University Press, 1967.
72. T. Shibutani, *Improvised News*, Bobbs-Merrill, 1966.
73. Katz and Lazarsfeld, op. cit.
74. J. S. Coleman, E. Katz and H. Menzel, *Medical Innova-*

tion, Bobbs-Merrill, 1966.
75. B. S. Greenberg, 'Person to person communication in the diffusion of news', *Journalism Quarterly*, 41, 1964, 489—91.
76. B. S. Greenberg and E. B. Parker, *The Kennedy Assassination and the American Public*, Stanford University Press, 1965.
77. Shibutani, op. cit.
78. T. Caplow, 'Rumors in war', *Social Forces*, 25, 1947, 298—302.
79. A. Inkeles and R. A. Bauer, *The Soviet Citizen*, Harvard University Press, 1959.
80. Festinger *et al.*, op. cit.
81. Shibutani, op. cit.
82. D. Lerner, *The Passing of Traditional Society*, Free Press of Glencoe, 1958.

Chapter 5 Communication as an influence process

1. R. Lippitt *et al.*, 'The dynamics of power', *Human Relations*, 5, 1952, 37—64.
2. T. Parsons, *Sociological Theory and Modern Society*, Free Press of Glencoe, 1967.
3. D. Cartwright and A. Zander, eds., *Group Dynamics*, 3rd edn, Tavistock, 1968.
4. H. Kelman, 'Processes of opinion change', *Public Opinion Quarterly*, 25, 1961, 57—78.
5. I. L. Janis and C. I. Hovland, 'An overview of persuasibility research', in Hovland and Janis, eds., *Personality and Persuasibility*, Yale University Press, 1959, pp. 1—16.
6. J. R. P. French and B. H. Raven, 'The bases of social power', in Cartwright and Zander, op. cit., pp. 259—69.
7. B. E. Collins and B. H. Raven, 'Group structure', in G. Lindzey and E. Aronson, eds., *Handbook of Social*

Psychology, 2nd edn, Addison-Wesley, iv, 1969, 102–204.
8. D. Katz, 'The functional approach to the study of attitudes', *Public Opinion Quarterly*, 24, 1960, 163–204.
9. Janis and Hovland, op. cit.
10. N. Lin, *The Study of Human Communication*, Bobbs-Merrill, 1973.
11. W. J. McGuire, 'Persuasion, resistance and attitude change', in I. de S. Pool and W. Schramm, eds., *Handbook of Communication*, Rand-McNally, 1974.
12. D. E. Butler and R. Stokes, *Political Change in Britain*, Macmillan, 1969.
13. D. McQuail, *Towards a Sociology of Mass Communication*, Collier-Macmillan, 1969.
14. D. McQuail, J. G. Blumler and J. A. Brown, 'The television audience', in McQuail, ed., *Sociology of Mass Communications*, Penguin, 1972.
15. J. D. Halloran, P. Elliott and D. C. Chaney, *Television and Delinquency*, Leicester University Press, 1970.
16. J. G. Blumler and E. Katz, 'The uses of mass communication', *Sage Annual Reviews of Communication*, 3, 1974.
17. J. G. Blumler and D. McQuail, *Television in Politics*, Faber, 1968.
18. J. Trenaman and D. McQuail, *Television and the Political Image*, Methuen, 1961.
19. McQuail *et al.*, op. cit., 1972.
20. E. Katz, 'Communications research and the image of society', *American Journal of Sociology*, 65, 1960, 435–40.
21. E. Katz *et al.*, 'Traditions of research on the diffusion of innovations', *American Sociological Review*, 28, 1963, 237–52.
22. Lazarsfeld *et al.*, op. cit.
23. Katz and Lazarsfeld, op. cit.
24. Katz *et al.*, op. cit.

25. E. Rogers, *The Diffusion of Innovations*, Free Press of Glencoe, 1962.
26. E. Rogers and F. Shoemaker, *Communication of Innovations*, Free Press of Glencoe, 1971.
27. Coleman, op. cit.
28. McGuire, op. cit.
29. Collins and Raven, op. cit.
30. W. Weiss, 'The effects of the mass media of communication', in G. Lindzey and A. Aronson, eds., *Handbook of Social Psychology*, Addison-Wesley, 5, 1969, 77—195.
31. E. Noelle-Neumann, 'Return to the concept of powerful mass media', *Studies of Broadcasting*, 1973, pp. 66—112.
32. B. Berelson and G. Steiner, *Human Behavior*, Harcourt, Brace, 1964.
33. J. T. Klapper, *The Effects of Mass Communication*, Free Press of Glencoe, 1960.
34. Berelson and Steiner, op. cit.
35. Collins and Raven, op. cit.
36. Blumler and McQuail, op. cit.
37. E. Walster and L. Festinger, 'The effectiveness of "overheard" persuasive communications', *J. Abnormal and Social Psychology*, 65, 1962, 395—402.
38. D. Byrne, 'Attitudes and attraction', in L. Berkowitz, ed., *Advances in Experimental Psychology*, Academic Press, iv, 1969.

Chapter 6 Mass communication

1. B. H. Westley and M. S. MacLean, 'A conceptual model for communications research', *Journalism Quarterly*, 34, 1957, 31—8.
2. D. M. White, 'The "gatekeeper". A study in the selection of news', *Journalism Quarterly*, 27, 1950, 283—90.
3. P. Elliott, *The Making of a Television Series*, Constable, 1972.
4. Ibid.

5. J. Tunstall, *Journalists at Work*, Constable, 1972.
6. C. Perrow, 'A framework for the comparative analysis of organizations', *American Sociological Review*, 32, 1967, 194–208.
7. W. Gieber, 'News is what newsmen make it', in L. A. Dexter and D. M. White, eds., *People, Society and Mass Communication*, Free Press of Glencoe, 1964, pp. 173–81.
8. H. J. Gans, *Deciding What's News*, Vintage Books, 1980.
9. Tunstall, op. cit.
10. T. Burns, 'Public service and private world', in Halmos, ed., 'Sociology of Mass Media Communicators', *Sociological Review Monographs*, 13, 1969, 53–73.
11. J. G. Blumler, 'Producers' attitudes towards the television coverage of an election campaign', in Halmos, ed., op. cit., pp. 85–115.
12. Tunstall, op. cit.
13. M. Cantor, *The Hollywood Television Producer*, Basic Books, 1971.
14. M. U. Martell and G. J. McCall, 'Reality orientation and the pleasure principle', in Dexter and White, op. cit., pp. 283–333.
15. Gans, op. cit.
16. Gieber, op. cit.
17. R. A. Bauer, 'The communicator and the audience', *Journal of Conflict Resolution*, 2, 1958, 67–77; reprinted in Dexter and White, op. cit.
18. I. de S. Pool and I. Shulman, 'Newsmen's fantasies, audiences and newswriting', *Public Opinion Quarterly*, 23, 1959, 145–58; reprinted in Dexter and White, op. cit.
19. Burns, op. cit.
20. C. W. Mills, *The Power Elite*, New York, Oxford University Press, 1956.
21. Elliott, op. cit.
22. B. Berelson and P. Salter, 'Majority and minority

Americans: an analysis of magazine fiction', *Public Opinion Quarterly*, **10**, 1946, 168–90.
23. P. Hartmann and C. Husband, *Racism and the Mass Media*, Davis Poynter, 1974.
24. Elliott, op. cit.
25. J. D. Halloran, P. Elliott and G. Murdock, *Demonstrations and Communications*, Penguin, 1970.
26. K. Lang and G. E. Lang, 'The unique perspective of television and its effect', *American Sociological Review*, 18, 1953, 103–12.
27. Elliott, op. cit.
28. R. E. Park, 'News as a form of knowledge', in R. H. Turner, ed., *On Social Control and Collective Behaviour*, University of Chicago Press, 1967, pp. 32–52.
29. Galtung and Ruge, op. cit.
30. Elliott, op. cit.
31. K. Rosengren and S. Windahl, 'Mass media consumption as a functional alternative', in McQuail, ed., *Sociology of Mass Communications*, Penguin, 1972, pp. 166–94.
32. D. Horton and R. R. Wohl, 'Mass communication and para-social interaction', *Psychiatry*, 19, 1956, 215–29.
33. F. Fearing, 'Influence of the movies on attitudes and behavior', *Annals of the American Academy of Political and Social Science*, 254, 1947, 70–80; reprinted in McQuail, ed., op. cit., pp. 119–34.
34. D. McQuail, *Towards a Sociology of Mass Communications*, Collier-Macmillan, 1969.
35. D. McQuail, J. G. Blumler and J. R. Brown, 'The television audience: a revised perspective', in McQuail, ed., op. cit., 1972, pp. 135–65.
36. McQuail and Gurevitch, op. cit.
37. W. J. McGuire, 'The nature of attitudes and attitude change', in G. Lindzey and E. Aronson, eds., *Handbook of Social Psychology*, 2nd edn, Addison-Wesley, 1969, pp. 136–314.
38. Weiss, op. cit.

39. McQuail, op. cit., 1969 and D. McQuail, *Mass Communication Theory*, Sage, 1983.
40. J. D. Halloran, *The Effects of Mass Communication: with special reference to television*, Leicester University Press, 1964.
41. J. D. Halloran, ed., *The Effects of Television*, Panther Books, 1970.
42. Klapper, op. cit.
43. Berelson and Steiner, op. cit.
44. J. D. Halloran, R. Brown and D. C. Chaney, *Television and Delinquency*, Leicester University Press, 1970.
45. Blumler and McQuail, op. cit.
46. K. Lang and G. Lang, 'Mass communication and public opinion: strategies for research' in M. Rosenberg and R. H. Turner, eds., *Social Psychology*, Basic Books, 1981, pp. 653–82.
47. Blumler and McQuail, op. cit.
48. W. Lippman, *Public Opinion*, Free Press of Glencoe, 1922.
49. Hartmann and Husband, op. cit.
50. C. Seymour-Ure, *The Political Impact of Mass Media*, Constable, 1974.

Chapter 7 Communication and society: a review of principal themes

1. J. W. Carey, 'A cultural approach to communication', *Communication*, 2, 1975, 1–22.
2. As shown, for instance, by G. Noble in *Children in Front of the Small Screen*, Constable, 1976.
3. See D. McQuail, *Mass Communication Theory*, Sage, 1983.

Chapter 8 Current directions in communication theory and research

1. A. Giddens, *New Rules for Sociological Method*, Hutchinson, 1976.
2. E. Wilson, *Sociobiology*, 1975.
3. M. De Fleur and S. Ball-Rokeach, *Theories of Mass Communication*, 4th edn, Longman, 1981.
4. E. M. Rogers and R. A. Rogers, *Communication in Organisations*, Free Press, 1976.
5. L. W. Porter and K. H. Roberts, eds., *Communication in Organisations*, Penguin, 1977.
6. W. C. Redding, 'Organisational communication theory and ideology: an overview' in D. Nimmo, ed., *Communication Year Book*, 3, Transaction, 1979.
7. G. Goldhaber, *Organisational Communication*, W. C. Brown, 1979.
8. J. M. Wiemann and R. P. Harrison, eds., *Nonverbal Interaction*, Sage, 1983.
9. M. Argyle, *Bodily Communication*, Methuen, 1975.
10. B. W. Eakin and H. G. Eakin, *Sex Differences in Human Communication*, Houghton Miflin, 1978.
11. G. R. Miller, ed., *Explorations in Interpersonal Communication*, Sage, 1976.
12. M. E. Roloff and C. R. Berger, eds., *Social Cognition and Communication*, Sage, 1982.
13. S. Weitz, ed., *Nonverbal Communication*, Oxford University Press, 1974.
14. D. E. Allen and R. F. Guy, *Conversation Analysis — the Sociology of Talk*, Mouton, 1974.
15. L. Berkowitz, ed., *Advances in Experimental Social Psychology*, vol. 12, Academic Press, 1979.
16. M. E. Roloff, *Interpersonal Communication — a Social Exchange Approach*, Sage, 1981.
17. E. Goffman, *Frame Analysis: an Essay on the Organisation of Experience*, Harvard University Press, 1974.

18. H. D. Duncan, *Symbols and Society*, Oxford University Press, 1968.
19. R. Schank and R. Abelson, *Scripts, Plans, Goals and Understandings*, Erlbaum, 1977.
20. D. K. Davis and S. J. Baran, *Mass Communication and Everyday Life*, Wadsworth Publishing Company, 1981.
21. H. J. Gans, *Deciding What's News*, Vintage Books, 1980.
22. G. Tuchman, *Making News: a Study in the Construction of Reality*, Free Press, 1978.
23. P. Golding and P. Elliott, *Making the News*, Longman, 1979.
24. M. Tracey, *The Production of Political Television*, Routledge and Kegan Paul, 1977.
25. P. Schlesinger, *Putting 'Reality' Together: BBC News*, Constable, 1978.
26. S. Chibnall, *Law and Order News*, Tavistock, 1977.
27. Glasgow Media Group, *More Bad News*, Routledge and Kegan Paul, 1980.
28. J. W. Johnstone, E. J. Slawski, and W. W. Bowman, *The News People*, University of Illinois Press, 1976.
29. T. Burns, *The BBC: Public Institution and Private World*, Macmillan, 1977.
30. L. Engwall, *Newspapers as Organisations*, Saxon House, 1978.
31. P. Elliott, 'Media organisations and occupations — an overview' in J. Curran *et al.*, eds., *Mass Communication and Society*, Edward Arnold, 1977, pp. 142–73.
32. P. M. Hirsch, 'Occupational, organisational and institutional models in mass communication', in P. M. Hirsch *et al., Strategies for Communication Research*, Sage, 1977, pp. 13–42.
33. M. Schudson, *Discovering the News*, Basic Books, 1978.
34. Much of this work has been reported in article form, especially in the pages of *Communication Research* during the last few years.
35. G. J. Goodhardt, A. S. C. Ehrenberg and M. A. Collins,

The Television Audience: Patterns of Viewing, Saxon House, 1975.
36. G. S. Comstock, S. Chaffee, N. Katzman, M. McCombs and D. Roberts, *Television and Human Behavior*, Columbia University Press, 1978.
37. J. G. Blumler, 'Looking at media abundance', *Communications*, 5, 1979, 125—58.
38. H. J. Gans, 'The politics of culture in America' in D. McQuail, ed., *The Sociology of Mass Communications*, Penguin, 1972, pp. 372—85.
39. G. H. Lewis, 'Taste cultures and their composition', in E. Katz and T. Szecsko, eds., *Mass Media and Social Change*, Sage, 1980, pp. 201—17.
40. E. Noelle-Neumann, 'Return to the concept of powerful mass media', *Studies of Broadcasting*, 9, 1973, 66—112.
41. E. Noelle-Neumann, 'The spiral of silence: a theory of public opinion', *Journal of Communication*, 24, 1974, 43—51.
42. K. Lang and G. Lang, 'Mass communication and public opinion: strategies for research', in M. Rosenberg and R. H. Turner, eds., *Social Psychology*, Basic Books, 1981, pp. 653—82.
43. J. G. Blumler and D. McQuail, *Television in Politics*, Faber and Faber, 1968.
44. S. Kraus and D. K. Davis, *The Effects of Mass Communication on Political Behavior*, Pennsylvania State University Press, 1976.
45. G. Noble, *Children in Front of the Small Screen*, Constable, 1975, is a good example.
46. R. Brown, ed., *Children and Television*, Collier-Macmillan, 1976.
47. E. Hedinsson, *Television, Family and Society*, Almquist and Wiksel, 1981.
48. E. Noelle-Neumann, 'Mass media and social change in developed societies', in G. C. Wilhoit and H. De Bok, eds., *Mass Communication Review Yearbook*, 1980,

pp. 657–78.

49. M. Robinson, 'The press as king-maker', *Journalism Quarterly*, 1974, 587–94.
50. K. E. Rosengren, 'Mass media and social change', in E. Katz and T. Sczecsko, eds., op. cit., 1980, pp. 247–63.
51. G. Gerbner, 'Living with television: the violence profile', *Journal of Communication*, 26, 2, 1976, 173–98.
52. P. M. Hirsch, 'The scary world of the non-viewer and other anomolies — a reanalysis of Gerbner *et al.* findings in cultivation analysis', *Communication Research*, 7, 4, 1980, 403–56 and ibid., 8, 1, 1981, 3–38.
53. M. McCombs and D. L. Shaw, 'The agenda-setting function of the mass media', *Public Opinion Quarterly*, 36, 1972, 176–87.
54. L. Becker, 'The mass media and citizen assessment of issue importance', in D. C. Whitney and E. Wartella, eds., *Mass Communication Review Yearbook*, 3, 1982, pp. 521–36.
55. Glasgow Media Group, *Bad News*, Routledge, 1977 and *More Bad News*, Routledge, 1980.
56. M. R. Real, *Mass-mediated culture*, Prentice-Hall, 1977.
57. A. P, Schmid and J. de Graaf, *Violence as Communication*, Sage, 1982.
58. T. Gitlin, *The Whole World is Watching — Mass Media and the Making and Unmaking of the New Left*, University of California Press, 1981.
59. R. E. Rice and W. J. Paisley, eds., *Public Communication Campaigns*, Sage, 1981.
60. J. M. Wiemann and R. P. Harrison, eds., op. cit., 1983.
61. M. Davis and J. Skupien, eds., *The Nonverbal Communication Literature 1971–1980*, Arno Press, 1981.
62. R. G. Harper *et al.*, *Nonverbal Communication: the State of the Art*, John Wiley, 1978.
63. M. L. Knapp, *Social Intercourse from Greeting to Goodbye*, Allyn and Bacon, 1978.

64. M. Coulthard, *An Introduction to Discourse Analysis*, Longman, 1977.
65. T. Hawkes, *Structuralism and Semiotics*, Methuen, 1977.
66. V. L. Leymore, *Hidden Myth: Structure and Symbolism in Advertising*, Heinemann, 1975.
67. Glasgow Media Group, op. cit., 1977 and 1980.
68. R. Barthes, 'The photographic message', in *Image-Music-Text*, Essays by Roland Barthes selected and translated by Stephen Heath, Fontana, 1977, pp. 15—31.
69. S. Hall, 'The determination of news photographs', in S. Cohen and J. Young, eds., *The Manufacture of News*, Constable, 1973, pp. 176—90.
70. J. Fiske and J. Hartley, *Reading Television*, Methuen, 1978.
71. C. Metz, *Film Language*, Oxford University Press, 1974.
72. D. Graber, *Verbal Behavior and Politics*, University of Illinois Press, 1976.
73. P. Thompson and P. Davenport, *The Dictionary of Visual Language*, Penguin, 1982.
74. A. M. Thunberg *et al.*, *Communication and Equality*, Almquist and Wiksel, 1982.
75. S. Chaffee and J. McCleod, 'Family patterns and adolescent political socialization', in J. Dennis, ed., *Socialization to Politics*, 1973.
76. G. Murdock, 'Large corporations and the control of the communications industries', in M. Gurevitch *et al.*, *Culture, Society and the Media*, Methuen, 1982, pp. 118—50.
77. P. Hartman and C. Husband, *Racism and the Mass Media*, Davis Poynter, 1974.
78. P. Beharell and G. Philo, eds., *Trade Unions and the Media*, Macmillan, 1977.
79. P. Golding and S. Middleton, *Images of Welfare*, Basil Blackwell, 1982.
80. S. Cohen, *Folk Devils and Moral Panics*, McGibbon & Kee, 1972.

81. S. Hall *et al.*, *Policing the Crisis*, Macmillan, 1978.
82. S. Hall, 'Encoding and decoding in the television message', in S. Hall *et al.*, eds., *Culture, Media, Language*, Hutchinson, 1980.
83. F. Parkin, *Class Inequality and the Political Order*, Paladin, 1972.
84. M. Edelman, *Political Language: Words that Succeed and Policies that Fail*, University of Illinois Press, 1977.
85. C. Mueller, *The Politics of Communication*, Oxford University Press, 1973.
86. R. Sennett, *The Fall of Public Man*, A. Knopf, 1977.
87. A. Gouldner, *The Dialectics of Ideology and Technology*, Macmillan, 1976.
88. As in C. W. Mills, *The Power Elite*, Oxford University Press, 1976.
89. Well described in M. Jay, *The Dialectical Imagination*, Heinemann, 1973.
90. J. Habermas, *Legitimation Crisis*, Heinemann, 1976.
91. G. Tuchman, A. K. Daniels and J. Benet, eds., *Hearth and Home: Images of Women in Mass Media*, Oxford University Press, 1978.
92. T. Millum, *Images of Women*, Chatto & Windus, 1975.
93. M. Ferguson, *Forever Feminine*, Heinemann, 1983.
94. M. Butler and W. J. Paisley, *Women and the Mass Media*, Human Science Press, 1980.
95. H. Baher, *Women and the Media*, Pergamon, 1980.
96. M. Gallagher, *Unequal Opportunities: the Case of Women and the Mass Media*, Unesco, 1981.
97. S. Hall and T. Jefferson, eds., *Resistance Through Rituals*, Hutchinson, 1976.
98. D. Hebdige, *Subculture: The Meaning of Style*, Methuen, 1979.
99. There has been much research and debate, but an early posing of the problem is to be found in P. J. Tichenor *et al.*, 'Mass media and differential growth in knowledge', *Public Opinion Quarterly*, 34, 1970, 158–70.

Or see D. McQuail and S. Windahl, *Communication Models*, Longman, 1982, pp. 70–74.
100. S. McBride *et al.*, *Many Voices, One World*, Unesco and Kogan Page, 1980.
101. J. Tunstall, *The Media are American*, Constable, 1977.
102. J. O. Boyd-Barrett, 'Cultural Dependency and the mass media', in M. Gurevitch *et al.*, *Culture, Society and the Mass Media*, Methuen, 1982, 174–95.
103. T. McPhail, *Electronic Colonialism*, Sage, 1982.
104. J. A. Lent and C. H. Gifford, 'The age of awareness in global mass communication', in B. Dervin and M. J. Voigt, eds., *Progress in Communication Sciences*, vol. 2, 1982, Ablex, 163–201.
105. For instance, F. Berrigan, *Access: Some Western Models of Community Media*, Unesco, 1977, or B. Singer, *Feedback and Society*, Lexington Books, 1973.
106. For instance, K. K. Reardon, *Persuasion Theory and Context*, Sage, 1981.
107. M. E. Roloff and C. R. Berger, op. cit.
108. P. Gould and R. White, *Mental Maps*, Pelican, 1974.
109. For instance, L. Donohew and L. Tipton, 'A conceptual model of information-seeking, avoiding and processing', in P. Clarke, ed., *New Models for Communication Research*, Sage, 1973.
110. E. M. Rogers, 'Communication and development: the passing of a dominant paradigm', *Communication Research*, 3, 1976, 213–40.
111. D. McQuail and S. Windahl, *Communication Models*, Longman, 1982.

Index